THE NATURAL BENT

Let early education be a sort of amusement; you will then be better able to find out the natural bent.

PLATO'S REPUBLIC

THE NATURAL BENT

The Memoirs of

Dr. PAUL B. BARRINGER

CHAPEL HILL
THE UNIVERSITY OF NORTH CAROLINA PRESS

Copyright, 1949, by Anna Barringer

MANUFACTURED IN THE UNITED STATES OF AMERICA

Van Rees Press • *New York*

PJ

FOREWORD

I FOUND it difficult to make my father realize that his life could contain any element of interest to anyone. Fortunately I was aware that he was, in seniority, the patriarch of our family, and that his contact with the past and his own active life had covered one of the most extraordinary phases of history in all time. Ultimately, he was persuaded, in the guise of a gesture of affection, to dictate some "recollections for his grandchildren."

Later, his friend, Dr. Walter A. Montgomery, had some incidents of North Carolina history transcribed. These random recollections given when my father was seventy-four years of age constitute the basis of these memoirs, with the inclusion of extracts from some letters which came to hand after his death in 1941. To arrange all this chronologically and to prune out repetition and genealogical matter of interest only to the family has been my own contribution.

In preparing part of this material, I was fortunate in having the valuable assistance of Miss Lena Barksdale, and later that of Mrs. Lucien L. Kinsolving. I wish to take this opportunity of thanking also for their generous assistance the editors of *Collier's Magazine*, who have permitted reprints from "Once a Week"; the Department of History of Duke University; *The Southern Medical Journal;* and the *Journal of Southern Medicine and Surgery* for reprints from articles; and the staff of the University of Virginia

Library who with unfailing courtesy and consideration have been most helpful in every way. Dr. Oscar Swineford of the Medical Faculty and staff of the University of Virginia Hospital has kindly reviewed the early medical data. Among my father's former students and friends, now deceased, I am indebted to Dr. William A. Lambeth, Dr. Roy K. Flannagan, and Dr. James K. Hall for their tributes.

It would have been impossible to achieve the completion of this task without the constant and generous assistance of my valued friend, Armistead C. Gordon, Jr., Professor of English at the University of Virginia, whose experience, ability, and appreciation have made this book possible.

Anna Barringer

Charlottesville
Virginia

CONTENTS

Part I

THE WAR AND THE BOY

I.	Milk-Teeth Times	3
II.	S'Quash	10
III.	The Big House	16
IV.	The Plantation	28
V.	Camp Follower	33
VI.	Uncle Victor	40
VII.	The Pinch of Necessity	48
VIII.	Wartime Industries	55
IX.	A Peculiar Institution	61
X.	First Railroad Adventures	68
XI.	Visit to Raleigh	78
XII.	The Laws of Man and Nature	85
XIII.	Stoneman's Raid	92
XIV.	A Visit from "Mr. President"	98
XV.	Our Reconstruction	106
XVI.	A Prisoner of War	111

CONTENTS

XVII.	General Rufus Barringer, C. S. A.	115
XVIII.	Harbingers of Peace	125
XIX.	Gate-Boy	131
XX.	A Trip to "Yankeedom"	137
XXI.	Mount Pleasant	143

Part II

THE WORLD AND THE MAN

XXII.	Bingham's School	151
XXIII.	The Four Musketeers	163
XXIV.	The Sports of the Gentry	168
XXV.	Kenmore University School	177
XXVI.	A Visit to My Future Alma Mater	186
XXVII.	The University of Virginia	193
XXVIII.	Faculty and Fracas	203
XXIX.	The Philadelphia Centennial	213
XXX.	The School of Medicine, 1876-1877	219
XXXI.	The Clinics of New York, 1877-1878	229
XXXII.	"The Grand Tour," 1881	233
XXXIII.	A Medical Student in Vienna, 1881	244

Part III

POSTSCRIPT

XXXIV.	Dr. Paul B. Barringer	257
	Index	275

PART I

The War and the Boy

I

MILK-TEETH TIMES

I AM TOLD that I was born on Friday the thirteenth, February, 1857. I have never taken the trouble to check the calendar, not being superstitious. The place was Harris's Hotel in the town of Concord, Cabarrus County, in western North Carolina. It was an unusual place for a baby to be born, but in anticipation of the extra space needed for an addition to the family, the roof of our house was being raised one story. The contractor was slow in his work, then as now, and my parents were caught with this great event at the local hotel, since hospitals and maternity wards were non-existent.

The time, as measured by events, was during the "Great Snow of 1857," which in North Carolina fell to a depth of thirty inches, producing great suffering and destruction of property. The roofs of many dwellings and barns were crushed in by this unusual and unanticipated weight.

A family tradition may throw some light on the severity of this winter. My mother's parents lived about thirty-five miles away. In spite of the fact that flakes of snow were already falling, my father, in his pride at his first son, determined to dispatch a messenger to notify them of my safe arrival. With an eye to the windward, however, he chose what was called in plantation lingo "a runaway horse and a runaway nigger." The runaway horse was a fractious saddle horse used only for fox hunting, and the Negro, known as Bill York, was "a natural bad man," who was always running away to the swamps and had given much trouble. When this pair of disreputables reached Beattie's Ford on the Catawba River, a large cake of ice coming down stream upset both horse and rider. The man took the farthest shore, which was on the side of the river in the direction of my grandfather's place, while the horse took the shore towards home and appeared at the stable door sometime during the night, without saddle or bridle. With any one else missing it would have caused much uneasiness, but Bill York's talents for survival were taken for granted, and rightly. Somehow, in the driving storm he espied a cabin light and came to the plantation of General Burton, by whom he was passed along until he reached the end of his journey. He did not return for six weeks.

In later life I was interested to observe that at the time of my birth the Indian Mutiny was in full swing, with all the changes in India which that subsequently induced, while Darwin was shaping that entering wedge of truth for the mental emancipation of mankind under whose beneficence we now live. In my own country, economic forces and political friction were gathering into a storm that was to sweep like a hurricane over the noblest experiment in freedom then existing and leave havoc and destruction in its wake.

My father, Rufus Barringer, who was a very successful young lawyer even then, had married Eugenia Morrison, a daughter of the Reverend Robert Hall Morrison and his wife, Mary Graham. The old family place which was to play such a part in my life was Cottage Home in Lincoln County, North Carolina, thirty-five miles west of the Barringer home in Concord.

My parents had one other child, my sister Anna Morrison, who was named for my mother's favorite sister and was two years older than myself. Though different in temperament, we were in all ways congenial and devoted. In selecting the cognomen which was to accompany the scion of this branch through life, for good or ill, my parents named me Paul Brandon after my grandfather, General Paul Barringer, and the family name of his wife, Elizabeth Brandon.

Concord, when I first remember it, was a village of some 1,000 to 1,200 inhabitants. It was "T" shaped, Main Street forming the top of the "T" and Depot Street the stem. Main Street extended from McDonald's cotton mill to Weincoff's tannery, and Depot Street ran from the middle of Main a distance of one-half mile to the Southern Railroad. The jail, presided over by Sheriff Stough, graced the right-hand point of the juncture of the two streets, and Harris's Hotel, my birthplace, graced the left.

On Main Street, in the direction of the cotton mill and placed well back from the street in the generous setting of the day, were the comparatively simple residences of my father and his brother, Victor Clay Barringer. Uncle Victor's wife, Maria Massey, was originally from Philadelphia. They had no children, and their house then and later was a second home to my sister and me. As a sprout I must have been rolled up and down Main Street, back and forth from one house to the other, always once and frequently twice a day; but of all this I remember nothing except my faithful nurse Phyllis.

On the line between these homes was "the office"—the name being a reminder of those rural offices which occupied a convenient site near the main house of every plantation, the point where the squire formally met the overseer for reports. This, however, was a law office, one half being used by my father and the other half by my uncle. It stood directly across the street from the first Methodist Church built in Concord, a brick building set far back behind a grove of enormous oaks which extended up to the Phifer and Gibson tracts.

I was not quite eighteen months old when, on June 28, 1858, my mother died of typhoid fever, then the great plague of summer and fall months. At that time the origin of this dreaded disease was utterly unknown. After her death our home was broken and the servants advertised for hire. However, they were returned to the Morrison home instead.

From then on, it was a childhood of constant visiting. The two bases of our lives, until we were old enough for boarding school, were in winter at Uncle Victor and Aunt Ria's and for holidays and summers, Cottage Home. Sometimes we went to Charlotte to my mother's sister, Aunt Harriet, wife of Mr. James P. Irwin. He was a man of great wealth and gave two city squares for the First Presbyterian Church and burying ground, now in the heart of town. But the real adventure was going to my Aunt Anna's—another sister of my mother—in Lexington, Virginia, for a two-year visit. Her husband, Major Thomas Jonathan Jackson, was the professor of Artillery Tactics and Natural Philosophy at the Virginia Military Institute. He was later known to history as General "Stonewall" Jackson.

The Jacksons had recently lost a little girl, their first child, Mary Graham Jackson, who lived less than a month. In looking over some old papers I find a letter from Major Jackson to my father, announcing her birth. Its brevity and clarity are of particular interest.

> Lexington, Virginia
> May 1st, 1858.
>
> My dear Brother:
> We have a little prodigy, one day old this afternoon. She calls herself Mary Graham Jackson. Anna is doing very well, and joins in love to yourself and Sister Eugenia.
> Your affectionate brother,
> T. J. Jackson.

In those days of slow and difficult travel Lexington, Virginia, was a long way from Concord, North Carolina, and I have been told that my trip required a long period of preparation, among the Barringers, Morrisons, and Jacksons. It was finally decided that my sister was to remain for the time being in Concord with the Victor Barringers, while my Aunt Susan Morrison should take me to Lexington. Phyllis, my devoted nurse, was left behind, and a white woman, Miss Kate Bassinger, accompanied me in her stead.

We went first by rail to Raleigh, then by rail to Weldon, North Carolina, and from Weldon to Richmond, Virginia, where easy travel began by the James River Canal to Buchanan, a village near Lexington. I have been told that we took along a nanny goat to provide me with milk, bought for this purpose in Richmond, and that the nightly serenades of the bullfrogs, an endless chorus from dusk till dawn, were most delightful, but of this journey I remember nothing. I could talk, though, for my aunt says in a letter that I greeted her with the remark, "We comed here in a cage, and horses pulled it."

Actually two stout mules—not horses—were hitched to the towline of the canal boat, and a man riding one of the mules kept them to a speed of three miles per hour. The boat was fifty by eighteen feet, with cabins standing up to six or eight feet over the midline for nearly its entire length. These opened on a narrow outer passageway which led to small decks fore and aft. On top was a deck over the full length where passengers sat until warned, "Low bridge," when there was a scurry for safety below. Next to the galley, a saloon used for dining and sitting completed the accommodations. Traveling from Richmond we were mounting steadily above sea level, and every five or ten miles we came to a lock into which the boat was warped and water turned in until we were lifted to the stretch beyond, then on again by mule power to the next lock.

The construction of the James River and Kanawha Canal, to link the coal fields and the Piedmont agricultural lands with the sea, was undertaken in Virginia soon after the Revolutionary War. Although projected in 1785, the James River and Kanawha Company was not organized until 1835, and the construction of the canal to Lynchburg was completed in 1840 and extended to Buchanan in 1851. Much of it was destroyed during the Civil War, but even before that period railroad development had begun to consign it to oblivion. In its heyday, however, the canal was an important link between railroads and stage lines.

In Lexington the Jacksons lived some distance from the Virginia Military Institute, where the Jackson Memorial Hospital now stands, but I remember almost nothing of my visit—only the sun-down gun and the lowering of the flag at the Institute, and I have a hazy recollection of some gigantic demon coming across the field. That must have been the Cadet Corps marching in column.

I do not remember my aunt during this period and, much to her indignation, I had to confess when I was older that I had not the slightest recollection of her famous husband! She told me that I was devoted to him, and that it was he who taught me a silly little rhyme that I have remembered all my life:

I had a little pig and I fed him on clover,
And when he died, he died all over.

I have no doubt that all of this is true. Stonewall Jackson's fondness for children was well known, and I was probably very happy tagging around after him, but I do not remember it, and by no stretch of imagination can I recall who taught me the rhyme.

I remained in Lexington for two years, and I remember the return trip very clearly. Aunt Anna Jackson took me back to North Carolina, and my sister Anna, who must have been brought up on a visit, was with us. Returning by canal boat we were going downhill to Richmond; so when the boat ran into what appeared to be the end of the canal, the gates were closed behind us and the water allowed to run out until we reached the level of the lower stretch. As I stood at the rear, holding Anna's hand, I was entranced to feel the boat going down with the opening of the sluices. The gates were of wood, and in spite of caulking, there were some small knot holes through which the water poured, sometimes showering Anna and me. I can even now see the rugged base of a knot still in the hole which divided this shower into two parts, and I in turn philanthropically divided the shower between us.

In Richmond we stopped at the Exchange Hotel, and there I had another experience which remains distinct in my memory. Gaslight was new then, and I was always wanting to be lifted up to see the flash and to hear the "pop" when someone put a match to the gas jet.

From Richmond, Aunt Anna took us down to Charlotte, North Carolina, to visit another of my mother's sisters, Aunt Isabella, whose husband, Daniel Harvey Hill, was soon to become a general in the Confederate Army. Aunt Isabella had a new baby and she told me that his name was Harvey. (He grew up to become President Harvey Hill of the North Carolina State Agricultural and Mechanical College at Raleigh.) I was much struck with the name Harvey and stood repeating it as I gazed at my new first cousin.

A week later I was confronted with another new baby, the son of my nurse, Phyllis, and was told that this child belonged to me and that I was expected to name him. I stood ransacking my brain but could think of nothing but the name of the James River Canal, which I had heard so many times on my recent trip, and the name of my youngest cousin, Harvey. So I pieced the two together and named him "Harvey James River Canal"! In spite of the name he survived, and as a child was known simply as Harvey, but after freedom came he dropped the "Canal," added an S, and became Harvey James Rivers.

Phyllis, who was part of my mother's dower, was the granddaughter of a remarkable character named S'Quash. Tradition must have made his a fearful name with Cottage Home Negroes, for when Phyllis ever said, "Lemme'lone now, doan you know I'se de gran-chile uv S'Quash!" there was no further argument.

II

S'QUASH

THE ABOLITION of the slave trade was voted by the United States Congress in 1790, but the importation of slaves was prolonged by the votes of two states, Massachusetts and South Carolina. North Carolina, which was never at heart a slave state, had always carried a tariff on Negroes. However, the law was finally passed in 1804, to become effective January 1, 1808, that no more slaves were to be imported. With this fact in mind, a group of gentlemen, General Joseph Graham—my great-grandfather—Judge Robert Johnston Shipp, Mr. Peter Forney, Captain Alexander Brevard, and Mr. Robert McDowell, who owned adjoining plantations, made up a purse of $5,000 in gold which Mr. McDowell was to take to Charleston and bring back two wagon loads of young Negroes. There were three four-horse wagons and Mr. McDowell on horseback.

The wagons had high plank sides and stretched on hoops was a canvas top, drawn at the ends front and back on a rope to tighten it and also to create a round hole for ventilation or vision. Starting out the wagons were filled with hay and other provender for horses and men. Returning, one wagon would be used for replenishment enroute. Such a caravan would make about twenty miles a day, camping by the road at night, in winter sleeping in, and in summer sleeping under, the wagons. This journey, which is about 268 miles, would therefore take at least a month for the round trip, going from Machpelah to Camden, South Carolina, and on to Charleston on the King's Highway.

The King's Highway still exists, and seems a simple, narrow, dirt country road, but it was then regarded as a boulevard, because it had no stumps, was kept crowned by labor from all adjoining property, and starting from Charleston was marked with mile posts each bearing Roman numerals.

It was about mid-December when this caravan set forth, arriving in Charleston during Christmas week. There Mr. McDowell found a hectic scene. The legal date limit, January first, was rapidly approaching, and new slave ships were coming in daily to get under the dead line. It was a buyers' market. His choice was to be about sixteen boys, from twelve to sixteen years of age, not more than three speaking the same language; for at this age, they were most adaptable and promising, easier to train, and when unable to use their own language would learn English without effort or resentment. Mr. McDowell, still undecided about his purchases when the sun went down, and in view of new slavers arriving, planned to shop further in the morning. The captain, anxious to close the deal, clear his ship and depart, became more generous. For that amount, he would give not only the sixteen boys but an extra, a grown man of splendid muscle and build. No, he could not be seen now as he was in the hold, but come tomorrow, early.

At six o'clock Mr. McDowell was on deck, as he wanted to be on his way. City fare and lodging were high, and provender for his horses was preposterous. Also January weather was far more uncertain and inclement than December. On board, the captain was cordial, the selected black boys were standing on the deck, and four sailors went below to struggle up with a massive human burden, "hog-tied," and dangerously quiet. A strange tension possessed the whole group, slaver and slaves alike. Only Mr. McDowell was undisturbed. "I wish to see him standing and free," he said. "No," said the captain, "you can cut him loose on the dock, but he has been loose on the ship once and that was once too often." So they moved on shore, Mr. McDowell cut the ropes, and the captive rose slowly to his full height. In spite of the cramps, galls, and filth of constant confinement, he was a commanding figure. His clear-cut, aquiline features were extremely dark, like a Moor, and his straight black hair and beard, matted and foul from neglect, were not kinky. He was obviously not a Negro. He stood there quietly, his eyes appraising Mr. McDowell. In that split second, he must have decided that this was for him the end of the journey, that there was no returning, and to cast in his lot with his masters. "I will take him," said Mr. McDowell. "What is his nationality?" "To tell the truth, I don't know," answered the captain. "This was our last trip, and we wanted no vacancies, so that when the last consignment was brought in we didn't ask questions. But I've always thought some slave dealer was settling an old score."

The potential truth of this statement has been borne out by history. With the approaching close of the slave trade, far more ships appeared on the Guinea Coast than could possibly be provided with cargo; so the slave traders made raids upon the slave barracks or barracoons. In doing so, they got a number of Arabs, themselves slave traders, and their wives, concubines, and children. At the last minute, it was "The devil take the hindmost." To avoid incrimination and to render the captives less dangerous, the Yankee slave traders divided these Arab families up amongst their various ships, and S'Quash fell to this trader. It was a terrible fate, but no more or less than his system had meted out to others. It was in the final settlement a case of "Winner take all."

Mr. McDowell paid off and led his group, without incident, to the edge of town, where his wagons were waiting. There the young Negroes, who had never before seen a wagon or horses, were terrified. They thought that the fore and aft openings of the canvas top were a sort of Gorgon's mouth and themselves some potential sacrifice; they had to be bound before being poked into security. The new captive showed no concern but strode to the head of the wagons, motioned the driver aside and took up the reins of the four-horse wagon with an experienced air. Mr. McDowell calmed the insulted driver, who, of course, was a man of position, but said he wished to see what this man could do for a while, and they started forth. Nine miles out on the King's Highway, the mile post, which should have carried the

Roman numeral IX, had been damaged and replaced with a simple 9, an Arabic numeral. The captive stopped the wagon and held out his hands, showing five fingers of one hand and four of the other, a total of nine, thus proving that he could read Arabic and understood at least simple arithmetic, no mean achievement for a slave. To make a long story short, S'Quash, as he was called in a phonetic effort at his real name, was an Arab of a family long engaged in the slave trade; he had the advantages of travel and education of his day and class in that he had been to Cairo and could read Greek as well as Arabic. Greek was probably his first means of communication, as that language was then a part of a gentleman's classical education. Whatever his past, he definitely now threw in his lot with the ruling class. He was assigned to the Graham plantation and in spite of not knowing any English was treated with unfailing, and you might even say, unctuous respect by the other Negroes, who usually enjoyed patronizing the new arrivals as "green" hands and country cousins. He was given work around the "big house," in order to acquire some English and the pattern of living in this strange land. Such was his ability that he ultimately became head man on the plantation, succeeding in time the white overseer. He held himself completely aloof from the Negro slaves and would neither live nor mate with them, staying in a hut by himself. Ultimately he came to General Graham and informed him that he had learned (by that mysterious grapevine route peculiar to African communications) that many plantations away there was a Dinka Negress and asked permission to marry her. The famous tribe of Dinkas, who were noted and valued for their physique and intelligence, came from what is now called Anglo-Egyptian Soudan, about the center of Africa and near the White Nile, between Fashoda and Khartoum. In their subtle Arabic caste system she was eligible as a wife and was purchased by General Graham at a substantial figure, $3,000, which was a top price. Needless to say S'Quash and his Dinka consort and their superior progeny became valuable additions to the Graham estate.

One day, an itinerant portrait painter arrived at General Graham's. In the fashion of the day he was riding on a horse and leading a donkey loaded with the necessary equipment of paints, canvas, and material for frames. For a month's board and lodging for himself with keep for the steeds and thirty dollars apiece per portrait (frames to be selected and extra), he painted portraits of General Joseph Graham and his wife, Isabella Davidson. While these were in completion he saw S'Quash, was greatly taken with his appearance, and asked if he might make a sketch of him. Permission was given and he made a sketch, which he considered unsatisfactory and left, and then another which he took away with him. I wonder what museum it might be in now, and who the artist may have been! The discarded picture was promptly relegated to the attic, where fortunately it was found later.

On the death of General Graham and the settlement of his estate, S'Quash and his family became the property of his daughter, Mary Graham Morrison, my grandmother, and went to live at Cottage Home.

Tradition has it that one of my great-uncles decided to go to Mississippi to raise cotton in the rich and profitable delta lands and collected all the difficult slaves and runaway Negroes in that section, taking S'Quash with him to keep order on the journey; also, that S'Quash made a similar journey a few years later with more undesirables, this time on his own. If this last be true, it was an extraordinary and ironical achievement for an African slave trader to have achieved a similar position of authority in his transplanted existence and without his freedom.

Phyllis's son, whom I had named so heartily Harvey James River Canal, was the playmate and "body servant" of my childhood. When he grew up, since he showed promise and intelligence, my father, though slavery was over, had him educated at Biddle Institute, a school for Negroes near Charlotte, North Carolina. He decided to go into the ministry and became "the Reverend Harvey James Rivers, D. D." One day I was questioned by one of the Graham cousins about a queer picture in the attic, "not quite white and not quite colored" and did I know anything about it? It was the portrait of S'Quash, and since no one else wanted it, I sent for Harvey and gave it to him, saying, "Harvey, you should have this for I am sure you are the only Negro in the United States who has the portrait of his great-grandfather who was an Arab slave trader." Years have passed. As far as I know Harvey is dead, and I wonder what has become of that portrait too.

III

THE BIG HOUSE

THE STATE OF North Carolina had not yet seceded from the Union, but in view of the imminence of war, there was a rush to get married in the early months of 1861, such as has been noticed in recent years. My aunt, Susan Morrison, was to marry Alphonso C. Avery of Raleigh, and all of the family were to assemble for the wedding at my grandparents' house, Cottage Home.

The horizon of my childhood was enlarged by another medium of transportation when my sister and I, with Aunt Anna Jackson, made our journey over the Plank Road which ran from Charlotte to Lincolnton.

These plank roads, often called "the farmer's railroad," were toll roads chartered by the state and a great improvement over the primitive corduroy road. The bed was graded, low places either filled in or supported by trestles, and cuts made through the steeper hills. To make a road eight or ten feet wide, four stringers were laid in parallel rows, the spaces between being filled with earth or other material, then the cross planks, three inches thick, were laid on top. These were not spiked down, as their own weight and the dirt shoulders on either side kept them in place. When such roads were new and kept in repair, they were a boon to stage coaches and heavily loaded farm wagons which had the right of way over lighter vehicles.

Directly in front of Cottage Home the Plank Road divided and joined the road from Lincolnton to Beattie's Ford, forming a large triangle filled with enormous oaks. The house, which was set back about two hundred feet from the front gate, was a large twelve-room country mansion with the white columned porch and ample windows of that day. Sheltered by a large grove of hickory, pine, and oak trees, it was approached by a central driveway which ended in a small circle before the house.

Here my mother's parents lived, the Reverend Doctor Robert Hall Morrison and his wife, Mary Graham, and here they raised their family of ten children. Three of their six daughters, Isabella, Eugenia, and Anna, married men who became generals in the Confederate Army, Daniel Harvey Hill, Rufus Barringer, and Thomas Jonathan Jackson. After the war their youngest daughter, Laura, married Colonel John Edmunds Brown; Susan's husband, Alphonso Avery, was a major and later a judge of the Supreme Court of North Carolina, but James Irwin, Harriet's husband, was too old for the service. Three of the four Morrison sons fought for the Confederacy; Major William Morrison was a victim of the war, and Alfred was too young to serve. Joseph Graham Morrison, when a sixteen-year-old cadet at the Virginia Military Institute, joined the army and became a courier for his brother-in-law, General Stonewall Jackson, and Robert Hall Morrison also joined at sixteen. He served on General D. H. Hill's staff, was wounded, later captured and imprisoned at Fort Delaware. All of this family were gathered, with a fair collection of grandchildren, in this spacious Cottage Home. Only two were absent, my father, who had recently married Miss Rosalie Chunn, of Asheville, and must have been on his honeymoon, and Major Jackson, who was detained in Virginia by the crisis of affairs.

I am unable to describe my aunt's wedding as, ludicrous though it may be, the only thing that I can recall is my first sight and taste of bananas and pineapples. It is difficult to conceive how they were obtained in this remote country place, but they were certainly some of the last fruits imported before the blockade, as Aunt Sue was the last of the brides to enjoy a New York trousseau. There was, however, another incident which was for me the beginning of the war.

On the right hand side of the front gate at Cottage Home stood a thirty- or forty-foot hitching rack, adequate to take care of a dozen or more guest horses, with a sawn "upping block" at each end by which the ladies mounted. Along the rack and about three feet from the ground were half a dozen sixteen-inch feed boxes, three on each side, for the horses of guests who remained for dinner.

Rumbles of impending war were becoming more and more ominous, and almost all the weapons in the South had been transformed from flint and steel to percussion cap, a very simple process in which the flashpan was removed, the firing hole bored out and threaded, and a short offset containing the tube inserted. Of course the hammer had to be changed in the blacksmith shop from flint carrier to a blunt nosed striker.

Most of the horses were unaccustomed to firearms, and it was considered good practice to give them suitable training at home. At first this was done by exploding only percussion caps on the transformed horse pistols; and to make this noise joyous to the horses, after firing three caps and having them rear and pull, a lump of sugar for each horse was dropped into the feed boxes. Dropping the sugar was my task. I walked along on the safe side of the rack, dropping the lumps, and I can still remember how the horses went for them.

This was no simple matter, for in those days lump sugar was as gold. Cones of white sugar about eighteen inches high and a foot in diameter, invariably wrapped in blue paper, were sawn into cubes some three quarters of an inch square. The sawdust of this operation, carefully garnered to be used on fruits, was the forerunner of the pulverized sugar of today just as the cubes, cross-cut by hand, preceded the modern dominoes which we call lump or loaf sugar.

When fifteen or twenty caps were fired, and every time each horse was fed one, two, or three lumps in proportion to his state of fright, this rite became expensive. It was kept up, however, day after day, until in a week or two those horses would come full charge to the feed rack at the crack of a pistol shot.

At Cottage Home I was to spend many summers of my youth and naturally the place and its people not only influenced my development, but were stamped indelibly on my memory during this most impressionable period of my life.

As I remember him, my grandfather, Reverend Doctor Robert Hall Morrison, was a man who looked the invalid, but he ruled the place with an iron rod. I never knew any man more rigidly just or more genuinely kind, however, when you got through his armor of nineteenth-century reserve and dignity. I soon saw that, in a way, his iron was all "bluff," and as I was not afraid of him, we grew to be most intimate. I have no hesitation in saying that I was his favorite among his many grandsons. He presented me with a treasured set of *The Bridgewater Treatises*, an illustrated set of early scientific writings published under the patronage of Lord Bridgewater, which I am glad to say I still have. He was born in 1798, but he lived to know my older children and died at the age of ninety-one.

He was of the Morrisons of the Isle of Lewis in the Outer Hebrides, a seasoned seafaring folk. From there my forebears went to Ulster and came with the first Scotch-Irish to America about 1700. First of the Morrisons to move to North Carolina was Old Jim, of true Isle of Lewis type, who came, I have heard, with the reputation that "he killed more red Indians and more red liquor than any man in Pennsylvania." On the long trip South, several of his sons settled in Delaware and in Virginia, and most of them became, like my grandfather, Presbyterian ministers.

He became deeply impressed with the fact that few candidates for the ministry came from his Alma Mater, the University of North Carolina. Therefore, realizing the necessity for a Presbyterian college as a nursery for the church and its ministers, he brought before the Presbytery of Concord on March 12, 1835, a resolution for the establishment of a Presbyterian college, in which Presbyterian doctrines should be faithfully taught and expounded. This was unanimously adopted, and Doctors Morrison and Sparrow were appointed the financial agents. They raised the sum of $30,000 and started the college in 1837. An uncle of Mrs. Morrison gave four hundred acres for grounds, and in compliment to him, the college was named Davidson, in memory of the donor's father, General William Lee Davidson, a Revolutionary hero who was slain fighting against Cornwallis at Cowan's Ford.

Doctor Morrison sensed the approach of the Industrial Era which would change values from physical strength to mechanical skill, so in addition to the necessary classical training for the ministry, young men were to put themselves through college by manual labor under directed training. At the same time, others less consecrated would have practical training in mechanics, et cetera. As a collegiate idea this did not work. The serious young men were too much exhausted for classical study, while the less serious were indifferent to the point of rebellion; so "manual training" was ultimately abandoned. Nevertheless, it left its impression, for today Davidson College, while retaining its sectarian character, has achieved high standing in science.

Under the strain of the presidency of Davidson College, my grandfather's health broke down, and he retired to Cottage Home. Later he recovered sufficiently to carry on his ministry and supplied the pulpit at Unity Church near Beattie's Ford, then at Castanea Grove, and finally took one Sunday a month at Machpelah Church near Vesuvius Furnace, the old home church and burying ground of my grandmother's people, the Grahams.

To my grandfather's duties as minister and planter were added those of postmaster, and according to the custom of the day he could pass letters through the mails for fifty or a hundred miles simply with his approval and signature. I have a number of such letters without a sign of a stamp. The mail was delivered by stage over the near-by Plank Road to the overseer's house, the stage driver blowing his horn half a mile down the road so that somebody would be on hand to receive it. From there the mail bag was taken, unopened, to my grandfather.

My grandmother, Mary Graham Morrison, was a different type from my grandfather. She was full of fun and laughter, yet withal a great disciplinarian. Her brother, William A. Graham, prominent in public life until his death, was one of the outstanding men of his day: member of the North Carolina legislature seven years, serving twice as its speaker, United States Senator, Governor of North Carolina, and Secretary of the Navy under President Fillmore from 1850-1852. While in that office he suggested and organized the expedition to Japan under Commodore Matthew Calbraith Perry and the mission of Lieutenant William Lewis Herndon to explore the Amazon, two achievements whose results have been among the most important of the nineteenth century. Strangely enough, neither of these expeditions was considered notable in my world at the time, and certainly the admission of the Japanese to the family of nations was no matter for pride. He was unsuccessful as the Whig candidate for Vice President and for nomination for President but was state senator for three terms, before, during, and after the Confederacy. In the later Reconstruction days he was again elected to the United States Senate but, like others, was denied admission.

My mother and her sisters visited him frequently in Washington, and I remember him very well—he lived until 1875. He was the only man left over from the old regime who carried knee breeches, a ruffled shirt, long silk stockings, and silver buckles down to my day. These were for dress occasions, and he cut quite a figure garbed in this rare holdover from ancient times.

Both my Morrison and Graham ancestors came from Scotland, lived for a time in Ireland, and were, therefore, dubbed "Scotch-Irish." They were—particularly the Morrisons—strict Presbyterians and came to western North Carolina on the same great tide of migration that brought my Barringer ancestor, "Old Pioneer Paul," of central European culture and devoted affiliation with the Lutheran church.

The early history of both the county of Cabarrus and the town of Concord were intimately bound up with the Barringers. Long before this region was settled hunters killed buffalo in what ultimately became Cabarrus County, and even within the memory of my ancestors the streams in this part of the Yadkin Valley were watering places for buffalo. The topography of the land forced the principal stream to divide and, following the custom of the time, both forks were named indiscriminately Buffalo Creek. Anywhere else eventually they would have been called East and West Buffalo, but here, a century before I was born, they were stamped forever as Dutch Buffalo and Irish Buffalo. It came about in this way.

Sometime before the year 1750, my great-grandfather, pioneer John Paul Barringer, traveling down from Pennsylvania with a train of five or six wagons, camped near a creek not far from the present site of Mount Pleasant, North Carolina, during the confinement of his wife. He was seeking a homestead and, liking the land there, decided to settle. Others looking around also found this marvelous valley, and in a few years the Derrs, the Barnhardts, the Melchoirs, the Phifers (originally Pfeiffer), and other families had spread over the Dutch Buffalo section. There were Palatines, Oberlander Swiss, some French, and a few of other nationalities. But the dominant language was German—hence the name Dutch Buffalo.

In like manner, the Scotch-Irish had already come, settling in large numbers on the other creek which was first called Scotch-Irish Buffalo, a name too heavy to be carried, so it was ultimately shortened to Irish Buffalo. As a consequence of differences in temperament, language, and church affiliations, these Dutch and Irish Buffalo settlements were always at loggerheads.

German was John Paul Barringer's native tongue as he had been born and bred in the Duchy of Württemberg, but he also spoke French. He was jovial, well-liked, and a first settler. He also possessed natural qualities of leadership, and was readily acknowledged by his German and Swiss neighbors as an important and influential man in the Dutch Buffalo community.

As captain of the militia, he was obliged from time to time to parade his company at Charlotte, the county seat of Mecklenburg, a county which then embraced the territory of the famous creeks, Dutch Buffalo and Irish Buffalo. Although his commands were given in halting English, his frequent reprimands were shouted in German or French. This quaint practice—particularly his orders to "Right veel!" and "Left veel!"—caused ribald merriment among the Scotch-Irish spectators which they made no pains to conceal. Such levity was most offensive to Captain Barringer, as it was to his entire company, and he determined that eventually the section of Mecklenburg in which he lived should be cut off and named "Lorraine," as a tribute to his Huguenot background. This was extremely important to him, but it was not until after the Revolution that he considered the time ripe to petition the North Carolina General Assembly to grant the severance. By the year 1792 he was ready; he had influential friends in the upper house of the assembly and his son-in-law, Caleb Phifer, was a member of the lower house, while a complaisant gentleman, Stephen Cabarrus of Chowan County, occupied the speaker's chair. Opposition developed, however, and the now patriarchal "Old Pioneer Paul," who was watching the proceedings with carefully disguised anxiety, realized that the voting would probably result in a tie.

With the wisdom born of long years of dealing with his fellows, he knew that the time had come to sacrifice a part of his plan in order to save the rest. He rose from his seat and casually sauntered over to the chair to whisper into the speaker's ear, "Cabarrus, you vote by uns—we name the county by you!" The vote was tied; Mr. Cabarrus's help was given, and my great-grandfather saw to it that his whispered pledge was kept. In 1793 the newly formed Cabarrus County sent its first delegates to the legislature.

The new county included the lands of the Scotch-Irish on the Irish Buffalo along with those of Old Pioneer Paul and his neighbors on the Dutch Buffalo, but it did not signal the close of contention between the two sections. That went merrily on for many years. In fact, those stubborn people could not even agree on the location for a county seat. Year after year county court was held alternately in one of the churches of the rival communities and, according to tradition, the sheriff was obliged to use his smoke house for the detention of prisoners.

Although the farm lands in this valley were exceptionally rich, there was a god-forsaken pea-ridge between the two creeks so poor that it was practically untenanted. Common sense dictated that the top of this ridge, which was easy to drain, large enough for all purposes, and equally accessible to both sections, would be the obvious site for the county seat, but only after years of wrangling did common sense prevail. The rival factions together staked out a town, built a court house and jail, and in deference to the end of a bad situation named their town Concord. These two strongly diverse strains were at last happily blended when Rufus Barringer, grandson of the German pioneer, married my mother, "the beautiful Eugenia Morrison, of Cottage Home."

Cottage Home had been part of the dower of my grandmother, Mary Graham, when she married Robert Hall Morrison; it was a rich six-hundred-acre plantation in the vicinity of her maiden home. There was not a single house on this property, and it was far from any thoroughfare; so in order to connect it with transportation, my grandfather bought the adjoining two-hundred acre tract lying between it and the Plank Road which ran from Charlotte and Lincolnton.

There was a small house on this new tract which I remember as the overseer's house, but when Dr. Morrison moved his family to the plantation, this small house became their home. He named the place "Cottage Home," and subsequently transferred that name to the much larger house which he built several hundred yards farther in, thus giving his permanent home a name which continually required an explanation.

This house had a four-room basement story of stone and two upper stories of standard frame construction, with four rooms each, opening upon a wide hall, and a fairly useful attic. To the north, about fifty yards distant from the corner of the garden, stood the carriage house and beyond it lay the barns. A lane from the latter, leading down to the branch, facilitated the watering of the stock. There were many riding horses, for in those days the entire countryside traveled by horseback and riding was not the item of luxury that it is with half of the riders today. (As a child, youth, and early practitioner of medicine, I averaged a thousand miles a year on horseback up to the time that I was thirty-five years of age.)

The well used jointly by the "big house" and "quarters," but approached from opposite sides, was some fifty yards to the south; and at an equal distance beyond the well the quarters began and, extending backwards, formed an "L" which swung around in the rear of the house. There were six or eight cabins, "hewn and chinked," with brick chimneys instead of those made of "mud and sticks" usual in servants' houses of that period. So substantially were these cabins built that some of them were standing within recent years.

The "summer kitchen" in the South was always placed at a literally ludicrous distance from the house to rid the latter of noise, heat, and flies, and this necessitated an incredible number of servants for satisfactory living. The one at my wife's home in Virginia was not only one hundred and fifty yards from the house, but the path led sharply uphill and was crossed by a fence, making it necessary for the bearers of food to mount and cross a high stile! The summer kitchen at Cottage Home was little more than half that distance from the house, and time and again I have seen Negro boys with batter cakes coming on the run. On a rainy day, bringing in dinner was a sight for the gods. A procession of ancient crones from the spinning room walked beside the houseboys and girls, the food bearers, holding big cotton umbrellas over the roasts and puddings, but not over the bearers.

The spinning room, lighted by large gable windows, was over the summer kitchen, and there all the superannuated women who were not knitting or watching babies carded, spun, beamed, and wove cloth of both cotton and wool. Downstairs, beside the kitchen, a room about twenty by twenty feet, there was another larger room which held two big looms. Old men also helped with the carding and weaving, and in winter this room was kept cozy with a five and a half by eight foot fireplace. Keeping a roaring fire required about as much time and attention as did the looms.

The dyes used were domestic indigo, walnut, cedar, broomstraw, and copperas. When I was a child they still had the small flax wheels and a flax break, but as cotton was already superseding flax, they rarely used flax wheels except to spin sewing thread. All the cutting and sewing for everyone on the place was done in the basement of the house, my grandmother herself doing the cutting and the Negro girls and young women the sewing.

Of the younger Negroes there were relatively few by this time, as seven of the sons and daughters of the house had married, each of whom usually carried away as household servants a man, his wife, and several children. As a result of this custom there was left on the home place a disproportionate number of the old and infirm, a fact which throws an interesting light on the economic absurdities of slavery, although at the same time such a condition made for a greater skill in crafts.

At this period, I was told later, there were some thirty slaves on the Cottage Home plantation of whom at least half were over sixty and, perhaps, eight under sixteen. Of course, to a child all adults seem old—those who are wrinkled and gray, incredibly so—and I still remember how this group of Methuselahs impressed me.

One of the most impressive was a favorite servant of my grandfather, "Uncle Abram," who was headman under the overseer on the plantation. He really was a Methuselah, but his voice was rich and deep, and he was immensely proud of his skill in calling the hands together for work every morning. First the overseer blew a rousing blast on his horn—and in winter he blew it well before daylight—then would come Abram's long, far-reaching call, and woe betide any able bodied laggard who failed to appear! Abram was originally owned by the Grahams. He was very proud of that fact, and he doled out to me a wealth of tradition concerning the family at Vesuvius Furnace. I learned from him that it was my grandmother who brought the richest land and the larger proportion of property into the family, and if I had heard only his side of my mother's genealogy, I would certainly have believed that, relatively, the Morrisons were very ordinary people.

"Old Phyllis" was another Graham servant who had come into the Morrison household with my grandmother, and she too was a great power on the plantation. To my immature mind she was raised far above the other hands because it was her prerogative to run the "stuffing machine" at sausage-making time. She was the mother of my nurse, Phyllis; they were respectively daughter and granddaughter of old S'Quash.

In addition to the company of the relatives and friends who often visited at his house, Dr. Morrison had the advantage of living in a community which was unusually rich in good neighbors. In front of his place on the Charlotte Plank Road lived Dr. Humphrey Hunter and also Dr. Sidney Johnston, the latter distinguished physician being a kinsman of the great Confederate general, Albert Sidney Johnston. Judge Robert Johnston Shipp lived still nearer, to the right of Cottage Home, and to the left was the home of Dr. Thornwell, a distinguished divine of South Carolina who came early in the war to Lincoln County as a refugee. The Hokes, McBees, and other well-known families lived near by in Lincolnton. Altogether they formed a community in which an invalid could easily meet with men of culture and world wide experience.

Among my grandfather's friends, as far back as the forties, friendly cooperation was practiced in the manufacture of alcoholic liquors, or "spirits" as they were called, twice a year; brandy from fruits in the summer, and whiskey from grain in the winter. Nearly every plantation owned a still, but Dr. Johnston had a twenty gallon blocked-tin still which he worked for the community. The Reverend Doctor Morrison owned a very cold spring. One of Judge Shipp's Negroes was famous for his finish on fine spirits. So the Judge, the parson, and the doctor united semi-annually in providing the spirits then much needed for *medicinal purposes.*

I once saw my aged grandfather pouring out a drink for Abram, who was almost as old as he was. As his wavering hand roamed back and forth over the glass, very little went in. "Marse Hall," Abram said, "what you pourin' in dar?" "Abram, this is spirits," my grandfather told him, and Abram replied, "Den dat's all right, Suh, but you was so keerful uv it, I thought it might be laudanum."

IV

THE PLANTATION

IN THOSE antebellum days it might be a number of years before the whole of an extensive plantation was cleared and made ready for cultivation. Forest growth was left standing until the land was needed for crops. Additional land was needed every few years, not always, as might be supposed, to increase the acreage under cultivation, but rather to maintain the status quo—the reason for this being that, because of the lack of suitable or even adequate quantities of fertilizers, cultivated lands rapidly deteriorated into the "old field" class. Such lands were then abandoned and a new clearing made. There was to some extent at least a rotation of crops, but soil conservation, as we understand it, was practically unknown.

It was, therefore, only a question of acreage and time before a plantation reached the exhaustion stage. Long before the 1850's many farms along the eastern seaboard had reached this impoverished condition, which is evidenced by the western movement from the older settlements into Kentucky, Tennessee, and the Middle West.

In western North Carolina at this time the problem of depleted soil was not serious—certainly it was not at Cottage Home, the plantation that I knew best. Although there were fields that had already been abandoned, there still remained a wealth of uncleared virgin land. Rich bottom land it was, too, on the original six hundred acres which lay a considerable distance from the big house.

So, when the overseer's horn, supplemented by Abram's lusty call, sounded bright and early on a winter morning, the hands might be ordered to hitch the mules to one wagon and steers to a couple of others, assemble their tools, and make their way to some uncleared acre. They would be gone all day, so the women prepared a lunch; a hot supper would await them on their return in the evening, but much work must be done meanwhile. The overseer led the way on horseback, and the cavalcade started.

Arriving at their destination, they attacked the forest as though it were some stalwart enemy. It was magnificent timber, oak, forest pine (now unknown), and hickory, of which nothing was saved. Only poles of sound hickory and forest pine were rolled to one side for winter firewood, the most choice of these being reserved for use in the fireplaces of the big house. All the discarded timber was dragged to a pile and burned.

Working a new ground, as it was called, was a master craftsman's job. First the trees were chopped almost through with the three-or-four-pound axe, the most important single implement on any plantation. Then they were thrown with ox chains and limbed. The stumps were left in the ground, but the top roots were cut away to a depth of some six inches. This was done with a coulter, a cutting instrument attached to the beam of a plow drawn, of course, by the patient steer. Behind came another long-suffering steer drawing the bull-tongue, an old fashioned plow, having a well-sharpened plate of iron—not steel—eight or ten inches long by four inches wide and one-half inch thick. Pointed slightly and bent at one end to resemble a tongue, it was bolted through a square hole at the other end to the carrier of the plow. Next came the twister—that was mule drawn. The metal part was keystone shaped, somewhat thinner than the bull-tongue, but resembling it except that it flared out into a wing at the upper end and was much narrower below; its average width was about six inches, and as it plowed it delivered nearly three-fourths of the earth on one side, and a good fourth on the other. Incidentally, I will say that there was only one cast mould-board plow on the place, and that was so large that it was drawn by four mules and used for "bedding cotton."

When the new ground was thus made ready for planting the first crop was corn. Next came oats, sown broadcast and plowed under with the twister. The following year, not as a fertilizing agent but as food for the hands, the field was put in cow peas, the planting being done in the following unique manner. Three twisters were used for the plowing; one following another, they dodged around the stumps and made, collectively, an eighteen-inch cut. An old man of skill and experience followed along behind the last twister trailing a tin horn through which he drilled the seed into the open furrow. This placed the peas in an eighteen-inch drill where, when they began to grow, they could be worked with a three-toothed harrow, later to be gathered and beaten out for food. Wheat was grown the fourth year and cotton the next. Then, unless the land was of unusual richness, it was turned out as "old field" and another field cleared in the same manner for planting.

Under such conditions it was impossible to use machinery, but the men attained a skill with hand implements that is practically unknown today. At cradling time, Judge Shipp, Doctor Thornwell, Doctor Sidney Johnston, and others sent their best hands to help with the harvest. To see a dozen husky blacks walking abreast across the wheat field and keeping time in their swing was an impressive sight.

In such a country where large areas were still covered with forests of oak, the mast constituted the main feed for the hogs. At Cottage Home the herd of hogs averaged one hundred head or more; these were allowed to range during the summer, but in the early fall of each year they were brought in to a new pen which was built several hundred yards behind the house. There they were fed corn until the soft acorn-produced fat was hardened; then they were killed. Even now I can remember that the lot in which the hogs had been confined was used the next spring for raising onions and the next fall for turnips.

In old plantation life, hog-killing time was a great occasion for the children. There was no mock sentimentality then—no idea of secluding the children, certainly not the boys, from such scenes. We boys went down as a matter of course and saw the hogs struck on the head to stun them, then "stuck," or stabbed, with a long-blade knife, and finally their throats cut. In a few moments—a very few moments sometimes—they were thrust, dead but still warm, into a hogshead of hot water. The water was kept at high temperature by a continual renewal of hot stones from a near-by bonfire. In less than half an hour we were given the freshly cut off tails; and I may say that the first three or four joints of a pig's tail, roasted in the embers and eaten without salt or pepper, is indeed a delectable morsel, one which I remember with pleasure to this day. The balance of the tail went to the pickaninnies. The next few weeks in the big house and the quarters were indeed memorable times for me, for in one place or the other I ate my fill of spare ribs, chine, jowl, liver, sausage, crackling bread, and all the unmentionables from tripe to "chitlins."

Looking back now, there are only two things which strike me as incomprehensible in that land of good living. One was the paucity of fruits, except berries, and the other was the scarcity of milk. In season, in the big garden at the right of the house, my grandmother had strawberries, raspberries, gooseberries, and currants. I never saw a greater abundance of these garden fruits anywhere, and there were some cherries but almost no apples or peaches. As to milk, it seemed as if they looked upon that as something exclusively for infants or the sick. I cannot recall ever having seen at most more than two or three cows in milk on the plantation. Instead of raising milk cows it was customary to buy them fresh. Nevertheless, as four of the Morrison sisters lived to the age of eighty or beyond, and my grandfather, the invalid of the family, was ninety-one when he died, we cannot say that they suffered from undernourishment or an unbalanced ration.

One of the most interesting things on the old plantation was the cotton gin, built by traveling ginwrights. The gin house was a one-and-a-half story structure, about thirty by sixty feet, and built of logs. One half of the lower floor was open with outside pillars rising to the second floor, the upper half story being used for storing cotton in the seed. At one end was the gin, driven by a belt from a revolving pulley below, the latter being driven by the traction of eight mules hitched to four revolving arms properly spaced below. A large horizontal toothed wheel, ten or more feet in diameter, revolving above the mules meshed into a "squirrel-cage" gear on a horizontal shaft (under which the mules walked), the cage gear being at one end and the pulley at the other. It was a simple mechanism, but it required a good wheelwright and his "chist."

Now I have to report a fact which in this day and time seems utterly incredible. When, after twenty years of service, the cotton gin had built up a dump pile of cotton seed that was fully as large as the gin house, my grandfather contemplated moving the gin to another site, as that seemed simpler than moving the rotting dump of seed which was considered useless rubbish. Even in 1864, however, some idea of the chemical value of this decomposing mulch had reached Cottage Home. Grandfather reluctantly ordered the dump pile removed and placed in the corn and cotton furrows. The results were so satisfactory that this plantation became thereafter the missionary of a new faith.

The object of real magnificence in this primitive cotton industry of the Old South was the cotton press. Because of the present inadequacy of suitable lumber in that section, such a cotton press as we had could hardly be built today.

To work the press a mule walked around and around in a sixty foot circle, hitched to one end of a revolving pair of oblique timbers joined above like a pair of calipers. These were balanced at their union on the summit of an immense wooden screw, eighteen inches in diameter outside the threads and threaded for a distance of twelve or fifteen feet. The nut through which this big screw descended was held up, twelve or fifteen feet above the ground, by immense timbers and in itself consisted of four white oak sections, two feet square and ten feet long. These four timbers were held together by ten- or twelve-inch square hickory and white oak braces and black locust wedges. When the big screw came slowly down, revolved by a sprightly mule, 500 pounds of cotton could easily be compressed into a standard bale.

V

CAMP FOLLOWER

DURING THE WINTER of 1861 my father had married Miss Rosalie Chunn, of Asheville, North Carolina, a cousin of Uncle Victor's wife. I was not taken to the wedding, but when I returned from Cottage Home to Concord my father's house was at least nominally my home during the short time that my stepmother lived. She was a lovely woman, and I grew very fond of her, but Uncle Victor and Aunt Maria's was still a second home.

Although Maria Massey, my uncle's wife, was born in Pennsylvania, she was brought as a child to Morganton, North Carolina, and I never in my life heard her called a Yankee. She was widely traveled, a painter of unusual merit, and one of the most charming letter writers I have ever known. Having no children of her own, she was like a mother to Anna and me, and surely she was a long suffering woman, for by all accounts I was a lively boy.

I was ready to try anything, and the following incident which occurred when I was about five years old is a fair example. I had seen old Ellen, a half-Indian woman, draw water at my Uncle Victor's well, and after watching her many times, I came to the conclusion that I could do it myself. So one bright afternoon when no one was in sight I made the attempt, and at first I thought I was wonderfully successful. I don't suppose the bucket was more than half full or I could not have drawn it up, and it was not until it reached the mouth of the well that the trouble began. My arm was not long enough to reach the bucket, so holding the crank with one hand, I leaned far over and hooked the fingers of my other hand under the bucket to bring it in, but that loosened my grasp on the crank and the bucket began to sink, whirling the crank with rapidly increasing force. I was angered at the humiliation as much as I was alarmed by the catastrophe, and closing in on the revolving crank handle, I tried to seize it. In return for my misplaced confidence I was carried, badly injured, into my uncle's house, and although I was attended by Doctors Fox and Bingham, the best physicians in town, I nearly died. They did not move me home for a week, and ever since I have borne a three-inch scar on my forehead.

Both my father and Uncle Victor volunteered immediately upon the outbreak of the war. My father organized a cavalry company, of which he was elected the captain, and which was later designated as Company F in the First Regiment of the North Carolina Cavalry. I recall seeing this company drawn up on Main Street in front of my father's law office, while he received a flag presented by a troop of girls and older women. I find from the records that the presentation was made on May 18, 1861, and the flag, as I remember it, was a small flag like the National flag except that it bore five bars in place of thirteen and had nine stars in the blue, thus representing on the bars the five original states which had seceded and on the field the total number of nine states of the Confederacy. The early wild-cat flags, such as the one presented to my father, were sent home to be treasured in many an officer's family. Ours is still preserved.

I distinctly remember being taken to see my father's company drilled in the suburbs of Concord near a cotton factory, and I recall the filial pride with which I regarded him as he rode at the head of his men. Having been a fox-hunting boy he was ultimately a superb rider.

In June, his men being in need of better mounts, he was ordered to take them to Asheville, where good mountain horses were available in abundance and where other companies of the

First North Carolina Cavalry were organizing and drilling. He of course led his company on horseback, while my new mother took Anna and me by train and stage coach to join him in Asheville. We went by the North Carolina Railroad to Salisbury and then by the Western North Carolina to a point twelve miles beyond, which I think was called Pioneer Mills. There we took the stage coach to travel through some one hundred and fifty miles of magnificent scenery to our final destination.

Today there are few people living who can recall traveling in the old English stage coach which was adopted in America, so it may be of interest to describe it.

The coach consisted of a strongly-braced platform united to the rear axle and "fifth-wheeled" over to the front axle. This gridiron-like platform was built on a running gear a little heavier than the average four-horse wagon "box and skein." The brakes on the rear wheels slid under this platform, and the braking mechanism, from foot lever to good black locust blocks, was superb for the mountain work for which it was constructed. Fore and aft on either side of this platform rose an enormous gooseneck steel spring, from which the body of the coach was suspended by multiple leather hangers, designed to make riding easy. The coach body held, according to width, from nine to twelve people. Three fat men could sit on the front and the rear seats, and an equal number of less substantial passengers on the removable middle seat, which when in use was anchored on a beam between the two doors. An immense leather-covered rack extended out four feet or more behind the coach to hold the cowhide trunks and other luggage. The driver sat outside with the mail bags under him and the seat of honor beside him. On some coaches there were three or four much sought after passenger seats above the driver on the front edge of the coach body. It seemed that the driver's chief occupation was the proper manipulation with his foot of the long brake lever to control the back wheels. He could almost bring his team to a standstill when he stood on the brake and used its full thrust.

They changed horses every eight or ten miles. Upon arriving at a changing point the driver handed his lines to a hostler who reached over and lifted a large pin from the forehound to loosen the pole and doubletrees. The team walked out and was quickly replaced. Ordinarily a team consisted of four good horses, but on this mountain line between Old Fort and Gray Eagle six horses were needed.

I remember little or nothing of this trip until we reached Morganton, where we must have remained for some time. I was taken to see friends and relatives in the neighborhood, the McKessons, the Tates, the Irwins, and best of all we went to Swan Pond, the old Avery homestead, and now the home of my aunt, Susan Morrison Avery. When we resumed our journey my seat was on top of the coach between my mother and Hetty, a maid whom we had borrowed from Cottage Home. The driver, like most of his kind, must have talked about bears, catamounts, wild cats, and other "varmints," for I recall that I would not have been surprised or very much scared had a sabre-toothed tiger appeared in the road. When I was older—for I made this journey many times in my youth—there was a stage driver of wonderful skill and character whose name was Spence or Pence. He always expected to see a bear somewhere in the twenty miles beyond Old Fort. I saw a bear only once, but I saw many pheasants, wild turkey, and a few deer. Most of the road bed was raised with surface earth, and in damp places it was corduroyed, but, nevertheless, by modern standards a journey over such a road would be regarded as trying, and even at that time it was hardly considered the height of comfort.

At Old Fort we took on two more horses, thus giving me a remembrance of my first six-horse team. Now instead of the steady trot we had maintained, we were reduced to a steady pull, with occasional descents where the stage driver literally stood on his brake. Unconsciously I was getting that feeling of awe which so often grew upon us as we watched the marvellous mastery of those old mountain drivers. We dropped our extra horses at Gray Eagle, a point now named, I believe, Black Mountain, and started down the easy grades to the beautiful Swannanoa River. This river of Cherokee Indian name, poetically translated "nymph of beauty," joins the French Broad River near Asheville and flows therefrom into the Mississippi and the Gulf. We followed the stream until we were near the old Cheeseborough place, now "Biltmore"; there we turned to the right and climbed up to Asheville.

Our destination in Asheville was the home of Mr. Chunn, my stepmother's father. I spent the summer there and was given the run of the place, several acres in extent, reaching almost to the French Broad. I learned to recognize the mountain peaks, Mount Pisgah and the Rat, Craggy, Beau Catcher, and others. It was on Beau Catcher that I first saw a flock of wild pigeons. I was to see one of their immense roosts in Amherst County, Virginia, ten or twelve years later, and then in a few decades this great American bird, so often noted in the old records, was extinct.

On this visit to Asheville I saw my first real Indians. A thousand or more "civilized" Cherokees lived in Cherokee County, some distance west of Asheville. When United States troops carried the bulk of the Cherokee nation to the old Indian Territory, these members of the tribe, having passed the blanket stage, were allowed to remain. They still retained their skill with bow and arrow and for special occasions preserved their special dress and peculiar ball games, but they were good citizens.

In the Chunn household was a Mrs. Patton, a sister of my stepmother, who had lost three children in one week of diphtheria, a calamity which as a practitioner of twenty years standing before the coming of antitoxin, I saw many times repeated. And there was Billy Hilliard, a boy about my age, who in a frenzy of rage said he was going to stick a fork in his eye, which he did, injuring it beyond remedy. Even then, I thought he had miscalculated the distance and did not really mean to carry out his threat.

In August my father was ordered to take his company to Camp Beauregard in Warren County, near Ridgeway. My new mother and Anna went to Ridgeway by train, a tedious journey with many detours, but for some reason my father wanted to take me with him, so I went with the troops. I rode in an ambulance by day and slept in a tent at night, my father's body servant acting as my nurse! In these days that seems an incredible procedure, but at that time most Southern gentlemen were under the delusion that a body servant was, between battles, a necessary attachment. They were going through the stage of mental evolution that preceded facing the facts. I enjoyed my camp experience. In Ridgeway we stayed with a family named Woodson and there I met my first five-year-old sweetheart, whom I have never seen since.

Soon those early, lackadaisical days of the war were over, and body servants, women, and children went to the rear for good.

The First North Carolina Cavalry was ordered from Camp Beauregard to Manassas, Virginia, where in the preceding July the battle of First Manassas, or Bull Run, had been fought. Soon after his arrival my father wrote a letter to Anna and me, as follows:

"Bull Run
"Octr. 30, 1861

"My Dear Little Children:

"Papa is at last where the *War* is. Tonight we camp on a battle field where a great battle was fought—when the Yankees came to kill our people & our people killed them. . . . I have seen the Big Guns on great big wagons with which they shot the Yankees and made them run away. There are so many people here come to the war (like Papa did) to fight the Yankees [again] if they come back . . . but Papa hopes the Yankees will never come back any more and that he can soon return home to see his dear little Rats & Mamma & Aunt Ria & Uncle Victor & all the friends. . . . Uncle Jackson [Stonewall] is here. Uncle Jackson asked so many questions about the children. There [are] some little cadets here too.

"Papa saw so many towns when he was coming here, and so many big Rivers and long Bridges & Railroads.

"There are no little children here. The war has frightened them all away. You must both pray that the war will never come near you & Mamma. Pray for Papa too—that the bad Yankees will not kill him; but that the Lord will preserve us all.

". . . [Do] my little children learn their lessons . . . ? Do they say their questions [Catechism]? Do they gather chips for Aunt Phyllis? I think sister Anna will soon knit Papa a pair of socks. I know she helps Mamma to keep house.

"Now my Dear Children, farewell. Papa prays for you very

often, and hopes you will always be good children and be good to each other & to Mamma and nurse her & wait on her when she is sick. You must write me a letter some of these days & tell me what you do—how many chickens . . . how many fattening hogs, how many calves and all about the other things at home. . . .

"Papa sends you ever so many kisses—You must give some to Mamma & some to Aunt Ria. Tell Uncle Alfred & Aunt Phillis & Elmira [servants] howdye. Mike, Jack & all the servants & all the men say, "Tell Pauly and Anna howdye for me." And now may the good Lord ever protect & bless you is your father's prayer. From

"Papa."

This letter, evidently written under great stress and probably with many interruptions, was followed by others equally affectionate and full of concern for our conduct and welfare.

VI

UNCLE VICTOR

AFTER HAVING trailed the army over a considerable part of North Carolina, I returned to Concord and began learning my way around my native town. I played around McDonald's cotton factory and the Court House and knew the street up and down between the two for that was where my friends and playmates lived. I was getting along very nicely when my uncle Victor came home on a stretcher. He had been shot through both hips at Manassas and appeared to be a hopeless cripple, but in another six months he was using a wheel chair and smoking one or two pipes after each meal. As soon as he began to ask for his pipe his friends knew that he was getting better, and I can still remember the heated arguments between "old man Wash" Allison and Uncle Victor over the relative merits of Sally Michael and Powhatan pipes. It was natural that with my father away I should see more of this brother of his who was to act *in loco parentis* to me for the rest of the war.

Victor at a very early age had entered the University of North Carolina. There in his sophomore year, because of some reflection that he resented made by the professor of French who was a New Englander, he got into a wrangle with this gentleman, who had hitherto been a good friend. Feeling that the difference in age and size—some twenty years and about a hundred pounds —justified some outside resource, young Victor supplemented his armament with an inkwell. The University authorities apparently took a sympathetic view of the case, as they simply suspended him for one year, and my grandfather sent him to finish his sophomore year at Gettysburg College, Gettysburg, Pennsylvania.

In due course, Victor returned to Chapel Hill and was graduated in 1848. Then he went to Washington and studied law with his elder brother, Daniel Moreau Barringer, who was at that time a Whig member of Congress. During his stay in Washington, Victor had abundant opportunities to observe some of the famous lawmakers in action on the floor of the Senate and the House and to know them personally in the homes of his brother and his uncle, Daniel L. Barringer. He became so impressed with Henry Clay, glorified as "the mill boy of the slashes," that although he was baptized simply as Victor, he then adopted Clay as his middle name, and that name has been perpetuated for several generations in the family. Another friend was Hamilton Fish who was Whig representative from New York.

About this time President Zachary Taylor appointed Daniel Moreau Barringer as United States minister to Spain, and the minister took with him, as his personal secretary, his red-headed young brother, now known as Victor Clay Barringer. They stopped in Paris, and the letters of young Victor there and from Madrid were published serially in the one weekly newspaper of Concord.

In Spain the new minister's secretary became a great favorite because of his youth, his gifts as a linguist, and, particularly, his red head. Soon, however, he was in trouble, both financial and feminine, and a convenient "weakness of the lungs" made it advisable for him to spend the winter in Morocco.

If his red hair had been a *casus mirae* in Spain, imagine what it was in North Africa! Without going into details, I will merely say that he went where he wished, and wherever he went he was always welcome. On camelback he traveled with caravans south to Fez and eastward along the coast almost to Libya. Being a natural linguist, he picked up colloquial Arabic with ease and was so popular with the natives that they made him a tribal mascot. He also learned as much of the structure of the language as the study of an Arabic grammar printed in French, without other instruction, could give to one who already knew Latin, Greek, French, German, and Spanish.

Returning to North Carolina a few years later, he married and became professor of belles lettres at Davidson College, but his temper being too tremendous for pedagogy, he soon resigned to practice law in Concord.

Of course when the war broke out he enlisted and, with the rank of major, became aide to General Ransom. It was at First Manassas that he received the wound which sent him home. His red head stood him in good stead, and although he was a wheel chair invalid for some years, he was able to resume his law practice about a year after his return. Throughout the war he was an agent of the Confederate Government and acting through blockade runners kept up a steady foreign correspondence.

After the war he was a member of the North Carolina Code Commission to codify the laws of the state; following that he was called to Washington to assist Judges Boutwell and Abbott in the codification of the laws of the United States. One day while he was engaged in that work, an old friend of antebellum days, Hamilton Fish, by that time the Honorable Hamilton Fish, Secretary of State, said to him, "Victor, don't you speak a little Arabic?" "I once had a smattering," Victor replied. Thereupon Mr. Fish explained that Ismail Pasha, Khedive of Egypt, had asked the State Department to send an American representative to the Mixed Tribunals of Egypt, the only conditions being that the nominee be a jurist of distinction and have some knowledge of Arabic. And so my uncle was appointed to the Mixed Tribunals, who sat as admiralty judges in Alexandria, their first duty being admiralty jurisdiction over the Suez Canal and as appellate judges in Cairo. Thus it was that he, who was never on the bench in his own country, became an American judge in Egypt and retained the title for the rest of his life. He remained in this service for twenty-five years and then returned to Washington, where he died a few years later.

In those youthful days I was too inexperienced to recognize that this relatively young uncle of mine was a great man, but I did recognize in him an intensity of purpose, a devoted loyalty, and an unconquerable will, which in later years I knew were qualities of the great.

My friendship with Uncle Victor gave me an early introduction to a lifelong habit. He had a dozen or more Sally Michael clay pipes, made somewhere near Morganton, with a full complement of two-foot hollow fig stems. Being familiar with the hookah used in the Orient, he once tried to make one himself, assisted by Aunt Maria and me, but he said that our nargileh was a poor performer and went back to his Sally Michael. We had no matches in the Confederacy then, but we always had an open fire, so after he filled his pipe it was my duty to take it to the fire and deftly place a burning coal on the packed tobacco. Often it went out two or three times before I could get it to him, so he sagely suggested, "Stick the stem in your mouth and pull—like this—when you are bringing it to me." As this new procedure added much pleasure to my duties I never failed to follow it, and by the end of a month I was blowing smoke out of my five-year-old nostrils in a way that would horrify any sister-in-Israel who might be present. So, I may say, I have been smoking rather consistently for more than seventy years! A "chaw" of tobacco, however, is different—that gives a real kick. A couple of years later, when I first tried one, there were dire results.

It was about this time that we acquired a new member of the family, a Negro man who had belonged to some member of the Washington family down at Little Washington, in North Carolina. Jim, for that was his name, was captured by the Federal troops and used by them as a servant in one of their hospitals; but in about a year, tiring of his so-called freedom, he ran away from the Yankees and came home. As he had some training as a nurse, Uncle William Graham (whose wife was a Washington) thought that he might be useful to Uncle Victor in his crippled condition. We bought him, and he started in his new home under the name of Yankee Jim.

I shall never forget my astonishment when I learned from Yankee Jim that Yankees were very much like other people; at least they differed in no marked essential—each one had two feet, two hands, and a head, like other folks. He thought they might be a little shy of heart, but the only way he could think of in which they really differed was that they were *scared to death of rebels!*

When my uncle was lying wounded at Manassas he saw a singular war trophy driven in to Confederate headquarters by a laughing soldier. It was a miniature spring wagon, containing a bass drum, kettle drum, cymbals, and all the string and reed instruments of a regimental band. Hitched to it was a very small pony, one of that mysterious breed that we in North Carolina call a "banker." These ponies are found running wild on Atlantic coastal islands from Cape Fear to the mouth of the Delaware. Up in Virginia and Maryland they call them Assateague and Chincoteague ponies, but we always referred to them as "bankers." This strange outfit was found after the battle, abandoned in a fence corner, and it caused much merriment among our troops. Then and there Uncle Victor determined to buy that pony for me. He wrote to the Confederate Remount Department, and in the course of time the pony turned up in Concord, led by a wounded soldier riding a crippled mule.

He was small even for a banker—less than ten hands high—and he carried numerous brands. On one flank was that of his original owner, on the other U. S.; on one shoulder C. S. and on the other CD, for condemned. Certainly he would never be lost for lack of identifying marks. He was four or five years old, active and capable, but positively the most obstinate and stubborn little brute that was ever wrapped up in the same amount of hide.

Riding was no luxury in those days—it was a necessity. Children of four or five were put on work horses and allowed to ride them down to the spring when they were brought in from the fields to be fed. By this time, therefore, I was accustomed to horses, and I learned to ride my new steed very soon. At first I rode him bareback, but this was very hard on my clothes, so they got me a quilted leather pad attached to a surcingle, on which were riveted two loops for stirrups. With these supports I could not be unseated, and I have often thought that such a device is a vast improvement over the stirrup in teaching children to ride. It does not come up like a stirrup.

On sight I named my steed Rebel-Victor, and this came about as the result of an earlier family row. Some members of the family were not at all in favor of the war, particularly my aunt Margaret Barringer Grier, who was twenty years Uncle Victor's senior. He, on the other hand, hot-headed and impetuous, was literally rabid. Somehow Aunt Margaret must have sensed coming trouble, for she later lost five sons in the war, and when the talk of war started she did not hesitate to upbraid her young brother for his strongly expressed support of the Confederate cause, always adding in a loud tone, "You are nothing but a rebel, Victor!" *Rebel-Victor* caught my fancy. I pondered it, and repeated it to myself in quiet moments. When my pony came his name was ready.

I had a small dog too, a black and tan terrier, named Snap. Although fully grown, he could not have weighed over ten pounds, and whenever I rode Rebel-Victor, Snap always trailed behind. He was my devoted friend, and when he died from the kick of a mule, I gave him a funeral which still brings me much satisfaction. Every child in the neighborhood was there, and Jimmy Anderson, the son of a minister, preached the funeral.

I used to ride out into the country to visit my relatives. First I rode to Bellevue to visit my aunt Katie Barringer who married General Means, and ere long I rode with a wagon to the home of my aunt Betty Barringer, whose husband was Mr. Edwin Harris. She was a little woman of rare intellect and culture, and it was her husband who imported from India a trio of the sacred or Brahman cattle, thus vastly improving the work cattle of Cabarrus County by adding at least 20 per cent to the daily plowing allotment of an ox team.

While I was staying there, Rebel-Victor was foundered. At home we fed him on hay with a mere handful of oats, but here the Negroes gave him the standard feed of "ten ears of corn," and it was too much for him. So they made a mud hole of soft, well-worked red clay, six or eight inches deep, and kept him standing in it for a couple of days. That cured him, and I rode him home, but I had to ride at a slow pace for several days.

One afternoon when I was riding in the lower part of Concord near Weincoff's tannery, I saw little piles of dried tanbark burning along the sides of the street for several hundred yards. I had never seen this done before, so on my return I asked Uncle

Victor what it meant. He said he did not know, but he seemed to be troubled. The next day I saw other smouldering fires, all of which were of something unusual, bits of old woolen clothing, onion hulls, all sorts of things that made a disagreeable odor. When I reported this to Uncle Victor, he and Aunt Maria talked it over and said it must be smallpox. He sent me immediately with a note to Doctor Scott, a refugee from Virginia newly arrived in the town. We applied the term "refugee" to residents of a war section, fleeing before the Federal armies, and even as a child I noticed that most refugees had families of daughters. We were very glad when Doctor Scott, who had been wounded and assigned to civilian practice, settled in Concord, for by that time the only physician left in the town was an octogenarian. Doctor Scott came over to discuss the matter with my uncle and aunt, and I was a close listener. I learned that the Negroes and poor whites thought foul smelling smoke was the best way to banish plague and pestilence, and that no amount of reasoning or persuasion could alter their age-old belief.

The result of this council of war was the decision that I should be vaccinated, and I welcomed it as any child welcomes the ultra and modern. The doctor stated that he had half a dozen or more scabs taken from the arms of healthy children, and as a special favor he would use on me the scab from his young daughter.

He then proceeded to take from his pocket and wipe on his handkerchief a small edition of a Roman broadsword. He scraped my upper left arm until he got off all the dirt and dermis, epi and otherwise, and brought about a pink discharge of fluid over the entire surface nearly as large as a dime. On this he placed a little of the precious balm and rubbed it in with the flat of the same handkerchief-disinfected broadsword. I stood it very well, thinking that was part of the game, and for about a week nothing happened. Then I had an arm to remember, with a permanent scar the size of a silver dollar.

That smallpox outbreak proved to be a very serious epidemic. There were many funerals and many disfigurements. This reminds me of a remark my grandfather made when he was a very old man. It was about 1885, when I had been a practicing physician for nearly ten years. A young girl came bouncing into his room, and he turned around to me and said, "Isn't her complexion magnificent? Do you know, son, that until I was old enough to vote I rarely saw a woman that was not pock-marked!" As he was born in 1798, I could readily see that the time he mentioned coincided quite well with the incidence of "inoculation" and "vaccination" in rural communities.

All through the war I, like everyone else, had chills and fever. The blockade was responsible for quinine being two hundred dollars an ounce in gold. We never met anyone who had any; we drank boneset tea. I have often gone fishing and been unable to tell from my cork whether I had a nibble or a chill.

Of course we did not escape suffering now and then from scabies or itch, which the Negroes called "the seven year itch." We were fortunate, however, that it did not come sooner, for we had heard of cases elsewhere before there were any amongst us. Because sulphur was imperatively needed for gunpowder, it was very hard to get, even for medicinal purposes. I was cured very promptly by washing in a soup made from boiled pokeberry root. This I learned later was *phytolacca decandra* which has a poisonous stem and leaf, although the young shoots have been used by man since time immemorial as "spring greens." The Negroes must have known some kindred plant in Africa, as their longing for this form of greens was inordinate, far greater than that of the whites.

With wounded and sick soldiers coming home all the time, it is indeed strange that we in Concord escaped lice, but we did until nearly the end of the war. Then they came with the Federal Army, and they were the kind that we called "grey backs" and now call "cooties." I remember two Yankee orderlies, tented in our yard, racing "grey backs" and betting on the result. The contestants were placed between two knitting needles, and the course extended from one red spot on the deuce of hearts to the other. I was a fascinated spectator.

VII

THE PINCH OF NECESSITY

ALMOST AT ONCE we began to feel the pinch of war. White sugar disappeared immediately; not only were there no more lumps for gun-shy horses, but there was no sugar for the table. There was, however, an unlimited quantity of sorghum syrup, and around the barrels of sorghum a thick crust of brown sugar often formed. This was carefully scraped off to be served with coffee and berries, the fluid product going to the servants. They called it "long sweet'nin'" and the other "short sweet'nin'." To provide a constant supply new cane was planted every year. It was noted even then that the crystalizing power of some sorghums was much greater than that of others. I remember hearing this difference discussed.

The imperative demand for sweets soon brought the omnipresent "bee-gum" to every yard and orchard, for that was what we called our homemade beehive. Made from a hollow black gum tree, which was often eighteen inches or two feet in diameter, this hollow log required very little chiseling out. It was simply cut in two foot lengths, a board nailed on top and a hole bored near the bottom, and it was ready for the spring swarm. Our wild bee, as is well known, was the European bee brought here about 1720 by the Palatine Germans who settled above Fredericksburg, Virginia. Every swarm in the spring was greeted with the beating of tin pans, the blowing of horns, and every

THE PINCH OF NECESSITY 49

other noise-making device that could be thought of. Superstition dies hard. We had the idea we could not secure the swarm unless we made so much noise that the workers would be unable to hear the call of the queen bee, but all that noise was useless, as the queen is found to be practically a deaf mute.

In a very short time I noticed that matches had disappeared, and I have learned that at the outbreak of the war there was not one match factory in the South. However, flint and steel had passed out of use so recently that many of these old relics, which were sticking around in closets and hidden recesses in attics, were taken out and returned to use. During the first year of the war I must have seen fifty "old-timers" using these, as we now use lighters and with far more certainty of results than the average lighter will render. They held the "spark," a fungus called punk which grew on oak trees, for lighting pipes and the already rare cigars. The cigarette of that day, wrapped in a corn shuck, was still a mere fad; it could not be lighted easily from punk. I learned later that the punk was usually soaked in a much diluted solution of saltpeter which everybody kept as standard equipment for hog-killing time.

Not every family had preserved the flint and steel, and even if they had, the fire on the hearth was husbanded as meticulously as ever it was in the old Vestal days. Although there was no curfew (cover-fire) sounded, the rite was enacted at a convenient hour in every household. Someone drew the andirons forward and turned the back log to face against the white brick. He covered the log with embers, shoveled ashes on top, and went to bed confident of starting a new fire in the morning. Sometimes the Vestal fires failed, or perhaps the morning spark had not been nursed with sufficient care by the boy whose duty it was to tend it. When that happened the boy would be soundly flailed and sent posthaste with a flowerpot to borrow fire from a more fortunate neighbor, a simple errand in town but out in the country the neighbor might be a mile or several miles away. They used to place a piece of slate in the bottom of an earthen flowerpot to regulate the size of the hole, fill the pot with burning embers covered with ashes, and carry it suspended from a green pawpaw twist. Sometimes they had paperbark flowerpots woven in the shape of a pear for convenience in carrying and soaked in water for safety, or covered inside with a layer of wet red clay.

At Cottage Home we would send a Negro on a mule to Judge Shipp's or to the Reverend Doctor Thornley's but if these sources failed the man would have to go to some of our much despised "fox-hunting, whiskey-drinking" neighbors. I often wondered how it was that the ungodly seemed to keep fire better than the pure in heart.

Long before the war was over matches came back, but they were not the boxed kind that we were accustomed to use. The new matches came in blocks of wood, sawn nearly through with an old cotton-gin saw, and you broke your sulphur match from the block. Aside from the smell, which would disinfect a ballroom, and the fact that they got your fingers full of splinters, they were not bad matches.

Soap was another imperative necessity. In every family the fats were conserved, but soap cannot be made without alkalies, so for home and plantation use the ash hoppers were extended. When new ground was cleared for agricultural purposes the ash hopper was carried to the forest. A pine log some six or eight feet long was channeled on the upper side to within a foot of one end, and in this channel were laid, at an angle of forty-five degrees, clapboards some four feet long. Ashes from the burning of the logs were shoveled into this ash hopper, and the rains of heaven leached out the potash which, running down the inclined channel, was delivered into a stone tub, or some other receiving vessel made by hewing out a log at least two feet by four in dimensions. The ash hopper near the house usually drained into a pre-war cast-iron ham boiler, and in the South many were the children who perished from drinking lye from these tempting reservoirs of peril.

As the blockade grew tighter, whale oil became very scarce. Our beef tallow was saved for greasing cartridges, and fat was needed for soap making, so we were unable to make good candles. The de luxe candles of those days were called candlettes, and they were made by dipping a long strand of cotton into a mixture of beeswax, mutton suet, and lard until it became as thick as a lead pencil, when it was coiled into a roll. When

THE PINCH OF NECESSITY 51

lit, it gave a flickering smoky flame that was very hard on the eyes.

It seemed to me that an infinite number of little things were missing, such as toothpowder, for which we found a substitute in ground sassafras bark and chalk. We made a unique shoe polish by mixing lamp black with the ripe cortical pulp of the abundant chinaberry, and we made good ink from oak balls and burnt copperas.

Soon no more tea and coffee was brought through the blockade, and everybody was forced to use substitutes. We had tea made of sassafras roots, cleaned and dried, and we jokingly called our product "Grub Hyson," after a famous tea which was much in vogue before the war. For coffee we parched rye and wheat and browned sweet potatoes, making a mixture which was cut into quarter inch cubes before drying. Aunt Maria Barringer, when the blockade closed in, was fortunate in having a full bag of Mocha and half a bag of Java, but before long half of that was gone, and to preserve the precious remainder she also was obliged to use "ersatz." However, when she entertained a lieutenant, she had the cook add three grains of mixed Mocha and Java to the usual brew; a captain got five grains; a major, ten; a colonel, fifteen; and a rare brigadier general was given twenty of the precious grains.

Other shortages threatened of which I, as a child, saw only the signs and could not realize the seriousness. Paper was getting so scarce that my elders feared that even the dreaded deathlists might cease to come. Then it was discovered that wall paper could be used, and if properly removed from the walls and bleached, it could be printed on both sides. At the last, they used wall paper that could not be bleached, printing on one side only. I still have one of these old journals. Framed under glass it shows pink flowers on one side, while the bloody harvest of war is recorded on the other.

There was little opportunity to replenish such supplies of writing paper as were on hand when the war began. As the years passed my father wrote us letters on torn scraps of office paper and sometimes on the letter head of his division, but even that paper was of very poor grade.

Anxiety for the men at the front was ever present; many of them came home wounded, and there were many funerals. As the years passed, nearly all the women, mourning for some member of the family, dressed in black. All the young and strong men had long since joined the army, only old men and cripples remained at home, and the plantations were run by Negro men and boys of twelve or fourteen. All bronze church bells were taken down to be melted and made into howitzers or gun caps, and the sabbaths were silent. We—patriarchs, black-robed women, and children—went unbidden to church, where even in the hymns there was a note of sorrow, and the Negroes in the gallery became solemn under the universal strain. Things were surely serious when the Negroes looked solemn.

However, I cannot recall feeling depressed, nor do I remember that any of the other children were. Our conduct was normal and lively as usual.

As the war progressed the stringency deepened. Food portions were small and there was enough to eat, but the best went to the soldiers in the field. We had plenty of cotton as long as there were hands to work it, and we had wool from our sheep, so the looms, the spinning wheels, and cards were never idle. At Cottage Home all the looms were kept going day and night throughout the four years of war. They even rigged up an old, discarded loom and used that steadily.

Everyone worked at Cottage Home, white and black, young and old. We children could scrape lint, the forerunner of absorbent cotton, desperately needed in the hospitals. I worked at that nearly every morning, and in the afternoon I went out with the other children and gathered sweet gum balsam. The benzoic acid in these oleoresins was the most suitable material known for treating wounds before the coming of asepsis.

The Federal Government declared all drugs contraband of war, and almost no morphine or quinine came through the blockade. As a substitute for the latter, as I have already stated, we used boneset tea, which helped but did not cure malaria. To supply opiate we grew our own poppies, making incisions into the sides of the ovaries of these plants and with the flat of a case knife scraping up the exuded gum. The knife was then scraped off on the edge of a glass jar, and thus we found that we could raise gum opium that was 10 or 12 per cent morphine.

There was a poppy bed in every garden planted for this purpose, and when I was seven years old I worked daily for the soldiers, scraping the inspissated juice of the poppy from the bulbar ovaries which had been punctured a few days before, and, like everyone else, I worked under the eternal mandate, "Don't taste it!" On some fifty poppy heads it was a morning's work to get a mass about as big as a small peanut.

The time came when no more Chilean nitre could run the blockade, and the South must depend on its own resources for this essential element of explosives. It was then that the urine cart began to make its rounds, collecting the night's urine and hauling it to the boiling vats, where the urea and other nitrogenous constituents were extracted and shipped to Augusta, Georgia, for the manufacture of gunpowder. That plant was never more than a few days ahead of the needs of the firing line.

Later on the need became so great that many old cabins which stood up on four corner posts were raised by levers, so that men could crawl under them to scrape the ground for the thin layer of nitrogen charged clay at the top. As wondering children, we saw men crawling under old barns to scrape up the dry dust, and we saw old plaster taken from the walls and leached in the ash hopper. We heard that in Virginia and Kentucky searching parties invaded the caves where bats roosted to scrape the bat manure from the floor. All such gleanings were likewise sent to the plant in Augusta.

Looking back at it now, I can see the reason for that persistent and unceasing call to save and extend every natural resource in every section of the South. The need was desperate and the toil in the homes, the fields, and the improvised factories was unceasing.

In North Carolina, Wilmington was our sole open port, but it gave us little relief. The blockade runners brought in munitions and such light things as papers, magazines, and books. Uncle Victor subscribed to the *London Times,* and he literally wore out every copy, so hungry was he for European news. He also bought an ornately bound and illuminated copy of Johnson's

Rasselas, and as that came early in February, 1865, in time for my eighth birthday, he and my aunt gave it to me as a birthday present. They wrote my name in it and made much of it. I was pleased until I was informed that I must learn enough of it by heart to get Johnson's peculiar style!

VIII

WARTIME INDUSTRIES

IT WAS actually the United States Navy which won the Civil War, for its relentless blockade strangled the South's victorious armies. A country, basically agricultural, when caught in such a blockade is forced to use all its scant industrial power to supply its army, therefore the people at home must suffer severely. They devise all kinds of makeshifts to relieve the distress, and unwittingly I saw all this while living at Concord.

The demand for leather for the army, and secondarily for the home folks, grew far beyond the previous supply. Now, in cutting a new ground, some of the white oak and post oak bark was always saved for the tanning vats which were dug out everywhere. Every form of hide was tanned. Furs previously secured only for their natural use and tacked on the end of the smokehouse to dry were taken down, the hair clipped (for the hatter), and the skin tanned. In some places they even went back to the old method of brain-tanning for deer skins, coon skins, opossum, and others. In other words, when you killed a deer you took out his brains and salted them to cure his hide. It is needless to say that during the four or five years of war game everywhere increased greatly.

Another industry that increased markedly during the war was ropemaking. A great many plantations instituted primitive ropewalks. The crude "whirling hooks" were run by hand under a small shelter and the walk extended forty or fifty yards in the open air. That it was not an absolutely new art, however, is proven by the fact that only the old Negroes seemed to know it. To see them walking backwards, paying out tow to the growing line, was a fascinating sight. This tow was home-grown from Kentucky seed and was used with very little heckling; in fact, I don't remember that for rope tow there was much more done to it than to run it through a sorghum mill and beat it a little bit. Many years after the war I saw one of these old ropewalks at my father-in-law's home in Charlotte County, Virginia. It must be remembered, however, that making tow ropes in North Carolina was a war measure; our old Negroes were much more skillful in using cotton to make "plow lines" and "traces" for farm use.

The grist mills began to wear out. The peculiar stone masons who could cut the burrs were foolishly sent to the war and killed, so the old experts at home were kept busy and even then were not equal to the demand. Poor folk reverted to the old-fashioned primitive mortar and pestle made by burning out a two-foot section of white oak cut off about four feet long. Damp earth was smeared around the outer six inches and a fire built on top which was fed and tended for some days. This would give a mortar a cavity eighteen inches in diameter and some two feet deep, hard-faced from the burning. In this, corn, cow-peas, and even peanuts were mixed and coarse meal used, with flour added, to hold it together. Looking back at it, I can imagine no better foods than some of these mortar mixtures.

This innovation of industry with shortage of iron brought about some singular inventions. The pre-war crowbar was sent to the blacksmith shop and one end shaped into a "bit" that would bore a two and a half-inch hole. This "bit" was constructed wholly on an anvil, twisted when hot in the vise, and the threads shaped on the point with some highly treasured old triangular file or a new file brought in by the blockade runners and worth its weight in gold. With these "bits," pine logs were bored from each end, giving lengths of from ten to fifteen feet, and these placed end to end were used in conveying water from the springs and pumps. One end, of course, was made cone-shaped to fit into a conical cavity in the other. A band of iron, made from some rusting old "cotton tie," was often driven in one end of the log to prevent splitting. It is needless to say that such pipe could not easily turn a corner.

I could add many other industries which, having long since disappeared, were revived in the South—hatmaking from rabbit, coon, and muskrat hair, with blocks carved by cabinetmakers out of black gum. Tea plantations were set out in South Carolina and Florida, as well as the opium industry already referred to. Looking back at it, it is of interest to recall that these industries sprang up around the homes of culture and erudition. I was always impressed each time I visited the homes of my uncles, Edwin and Charles Harris, in Cabarrus County, with the new things being developed there. Their father, Charles W. Harris, had been a professor of mathematics and the second president of the University of North Carolina about 1795.

I shall refer later to the minting of Bechtler gold, as this industry was not operating during the war, although Bechtler coins were then greatly treasured, and many contracts during that period specified that payment was to be made in Bechtler gold. No coins were issued by the Confederate Government, and its paper money rapidly deteriorated in value. I have often heard the story of a farmer who when offered $15,000 in Confederate money for his fine horse, replied gently, "I could hardly sell him for that, as I have just paid $1,500 to have him shod." In those days I saw many thin octagonal gold pieces bearing Bechtler's name and stamped with the value, one dollar or five dollars, and I recall one octagonal fifty dollar coin, fully two inches across, but I am not positive that it carried the name of Bechtler.

Still later, as war dragged on, the need for repairs on chimneys and the settling of brick corner posts, on which more than half of the dwellings of the South were built, called for brick. In a land where adult labor was unalterably tied to food production, to meet this need a system of brickmaking which called for nothing more than a few old men and "plenty of chillun" came into vogue.

Some spring branch on whose banks a recent freshet had left piles of good sand in a meadow of good clay (crawfish land) was chosen. At the center of the selected spot of level bottom land, some fifty yards across, a deep post hole was dug and an eighteen-inch post about seven feet long and sawed off square at the top was sunk about four or five feet deep in the soil. A young hickory tree some eight or ten inches through at the butt and over thirty feet long was cut down, trimmed up, and first carefully balanced across the post top. At the point where it balanced most perfectly, the hickory was squared on the bottom side with an axe, and then at the center of the squared spot a two-inch auger hole was bored which was fitted over a two-inch locust pin, sunk deep in a similar hole in the top of the central post. That gave a heavy balanced sweep, with about equal weight in the (one-fourth) butt end and the (three-fourths) sweep end. With a draw knife a six-foot section on the sweep was made true, and on this one of the many old high "logging wheels" of the South was slipped. These old wheels were always preserved when worn out and the opening in the hub enlarged for just such work. Holes and pins in the sweep arm allowed one to move the wheel in or out with a fixed traverse of some six feet.

In the broiling days of August and early September when crops were "laid by," the call came for brickmaking. The spring branch was diverted and turned into a circular trench which was dug around the central post. With the trench half full of water a yoke of steers was hitched to the end of the sweep and driven in a circle until the big logging wheel cut down almost to the hub. At a call from the old Negro headman the children rushed to the butt place and hung on like flies, while others mounted the central post and walked out on the top of the beam until their combined weight lifted the sweep enough to shove the big wheel in or out a foot or more. Then the sweep started again and ground up the outer edge of the ditch, and thus alternately, in and out, the clay and loam under the sweep were thoroughly kneaded. Then the branch was cut off and the fun began. An old Negro in little more than a breech-clout waded in and was handed a properly prepared brick mould and carrying board combined. By "properly prepared," we mean dipped in the water of a contiguous pool and then half filled with sand at the sand pile, next thoroughly shaken, and the sand emptied out. When the old man pressed the kneaded clay into such a mould, and "struck it" with his shingle, we had a soft brick of clay with a good outside facing of sand. This mould was then carried to a dumping ground, this ground itself covered with a half inch of sand and always having a southern exposure. You will see that this gave in the end a brick with all the sides covered with embedded sand during the drying out process. These brick moulds varied from two bricks to four bricks, and for the giant half-wits, six brick boards. The shouts and yells and songs of a crowd of well-fed Negro pickaninnies such as gathered at Dr. Sidney Johnston's brick field are well remembered. Often I would motion some little Negro out of the line and try his two-brick board and when satisfied try a four-brick, and on one occasion, straining and struggling I carried and properly deposited a six-brick board. It is hard to believe the number of brick, good brick, that can be turned out from such a yard in a day by this simple means.

The cutting of the pine cordwood had already been done for us during the previous winter, and when these bricks had dried in the sun to the proper state, they were carried by the same children on flat boards and handed up to the old man who "stacked." Old men and women "fired," using salt for the needed glaze or plain brick, as desired. Of course, it is an industry now obsolete, but man has no assurance that he will not some day return to something like it.

At this time came also a crusade for an increase in the domestic fowls of the Confederacy as a method of saving dried beef and pork for the soldiers in the field. Every plantation, every small farm, and most village lots had chickens, turkeys, guineas, and geese, and fully half of the plantations and farms had peafowls both for food and "fly brushes."

We must remember the conditions—woods, thickets, and jungles everywhere, and yet pastures near at hand. At that time fowls that fed on "grub and grass" were sheer profit, for all prospered. As a boy at Cottage Home, Bellevue, and the Harris places, the peafowl was a common bird on the table, appearing even oftener than turkey, for at many places wild turkeys were so close to the house that all our tame turkeys went wild. This was long the condition at Swan Pond, the Avery plantation.

When we look back at the origin of these fowls—the chicken from Asia, the turkey from far-away America, the guinea from

Africa, and the peafowl of southern Asia—all new to the soil, except the turkey, we can but wonder at how long and how well they survived when first grouped together. We now know that the ancestral diseases of one have spread to the other: the Asiatic chicken gave the American turkey the disease now called blackhead; the presence of the African guinea soon in some way played havoc with the peafowl on the same plantation unless segregated, which we know was impossible. Of course, the peafowl is now a rare bird kept only for ornament.

Nature's laws of life had long since made the geese and ducks practically international. As they migrated thousands of miles each year, they became immune to almost anything, with the result that the gray goose and the puddle duck (Mallard) were everywhere, the first primarily for the feather beds of invalids and old people and the second for the free Negroes. The Muscovy duck was then known, but rare.

IX

A PECULIAR INSTITUTION

THE NARROW SOCIAL relations of the church in the days of the Confederacy were noticeable even to a boy of eight. Seemingly the chief use made of the Bible was to explain the relation of master and slave. As I had read the Bible through before I was twelve, I probably was loaded on Genesis and Numbers before I was eight. At all events, I remember that I knew all the passages relating to slavery as they came along. Moreover, I always felt the difference in the atmosphere between my two most common homes with Uncle Victor in Concord and with grandfather at Cottage Home in Lincoln. As compared with all other outside relations, Uncle Victor's home was liberal; there was no dancing because there were no young people, and no card playing simply because my aunt took no interest in it and Uncle Victor did not like solitaire, but he had the cards to play it. He was to that extent an anathema. My grandfather was a liberal fundamentalist.

About once a year, or seemingly at no set time, a sermon was preached on slavery to master and slaves at the same sitting by Doctor Kirkpatrick, the Presbyterian minister at Concord. These slavery sermons were not called by that name, as far as I can recall, but without specific orders the gallery of the old square brick Presbyterian Church at Concord always seemed fuller than usual. The regular Invocation, Hymn, Reading of Scripture,

Hymn, Sermon, Last Hymn, and Benediction was followed. I do not recall what hymns were sung, but I remember they always seemed appropriate. For the Scripture Readings, Doctor Kirkpatrick always read those parts of Genesis 9-10 which referred to the damnation of Canaan and also of Ham. His text was usually general, but from later reading I am convinced that his main idea was obtained from First Corinthians 7:20-24. "Let every man abide in the same calling wherein he was called. Art thou called a servant? care not for it; but if thou mayest be free, use it rather. For he that is called in the Lord, being a servant, is the Lord's freeman; likewise also he that is called, being free, is Christ's servant. Ye are bought with a price; be not ye the servants of men. Brethren, let every man, wherein he is called, therein abide with God." At all events, he gave the idea that the moderation of the master called for a proper submission from the slave.

If it be wondered that a boy of tender years should remember such things, I will say that times are different. Then every child that could go to church had to repeat upon return the text, and a little later on in life he was required to give some idea of the discourse; and furthermore, in this line, I had had an experience.

A visiting young minister was invited to preach at Unity Church when my grandfather was filling another pulpit. Instead of giving a sermon on the general patriarchal relation of master and slave usually affected by old Doctor Kirkpatrick, the young theologian went back to Exodus 21:6, and revived the Old Testament with fervor. This was my first sermon on the subject, and I sat popeyed when he read out, "He shall bring him to the door or to the doorpost; and his master shall bore his ear through with an awl; and he shall serve him forever."

The next day, still thinking this over, and times apparently being dull, I got a long three-inch thorn from a honey locust tree (acacia) and taking my stand high up at the ginhouse door, I called to all the little Negroes in sight and proceeded in order to transfix each ear to the ginhouse door. When I got through the place looked like a miniature shambles. The girl children objected very little, for they all wanted their ears pierced for ear rings, and they were very particular to show me where to pierce and gladly broke off straws to put in afterwards to hold the perforation open. My own Negro boy, Nat, an older brother of Harvey, was marched up first and after his ears were pierced, to even things up he went out looking for others. It was quite an affair.

The results were extremely disastrous, not to the little Negroes, for I don't believe any one of them had either a fever or a headache from it, but some of the older Negroes told Aunt Anna. She told grandfather and I was put to bed for a whole day on bread and water, but the worst was yet to come. My grandfather, who practically never preached on anything but the Beatitudes, recognized this text from my application of it and asked for me. He then sent for the young minister and gave him "Hail Columbia" at the idea of approaching the subject in this way.

The result of all this preaching and biblical study was a fear of God as a personal entity amongst white and black, a feeling utterly unknown now. These preachers believed what they preached and their audiences believed what they said. When old Doctor Miller roared out, "Go, curse God and die," every man there believed that should he curse God he would die at once. A very different feeling prevails now, but the net result then was a general morality such as I have never seen since. The lighter sins—lying, et cetera—of course, were common, but otherwise the Decalogue was rigidly conformed to.

Negro marriages were always demanded, and if any loose relationships were detected the master himself ordered marriage. Wife and husband, of course, need not belong to the same master, nor in fact be owned by the same connection, although this was much to be desired. Very frequently the master would buy whatsoever wife a favorite slave had picked out amongst the neighboring slave women. If she belonged to one of no connection to the family this brought about much dickering and trading, but if she were not purchased the inevitable results gave to slavery one of its distinctive organizations, the nocturnal "patrol." For instance, Yankee Jim, who nursed my uncle day and night, fell in love at church with a girl named Mandy, belonging to Mr. McDonald a mile away uptown at the Cotton Mills. To go and come to her husband at night Mandy was given a pass which simply read, "Permit Mandy to pass at will after dark between Mr. Barringer's and Mr. McDonald's," or something like this.

Incidentally, I will state that Mandy was the only female Negro I ever knew to carry a pass, but the conditions in her case were peculiar. The rule was that married men whose wives were on neighboring and particularly remote plantations were allowed to go and come at night, without interruption, carrying a pass from their masters.

Naturally, as these Negroes wandered almost at will, others attempted the same performance and lied about the permit saying they had left it in their "chist," or some such story, but, as the reverberations of the Nat Turner Virginia Insurrection of 1831 were still in the air, such wanderings and opportunities for collusion could not be allowed. The result was that a Negro claiming a permit when he had none was always whipped, and illicit traveling by night became a matter of hazard, adopted only by the brave and the fleet of foot. The members of this nocturnal patrol were called by the Negroes "patterollers." In some aged minds the slave cabin ditty, "Run, nigger, run, the patteroller 'll catch you," may still linger, and even the next verse, "Dis nigger run and run so fast, he stuck his head in a hornet's nest," will again bring a laugh. All the fun, however, was not on the side of the whites. I can remember the inordinate glee with which a Negro named Napoleon recited how he had shown an old order on the Commissary to a white man in lieu of a pass and had it accepted because the white man could not read. Naturally, as a child, I got both sides of pretty much all that was going between these two phases of civilization.

Since life revolved from sunup to sundown, slaves were worked as long and as hard as was possible without injury to their health. That was an economic necessity, but at the same time Negroes were chattels too valuable to injure, and they were given strict medical supervision by the best physicians, often under yearly contracts.

When at the age of six or eight, slave children were brought into the house to "learn their manners," each one was usually attached to a grown person to fetch and carry for a year or more. The grown person, giving them light work and sending them on errands, made work for them, and the purpose of this was often misunderstood by outsiders. The children were pretty well tested by being tried at every kind of work on the place. Any child showing an aptitude for housework was seldom sent to the fields, house servants being much more valuable than field hands. Of course, the rod was used freely, but those were the days of frequent floggings even for the master's son.

At Cottage Home I never saw a slave whipped by the overseer, although I remember hearing that our overseer once broke the jaw of a "bad man" with a carriage spoke, but the victim was not our servant. Once I saw my grandfather have a half-grown boy severely whipped for stealing the mail bag containing mail, a legal offense. He was given "forty lashes less one."

In this day and generation Negro dialect is more or less standardized by being forced into a form in which it will be recognized by the average reader. This, of course, is a purely artificial standardization. Negro dialects grew out of the relative proportion of Negroes and whites in any given locality and the social status of the whites who came in contact with them. On very large plantations with enormous bodies of Negro field hands whose only relationship with the white race was made through the overseer and his aides, there was very poor English, but always English. The probabilities that any purchase made in Newport, Rhode Island, New York, Norfolk, Charleston, or anywhere else would embrace only Negroes having the same language were very small. The slave trade was maintained in Africa by constant raids on outlying territory and bringing in these prisoners for confinement in barracoons to await the arrival of a slave trader and his ship. Then these unhappy victims from anywhere and everywhere, having almost no language in common, were bundled aboard and taken overseas to a land where they were given orders in a strange tongue, but which tongue they saw at once was their sole hope of economic, intellectual, and spiritual advancement. Naturally they hung on the master's lips and those of his representative, the overseer, and the language of any plantation was a compound ratio between the proportion of various African tribes and the literacy of the overseer and his employer's home.

Of course, this applied only to field hands. The house servant learned his master's speech and the bigger the word the prouder he was when he had swallowed it, and the greater the pride with which he spouted it when he condescended to visit the field hand "quarters." To make a long story short, as a boy of eight or ten, I could tell the Negroes from the Hunter place, the Shipp place, or the Forney place by their accent even if I had never seen the Negro before. The Thornwell Negroes (refugees from South Carolina) were most distinctive; sounding much like the modern "Gullah" because Galla Negroes were largely taken to Charleston. The Shipp Negroes had long since come from Virginia, and the Forney Negroes had been moved from Pennsylvania in the preceding century when emancipation came slowly down the coast. In short, there were dialects influenced by tribe, influenced by master, and even influenced by state, so we can naturally see that Joel Chandler Harris, Armistead Gordon, and F. Hopkinson Smith could not exactly agree.

The use of the terms "Negro" and "nigger" was more a measure of the master's gentility than anything else, and most masters were gentlemen. There were only about three hundred thousand slave owners at the beginning of the war in a total Southern white population of seven and a half million. This naturally made them a class apart. On the other hand, the master's son, who was instructed never to let the plebeian word "nigger" pass his lips but stick by the patriarchal "Negro," had many difficulties. The Negroes themselves in slave times nearly all used the word "nigger" when in a rage and invariably used it if they suspected that the object of their compliment came from the Guinea Coast. A "Guinea nigger" could not, in fact, ever become a Negro; he was too low down in the scale, and he was seldom chosen as a house servant. On the contrary, the tall, light-colored Mandingo with the rich tenor voice was nearly always held in the house. I use the term "held" advisedly because I remember that it was the custom in slavery days to pass all young Negroes through the big house if it were possible. They were first placed as helpers to the cook, swinging peacock-feather fly brushes over the table, and running messages. The best ones were promoted and the very elect were kept. In this race the "Guinea nigger" had little chance. I also remember how the fame of the mistress as a housekeeper and manager added to the value and price of the slave desired. The Phifer house servants of Concord would bring almost any price on account of the fitness, but there were some who, at least in my Aunt Maria's opinion, did not rank so high.

After freedom when the Negro became educated, he immediately turned to "Negro," although the classical root from which the name was derived—*niger*—led straight to nigger. The fact that the master class used Negro, and it only, fixed the name with him "forever."

X

FIRST RAILROAD ADVENTURES

MY STEPMOTHER continued in delicate health after the birth of her son, Rufus Chunn, in March, 1862; also the baby did not thrive. Naturally my father was most anxious to come home on a visit, but because of the seriousness of the military situation, he was unable to do so. In this connection, I have a letter written to Captain Barringer by his brother-in-law, General Stonewall Jackson. In it he gives news of all the brothers-in-law, and it is probably one of the last intimate letters he wrote before his tragic death, on May 10, 1863.

> "Corbyn's Farm
> Caroline Co. Va.
> Feby 11, 1863.

"My dear Captain,

"Your letter of the 5th instant has been received, and your request will receive special attention. I am not sanguine of success, but an available opportunity may occur.

"I regret to hear of the continued delicate health of Mrs. B & child.

"Joseph Morrison has gone home to see his mother who is seriously ill. Capt. Avery has also gone on leave of absence of 25 days.

"Gen'l Hill has been assigned to duty in North Carolina.

"Mr. Irwin and Sis with their children were at Cottage Home

at last accounts. I hope that they will be there when Anna and Paul arrive there.

"Should you come near me I hope that you will not pass by without calling.

"Very truly yours,
"T. J. Jackson

"P.S. Gen'l Stuart has arrived since the foregoing and he desires getting you appointed on his Military Court of which he has the promise. Say nothing about this as the court is not yet secured.

"T. J. J."

During the following April, my father still being unable to come home, my mother made the difficult journey to Hanover Court House, Virginia, to visit him. He had been ordered there for rest and recreation after hard service around Fredericksburg and further brilliant achievements in defending the stores at Hanover Junction.

Quoting from a letter that he wrote to Anna, "Tell Paulie," he says, "I hope soon to get one of those grand letters he has been talking of writing me." Instead of laboring to write him a letter, however, I visited him at Hanover Court House in September when he was recovering from a severe wound sustained at the Battle of Brandy Station in June, 1863. This, he told me later, was probably the largest cavalry engagement of the war, some 12,000 to 15,000 men having been engaged on each side. Following this engagement he had received his commission as major.

I had spent the greater part of that summer in Asheville with my mother and the other children. We visited her father, Mr. Chunn, and I think it was the last time that I stayed at that old place, for shortly after this, Kirk's "Tories," or Kirk's "Lambs" as they were often called in apprehensive derision, threatened Asheville from the west. These mountain people of Southern stock were Union sympathizers and in the absence of Southern troops they were preying openly upon their Confederate neighbors. Perhaps it might not be amiss to add that their Southern neighbors had set them a good example in unneighborly treatment. The Confederate authorities sent officers, a small engineer corps, and four guns to defend Asheville against these guerillas. In order to do this effectively, they bought both the Chunn and Chapman places, and either burned or tore down all the houses on and around the apex of this little peak in the city. They erected there a star-shaped four-gun battery, garrisoned with regular Confederate artillerymen. Mr. Chunn moved out of town on the prolongation of Main Street which passes the Court House. I went back there several times while the peak was garrisoned, and if I remember aright, it was called Battery Porter. At the close of the war it was confiscated by the city of Asheville and called Battery Park. A Mr. Coxe, who was then a resident of Asheville, doubted the validity of the city's title, so he went to Washington, patented it, acquired a better title, and built there the now famous Battery Park Hotel.

My mother, who had a tubercular tendency, was not well during the summer, and after her return to Concord in the fall, her health failed rapidly. Doctor John Bachman, a Lutheran minister of whom I shall have more to say, had known the Chunns well during her youth, and when he was in the vicinity of Concord organizing the Lutherans for war, he visited her several times before her death. Having lost two daughters from tuberculosis, he was able to realize her hopeless condition before the family could do so. In Aunt Maria's diary is a poignant account of his administering the last rite of communion to this slowly dying friend on New Year's day. She died early in January, 1864, her death being hastened probably by the anxieties of war combined with the necessarily narrow balance in rations. My father, then Lieutenant Colonel Barringer, came home on a twenty day furlough, arriving three days before she died.

Again I was motherless, and now more than ever the home of Uncle Victor and Aunt Maria was for me one of the two stable spots in the universe.

The other haven, of course, was Cottage Home. My Aunt Anna Jackson and her little daughter, Julia, had moved there after General Jackson's death. My grandmother was seriously ill when Aunt Anna arrived, and as she died soon after, Aunt Anna became the mistress of the house. A gentler, but at the same time more efficient, mistress of a plantation never existed than she.

Again I returned to Asheville when my baby brother was taken to his grandfather's home. Returning, I stopped at Morganton as before to visit Aunt Sue Avery at Swan Pond and some other relatives at Pleasant Gardens. Wherever I went I saw the sad harvest of war, wounded and dying soldiers.

After my return to Concord, I visited the Irwins in Charlotte and while there Uncle Irwin went to Davidson College to see Aunt Isabella Hill. As I had never seen the college that my grandfather founded, on our earnest appeal, he took his son, John, and me with him.

We went by the A. T. & O., which being translated means the Atlantic, Tennessee and Ohio Railroad, the route that was "eight hours long and forty miles short," and there was one daily combination train to make the journey. That railroad bespoke the spirit of the times. They never intended it to stop in Ohio. It was headed, like all western roads of that time, for the Pacific, but it lived and died in its original length. The stations were five or six miles apart, and at several of them the train stopped for an hour or more.

I never enjoyed a trip more in my life, for during these long stops, Uncle Irwin got out and showed us the train, the water tank, the depot, and the by-pass (switch). Above all he showed us the engine which was of the old eccentric and link-driven type, and the upper part of the smokestack was almost as great in diameter as the boiler. These engines burned nothing but wood, rich resinous pine wood, and sparks from the smokestack often set fields afire unless the sparks were controlled by a sifter of fine mesh set in the upper part of the smokestack.

The thing that interested me most was learning how the boiler was filled from the reserve tank on the tender. When one of these little pony engines was delayed too long on the by-pass or switch, its water was used up by the constant blowing off of steam. Then the engineer, much alarmed, cut loose his engine which was three-fourths smokestack, threw one end of the switch, and charging out on the open track, ran up and down for about twenty minutes, a mile or so each way. I had watched this proceeding and thought it was very exciting. Now I learned that it was done to work the pumps, which were fastened one on each side of the piston drive, so that they would pump the reserve water from the tank into the boiler. As soon as the boiler was full the engine returned with cool satisfaction to pick up the train. I was almost a man before I saw the mechanism, now called an injector, which obviated this nuisance, and if I remember aright, the first injector I ever saw was called "the little giant."

The rails consisted of eight by ten oak beams, joined by spiked braces on the outside. On top of these was a flat iron rail three-quarters of an inch thick, four inches wide, and thirty or more feet long, held on by occasional spikes with countersunk heads. These wood-iron rails were held about five feet apart by strong wooden braces, countersunk into the beams. This was all very well for five- to ten-ton loads and a few years of service, but in time the spikes sunk through the rails ceased to hold, particularly at the ends.

First there would come a flap-flap, flap-flap, in every conceivable tone and pitch, caused by the revolving wheels of the train hammering down the end of the strip rail where the spikes had ceased to hold. The ultimate was reached when the end spikes were thrown out, and the ends of the iron rail stood up, perhaps on a cold day as much as eight or ten inches. Then catastrophe was close at hand. Soon some wanton rail rose up above the center of the oncoming wheel, which passed under it, while the iron strip, having nowhere else to go, pierced the floor of the car, and for a few seconds thrashed around wildly inside, often coming to rest on a corpse. Some passenger, who was not instantly killed, named the rail that bit at him but failed to make fatal contact, a "snake head."

When Uncle James Irwin placed John and me in the front part of the car, remarking that there we would be safer from "snake heads," I was greatly disappointed, for my biological interest was aroused as I had never heard of a rail snake head. I may add that I never saw one, for by this time these thin rails were being taken up and sent to Norfolk where some of them were used in the defensive armament of the Confederate ironclad, *Merrimac*.

FIRST RAILROAD ADVENTURES 73

There was first-, second-, and third-class travel in those days. Holders of first-class tickets stuck them in their hats, went anywhere, and sat where they pleased. Second-class ticket holders might be called upon by the brakeman or conductor to get out at any woodyard and help pitch pine wood on the tender. Holders of third-class tickets fully understood that they would have to get out at *every* woodyard to supply the tender, their only notification being a peculiar blow of the whistle. These third-classers might even be called upon to get out and aid the laboring engine by pushing the train up a steep grade.

Uncle James left John and me at Davidson with Aunt Isabella, and as the back of her lot overlooked the station, we had a glorious few days, starting frantically whenever a train came in and rushing down to the station to examine the engine with Randolph, Joe, and Eugenia Hill trailing close behind us. On one occasion we were allowed the privilege of riding on the tender when the engine ran up and down the track pumping water for the next five- or six-mile run.

During this visit to my mother's oldest sister, Aunt Isabella Hill, I came to know her well for the first time. As a young girl visiting a kinsman, Reverend James Morrison, in Rockbridge County, Virginia, she had met Daniel Harvey Hill, who was teaching mathematics at Washington College (now Washington and Lee University) in Lexington, Virginia. At West Point he had been a classmate and friend of Major Thomas J. Jackson, who at that time was a professor at the Virginia Military Institute, also in Lexington. When they were married, Major Jackson was groomsman, and it was there at Cottage Home that he met his future wife, my Aunt Anna. Now he, already famous as Stonewall Jackson, had died at Guiney's Station, and Aunt Isabella's husband had risen to the rank of lieutenant general in the Confederate Army.

Aunt Isabella told me much of the early life of my mother and that of my aunts. In the Morrison family there were six girls, coming as it were in pairs with a son or two between, and in each pair of girls there was one who had a good ear for music and one who could draw. Aunt Anna Jackson, for instance, had an overwhelming fondness for music, and my mother, Eugenia, drew beautifully. We have a few specimens of her girlhood drawing, and they are most unusual. The four older sisters, Isabella, Harriet, Anna, and Eugenia, were educated at the Salem Female Academy conducted by the Moravian Church at Salem, North Carolina, and I never saw more beautiful handwriting than theirs. This old institution, established in 1772, is still in existence as Salem College at Winston-Salem, and I hear that it still maintains the high standard of scholarship for which it was originally noted. The two younger sisters, Susan and Laura, were educated at a school called Edgeworth in Greensboro.

Sometime after my return to Concord an incident occurred which again aroused my newly-awakened interest in railroads. One day Uncle Victor was lying propped up in bed so that he could write on a tablet held on his knee, when four men whom he was evidently expecting marched into his room carrying a stretcher on which lay a much bunged-up and bandaged specimen of a man. They placed the stretcher alongside my uncle but facing the other way. This bade fair to be a circus of some dimensions, so I took my seat behind my uncle, ready to bring his pipe or pencil. It turned out to be the case of a man injured on the railroad, and this man's story was pathetic as well as interesting.

Young, hale, and hearty, he had been assigned to night work on a freight train in the wintertime, because he was what we would now call a conscientious objector. He did not seem to realize that somebody had to do this work, and if he refused to fight at the front in this time of trial, he must do some of the hazardous work at the rear. He made the story of his accident so graphic that I was literally standing on tiptoe before he finished.

It was a wintry night, and he was running on the North Carolina Railroad between Charlotte and Salisbury. His freight was a long one, going downgrade, and he was back in the caboose when he heard the engineer's signal for less speed—three short blows of the whistle. (This was, of course, long before the days of the air brake controlled from the locomotive.) He put on the brake at the front end of the caboose, then climbed to the top of the first freight car and tightened that one, and started to

FIRST RAILROAD ADVENTURES 75

walk along the top of the rolling, rocking train. But the little two-foot platform was covered with ice, so he had to get down and crawl to the end of that car, then get up and jump to the next one, adjust that brake, and again crawl forward. He knew that there was a bad curve about a mile ahead, and he was already picturing the wreck that would certainly occur if he did not put the brakes on with greater speed; so, hearing another imperative call from the engineer's whistle, he got up and tried to run. That was impossible; he fell and had to crawl again.

The braking device on these early freight cars consisted of brake-shoes, levers, and chains underneath the car ending in a mitre gear. From this rose a two-inch iron rod extending about three feet above the end of the car and crowned with a sixteen- or eighteen-inch cast-iron wheel, resembling the steering wheel of an automobile. The brakeman must grab this, turn it until the brake was tight, and then hold his gain by shoving a ratchet into a notched wheel below. The brakeman had to keep those ratchets loose, but this man complained that every one of them was frozen in place.

Urged on by the constant appeals of the frantic engineer, he made his way about halfway up the long train. Then another desperate signal came, and he decided to use his brake stick. This was a two-foot stick, a little larger than a broom handle, which when inserted into the wheel doubled his leverage. The finale came promptly; the brake stick slipped, and the brakeman rolled off the side of the car.

Nature was kind in having cast sleet and frozen rain on all the saplings beside the roadbed, and, fortunately, the man fell where one of the limbs had bent over so far that it scraped the side of the car. Falling at that exact spot, he broke only one leg and one arm instead of his neck.

The man had evidently been thinking a great deal about his accident. He knew that the railroad was owned by the state, and he said that he wanted to sue the State of North Carolina for damages. At that, Uncle Victor rose in his wrath and told him that he had no more chance of winning such a suit than a soldier at the front would have if he sued the Confederate States Government and tried to collect damages for wounds received on the battle field. Uncle Victor reminded his visitor very acidly that he had been assigned to that job because of his scruples against fighting for his country and said that he had better thank his stars for the sleet that gave him a comparatively safe landing place. And so a would-be client was shown the door.

Others came in these troubled times for counsel and friendly advice in their misfortunes, and one of them I remember particularly because her visit aroused my interest in another wonder of the age, the telegraph. She was a Mrs. Young, a friend of the family, who had been notified by the Confederate authorities that her husband had been seriously wounded. The letter had been delayed for about a week, so Uncle Victor advised her to telegraph for further information to the hospital to which her husband had been taken. She said that she wanted to do that but had been unable to find the telegraph office. I spoke up and said that I knew where it was and I could take her to it. So off we went with a telegram, written with Uncle Victor's help.

We found a young soldier in charge of the telegraph office; he was stumping around on a peg leg, and I remember just how his leg looked. It had been cut off just below the knee, flexed backward, and his kneecap placed on a pad between the diverging limbs of a white oak sapling with some of the bark still on it. It astonished me how readily he moved around with this, to me, barbarous apparatus strapped to him. Placing the message before him, he made some mystical sounds with the key and then proceeded to telegraph. The apparatus consisted of an open brass framework, some eighteen inches long, four inches wide, and six inches high, having at one end a narrow roll of paper, six or eight inches across, which was pivoted on the machine. I noticed that when he pressed his key down quickly, this moving ribbon of paper showed only a dot, but when he held the key down for a fraction of a second, a distinct line appeared on the paper, and the length of the line seemed to be significant. He said that he kept the script copy on file as a proof of service.

We waited about half an hour before he told us that Richmond was calling, and he should soon have the message. He fixed his machine in order to receive the dots and dashes which soon began coming in, and I can remember to this day the pathos with which he exclaimed, "Oh, Mrs. Young! I am afraid I have bad news." The news was indeed bad; Mrs. Young's husband was either dead or in a hopeless condition, I do not remember which. But I do remember that the young soldier was not looking at the receiver when he cried out, and I did not understand how he could anticipate the message before it was written down. When I told Uncle Victor about this, however, he was much interested. He had heard, he said, that now they were beginning to read the instrument by sound.

XI

VISIT TO RALEIGH

THIS WAS CERTAINLY a year of travel for me. I had already been out to Asheville, down to Charlotte, and up to Davidson, and now I was sent east to Raleigh to visit my uncle, Daniel Moreau Barringer. I probably went as the bearer of tender family messages of concern and good will, as Uncle Moreau had fallen and broken his leg, and for some time he, like Uncle Victor, had been a wheel-chair invalid.

I did not, however, go directly to see him, for I stopped off in Greensboro and paid a short visit at the home of my uncle, William Barringer. He was also my father's brother and was one of the most magnificent-looking men whom I have ever seen. He, over six feet in height, was the only really tall Barringer, the other brothers ranging from five feet six to five feet eight inches. He was the only Methodist in the family and was a minister in that denomination which he had joined after attending a camp meeting at Rock Spring. His wife, a woman of unusual grace and dignity, Lavinia M. Alston, came of the "fighting Alstons" of Chatham County, distinguished people in Colonial and Revolutionary days and always good sports. Uncle William was at that time engaged in the construction of Greensboro Female College, of which he was agent, manager, and prospective president. It was in that building that he subsequently met his death when he fell three stories to the ground while installing a six-inch

VISIT TO RALEIGH

telescope in the little observatory on top. He was absent from home at the time of my visit, and his eldest son, John, was away at school, but I met the other children, Paul, William, Victor, and one daughter, Ella, then a baby.

Oddly enough, it was in this ministerial household that I received my first introduction to the ancient art of cockfighting. Perhaps Uncle William's prolonged absences from home in the interest of the college had made it possible for John to embark on the biological venture of cock breeding. I saw no fights, but we children roamed around, admiring the old cock in the yard which was of the Alston breed as well as all the promising young "stags" which John kept around at the outlying Negro cabins. At all events, when I left Greensboro I knew something of the history of cockfighting and how the breeds differed, particularly the Alston Black, the Shawl Neck, and the War Horse, the three breeds that John and his brother affected. Somewhat later in life I was to find this information useful.

I had another stopover on this hundred mile journey and that was at Company Shops, the old name for Burlington, which, no doubt, that thriving city has long since forgotten. Here they built engines, cars, and even boilers for the railroad then extending from Goldsboro to Charlotte. I saw passenger cars, flat cars, and box cars in various stages of construction, and I spent a glorious day with a Mr. Andrews, who was some family connection of ours and who knew the railroad business from the ground up. I had heard of turntables, and I saw my first specimen at the roundhouse here, and to find that I could, by my own unaided efforts, turn this enormous pivoted mass was most gratifying. Already, I felt myself a man.

This Mr. Alexander Boyd Andrews had been in the First North Carolina Cavalry, serving under Generals Wade Hampton and J. E. B. Stuart. He was almost mortally wounded but recovered and was retired in 1864. He returned to really fight behind the lines in railroading which was desperately needed. After the war he achieved great success and was ultimately one of the presidents of the newly-formed Southern Railway.

Again we took the train (I do not remember who accompanied me, but someone did), this time for Raleigh and Uncle

Moreau's home. This uncle was my father's oldest brother, a former minister to Spain—where Uncle Victor had been his secretary—and he had served as a Southern peace commissioner to Washington in the spring of 1861. Too old for military service, he was active in public life until he fell and broke his leg.

I was met at the station by my cousin, Lewin Weathered Barringer, a boy of fourteen or fifteen who was very pleasant. When we reached the capitol he let me get out of the carriage and walk around that simple but noble bit of Doric architecture and also pointed out the governor's mansion which then faced the end of a wide street, now called Fayetteville Street. Here we turned to the left and came to Uncle Moreau's house which both outside and in—particularly the latter—clearly showed its master's many years of foreign residence and travel. I must confess, however, that the paintings, bric-a-brac, and Oriental rugs with which the house was furnished did not appeal to me nearly as much as did the wide variety of figs which grew outside. He must have had a dozen varieties, yellow, brown, and roseate, on the half acre or more allotted to this fruit. Outside of a botanical garden, I never saw so many varieties elsewhere.

The boys raised pigeons, and here I first became acquainted with the homer or carrier pigeon. Lewin bred these, and they were allowed to range free, so his younger brother (then called Rosie), in order to bolster his self-respect, had a pair of fantails in a cage.

Rosie and I had a fine time together. This boy, Daniel Moreau Barringer, Jr., two years younger than I, was my closest lifelong friend. There was also my cousin, Lizzie, a beautiful and charming child. Their mother, a great beauty, was Miss Elizabeth Weathered of Cambridge, on the eastern shore of Maryland.

Uncle Moreau was sufficiently recovered from his accident to be able to walk a little with the help of a cane. Many prominent men and women called to see him, and I have greatly regretted that I was too young at that time to remember the names of most of them. I recall having my first sight of a governor—it was a word to me, nothing more—and I think it was Governor Zebulon Vance. He did not come by the street but strolled over through the connecting grove. Uncle William Graham came, and

I remember Doctor Charles Philips, whose sons I was to know later, and the great and dignified Judge A. S. Merrimon, all of whom were extremely gracious to me.

Looking back at that visit after the lapse of considerably more than half a century, I am gratified to know that the man whom I remember best of all was my uncle's devoted servant, known to us children as "Uncle Jerry." When Jerry was a small boy he was given by my grandfather, General Paul Barringer of Bellevue, to Uncle Moreau as his body servant. In that capacity Jerry accompanied his young master to Europe on the "grand tour," was with him in Spain while he was United States minister at Madrid during the administrations of Presidents Taylor and Fillmore, and returned with him to the United States, preferring the benevolent slavery that he had always known rather than freedom amongst strangers. After the passing of the Thirteenth Amendment he remained with Uncle Moreau until the latter's death at White Sulphur Springs and then became a barber in Raleigh. I have heard that he not only amassed a good estate, but also left a family of self-respecting and much respected sons and daughters.

I cannot recall what name he took after leaving the family, but, notwithstanding the respect and affection he bore his old master, I am sure it was not Barringer. That would have been against tribal custom, because the Negroes feared that in the event of a Southern victory in some future war against the North, the old slaves could then be more easily found and reclaimed. For that reason they took names from the family connection, rather than the former master's own name. I may say that nearly every family name on earth was adopted except one. There are today Negro families named Brown and Green and White—but never Black. I never knew a Negro named Mr. Black.

I returned to Concord somehow a wiser, but also a wickeder, boy. I had had Methodist and Episcopal influences ingrafted on my rigid, hard-boiled Presbyterian concepts. I had heard of cockfighting, and euchre, and even graft!

Now, alcohol was different. I had known that from my earliest days, but I had known it as whiskey and brandy in cut-glass decanters decorating the sideboard. I must have seen such decanters at Uncle William's and at Uncle Moreau's, for had this symbol of dignity and hospitality been lacking there, I would certainly have missed it.

Once or twice in my life, suffering from a "maldetum" caused by eating green apples or raw sweet potatoes, I had been made to take a teaspoonful raw from one of those decanters, and as a result the idea never entered my head that anybody ever took that stuff for anything other than rite or ritual. However, I noticed even in those days that when Uncle Victor, "Old Wash" Allison, and Judge Ruffin put a decanter on the table between them and started to talk, they seemed exalted and I became all ears. I think I can state at this remote date that they always talked better when they gathered around this vitreous fetich.

It must have been soon after my return from Raleigh that my sister Anna came home. We had been separated a good deal during our short lives, and I remember the year or more that we were together as one of the pleasantest periods of my childhood. Of course, reminders of the war, its sorrows and work and privations surrounded us, but we were so young that we remembered little of any other life. Scarcely touched by the gloom that enveloped our world, we were companionable and happy with our playmates. Our father's house was rented, and although Uncle Victor was practising law, he did not go to his office. We used the office as a playhouse, Anna and I, the Foard and Phifer children, and others in the neighborhood. Anna used to entertain us with her stories of the "Tories," as we called the people who lived in the South but were Union sympathizers.

I went to school at the other end of town with the Foard children, the Phifers, the McDonalds, and the Allisons. Our teacher was Miss Margaret Long, who was employed as governess, I believe, by "Old Man Noah" Foard, the father of a large number of children. Although I had always played with other children, this was my first introduction to the group relations of childhood. Within a week I found that I could lick any boy in school except Hiram Foard; so he and I, each afraid of the other, united and ran the school.

Before I was eight years old I could read simple stuff fairly easily, but, on thinking it over, I cannot recall that there was much simple stuff in Uncle Victor's library. Even in those days, however, there was bootleg literature; I could get from Hiram Foard, Sut Lovinggood's stories, entitled, if I remember correctly, *Yarns* and *Georgia Tales*. I was reading the former when Aunt Maria caught me; horrified, she carried the book to Uncle Victor, and he nearly died laughing. He told her it was worse on the outside than in.

Needless to say, for the young in a Presbyterian family, learning to read had but one end—the attainment of perfection in the Shorter Catechism of the Westminster Confession. I went to Sunday school and to church in the morning and then spent part of Sunday afternoon wrestling with some of the abstruse questions of this great little work; for regardless of the premises, I must confess that I know of no work to compare with it in clarity of definition.

One Sunday afternoon, having just finished up *What Is Effectual Calling* or *Prophet, Priest and King*, or some other tough one, I was released for my first leisure of the day and went out on the front porch. I heard children's voices singing on my left and walked over to old Doctor Gibson's. Following the sound, I entered where Miss Mattie Gibson was holding her Singing Bee, or whatever she called it. Anyway, they were singing hymns, and I edged in and found a seat.

Miss Mattie was standing in front of eight or ten children, beating time, and she wore a hoopskirt. I don't know how old Mattie Gibson was then—eighteen perhaps—at any rate she was grown up enough to wear hoopskirts, and to me, a boy of seven, that made her seem almost an old woman. All the ladies I knew wore hoopskirts—those things made of steel under their outside skirts—and the outside skirts were four to five yards in diameter and three inches from the ground. I suppose I thought ladies grew in that peculiar bell shape. To see one of them walk down in the middle of a church aisle, turn at right angles, and with her hands make compression amidships until her skirt shot out long and narrow fore and aft, diminishing until it was narrow enough to negotiate the pew entrance—and that without any seeming discomfort to the lady or evidence of the steel—never failed to arouse my profound astonishment.

As I say, we were singing hymns, and pretty soon we came to one that I always detested. Why I cannot say, but perhaps others felt the same way, for it is seldom heard today. It ran something in this wise:

> I want to be an angel,
>   And with the angels stand,
> A crown upon my forehead,
>   A harp within my hand.

We had not quite finished the final unction on "hand" when a flash of lightning seemed to invade the very room. I learned afterwards that it struck one of Sandy Smith's oaks, just over the fence beyond the window. But I was not looking out the window; I was looking at Mattie Gibson. She went pale and for a moment stood paralyzed, doubtless remembering that "steel drew lightning." She quickly recovered herself, however, and regardless of place, perfect performance, or prudery, she then and there got out of that steel magnet!

This was my first great disillusionment. I now knew that ladies were human and biped. Dejected, I went home saying to myself, "I want to be an angel—but some other time, Lord, not this day."

XII

THE LAWS OF MAN AND NATURE

WHEREVER I WAS I found a good deal to interest me in my surroundings, including the punishment meted out for misdemeanors and crime in my native town of Concord. Although I was not supposed to do so, I used to inspect the whipping post and stocks on my way to school. These stood in Sheriff Stough's back yard which was surrounded by a picket fence and guarded by an enormous, and seemingly very fierce, bulldog. I was careful to choose those times when the dog was tied up to look through a gap in the fence, and once, finding a good opening, I slipped through the fence . . . and stood inside . . . and wondered.

I had seen many a culprit, both white and black, whipped, viewing these whippings surreptitiously from an attic window in the house of our neighbor, Dr. Bingham. The sentence then current, "forty lashes, save one," followed the old English phraseology. I never saw the stocks used, that apparatus being too tame for wartime. Nor did I ever see a hanging. It was customary for a condemned felon to ride to the gallows in a wagon, sitting astride his coffin, and once I arranged to be down at Hiram Foard's when a poor devil passed by in this miserable fashion to his hanging.

The methods of those days may shock us now, but the results were superlative. I daresay, allowing for increase in population, there are ten murders today for every one that occurred then and far more thievery.

For manslaughter there was a terrible punishment; I never saw it inflicted, but I knew the ritual. In Colonial times the convicted man was branded on the forehead with the letter "M" by the sheriff holding the branding iron in place as long as it took him to cry three times, "God save the King!" This punishment was still legal and was practised in the 1860's, the only difference being that the "M" was branded on the palm of the hand instead of the forehead, and "God save the King" was changed to "God save the State."

There was one older man who always wore a large black hat pulled well down over his forehead. I saw him only once or twice as he seldom came to town and then only on most pressing business. He was the owner of a large and successful plantation near by where he spent his life apart from his fellow man, for he bore the letter "M" branded on his forehead.

When Uncle Victor was practising law in his homemade wheel chair and being rolled to the Court House by Yankee Jim, he had one client who was undoubtedly a murderer. Although my uncle bounced the jury of seniles into permitting the man to live, he could not save him from the pain and humiliation of being branded. When the ordeal was over Sheriff Stough rushed the man to the doctor, and I learned from the little Scott girl how the doctor exerted his magic on the branded hand. (It is a matter of deep regret to me that I cannot now recall the name of this little girl—I think it was Alice—as I was much in love with her at the time.)

I remember another incident which occurred a few years later. I was with my father at some political meeting and, becoming bored with the speeches, I wandered away. I saw a man who had driven into town in a wagon with a strange burden. It was a rusty iron cage caked with clay and in it, equally foul, was the remains of a human skeleton. Long ago it had been buried at the crossroads outside of town. Erosion and some recent heavy rains had washed away the bank, revealing this horror. What the crime was for such a penalty I do not know, but to be hung alive in an iron cage, and there to linger until thirst, starva-

THE LAWS OF MAN AND NATURE   87

tion, and the elements took their toll, and then to be buried at the crossroads was a medieval penalty, appalling to discover in this country. Although passionate homicidal punishment may take terrible forms, certainly judicial punishment by slow and lingering torture was never, within the memory of living man, countenanced by our law.

Sheriff Stough's dreaded bulldog figured in one very pleasant episode. I had to pass the sheriff's house when I went down every morning, with a little bag over my shoulder, to bring Uncle Victor's mail, and almost daily I tormented the dog by beating a shingle on the picket fence. One day as I approached, shingle in hand, I saw to my horror that the gate was open, so I beat a hasty retreat for some little distance and then prudently crossed the street.

This brought me in close contact for the first time with an old man whom I had frequently seen but never spoken to. He was Mr. Rheinholdt Sutter, a small, dried-up, wizened old man who was fully ninety-five years of age. Having watched my manoeuvre from his chair on the porch, he poked fun at me. I finally told him that he looked older than my grandfather, and he asked who my grandfather was. When I told him Doctor Morrison, who was then approaching seventy, he replied that he was old enough to be my grandfather's father, and then he said that he was old enough to be my Uncle Victor's grandfather, which seemed truly remarkable to me. He went on to tell me that he had known my great-grandfather, John Paul Barringer, very well, adding, "Old Pioneer Paul surely was a bearcat!"

This expression puzzled me, so when I went home I asked Uncle Victor what it meant. He explained that it was an old-time border term for a man who had the strength and endurance of a bear with the swiftness and alacrity of a cat. From that day it was a fixed idea in my mind that John Paul Barringer, whose name I had known merely as that of my great-grandfather, had actually been a bearcat and, therefore, an ancestor to be proud of.

Years later I learned that old Rheinholdt Sutter was close kin to John Augustus Sutter, whose discovery of gold at Sutter's Mill in 1848 precipitated the California Gold Rush of '49. I have often wondered if Sutter's knowledge of gold which enabled him to recognize his find might not have been acquired during some visit to Cabarrus County. Although I do not know that he was ever there, I do know that at an early date gold had been found in this county.

In 1799, a boy found a nugget which weighed about seventeen pounds. He took it home as a curiosity and for the next ten years it was used as a doorstop. At last, having heard several people say that it might be valuable, the owner took it to Fayetteville, more than one hundred miles away, and showed it to a jeweler who said he believed it might be gold. He offered to buy it, and after some haggling the owner let it go for $3.50. Other nuggets, ranging in weight from one to four pounds, were found all through that region, in Mecklenburg and Stanley counties as well as in Cabarrus. There were also larger nuggets, one of ten pounds, another of twelve, and the largest of all weighed twenty-eight pounds. By 1829 feverish interest in native gold had developed in the western part of the state. While visiting his old home that year my great-uncle, William A. Graham, observed in a letter to a friend that he had, since his arrival, "heard of scarce anything . . . except Gold. Nothing before has so completely engrossed the attention of all classes. The discoveries have indeed in many instances almost wrought miracles . . . bankrupts have been restored to affluence, and paupers turned to nabobs."

This western North Carolina gold was used by Christopher Bechtler in making the Bechtler gold coins which for many years were in general circulation in parts of North and South Carolina, Virginia, Kentucky, and Tennessee. Each one was stamped with his name and the value, $1.00, $2.50, or $5.00. He put a United States gold coin on his scales and weighed an equal amount of pure gold without alloy for his coin, and probably for that reason the government allowed his private mint to continue. He was a German from Baden, a skilled metalworker and jeweler, who came to Rutherfordton, North Carolina, about 1830.

About 1865 we had a visit from Dr. John Bachman, the pastor of St. John's Lutheran Church in Charleston, South Carolina. No human life was ever more influential in shaping another's than his was in shaping mine. My Uncle Victor was a philosopher, lawyer, and linguist, but he had no scientific training and did not have much of the scientific method of approach in observation and record. This I love, and old Bachman gave me my first taste of it. He was a philosopher, botanist, zoologist, and astronomer whom chance had condemned to the ministry. Nevertheless, he fitted the functions of the latter ideally, because he was a man of extreme reverence for that great Power that shaped heaven and earth. He was full of the milk of human kindness, but in his life the ministry was submerged.

He was basically a naturalist. He wrote *The Viviparous Quadrupeds of North America* in collaboration with John J. Audubon, the great ornithologist. Two of Bachman's daughters married two of Audubon's sons and contributed their talents and training to the rendering of many of the illustrations in that great work, especially in the drawing and coloring of flowers. The old doctor seems to have been the personal friend of almost every living biologist and had, at the age of sixteen, met Humboldt on his trip to America. Thanks to this acquaintance and to a later friendship with the Earl of Derby, the great patron of science, Dr. Bachman was elected Foreign Correspondent for the Zoological Society of London. When I knew him, he must have been about seventy-five years old, having been born in 1790. I had no fear of old men, so common in children of that day, and as a result I became very intimate with many of them to my lasting benefit.

Like so many Charlestonians, old Bachman went to the mountains of western North Carolina in the summer. There he and his family knew my stepmother in her youth. In the spring of 1865, when visiting the Victor Barringers, he learned by "grapevine" telegraph that the Union General Stoneman, who was then raiding in North Carolina, had heard that he was in Concord and was detaching a scouting party to pick him up.

Dr. Bachman was originally from Rheinbeck, New York, on the Hudson and had come south because of his health. He had an influential and devoted congregation in Charleston and in November of 1860 had delivered a heartily received sermon on Love of Country which was the next duty to Love of God. "If," he said, "our rights had been protected in the Union, we would not desire a political change, but... those pledges had been violated and a mightier law than the Constitution substituted. It is better like Abraham and Lot, to separate, when we can no longer live in peace."

I have been told that when the legislative convention was meeting and found themselves by chance without a minister to open the proceedings with prayer, Dr. Bachman, passing on the street, was called in. Whatever the circumstances, when South Carolina passed the Ordinance of Secession, Dr. Bachman gave it God's blessing. For this reason he was a marked man with a price upon his head. To escape the danger from Stoneman's party, my Uncle Victor assigned to him a trusted Negro who was a good cook, a mule, provisions, bedding, and myself, delighted to go as companion and messenger. And we went, so to speak, underground. A small boy would be less suspect than an adult as means of communication, and I was perfectly capable of covering the country on my own. We left in the night, going down into a canebreak on Aunt Lydia Harris's farm, where we stayed for over a week, reports from the outside coming in every other day. The nights are cold in early spring, and the tent was so small that we solved several problems by my sleeping on the foot of his cot.

I had an enchanting companion. He taught me the five thrushes that were common there; the mocking bird, the catbird, the robin, wood thrush, and thrasher. He taught me to recognise six woodpeckers by name: the great woodpecker (now disappeared), the red-head, the yellow-hammer, the sap-sucker, the hairy, and the downy. One day he found a stray garter snake (Utania), and the Negro later dug into a pit of snakes, emerging from their winter torpor. He taught me the difference between the venomous and nonvenomous snakes, showing the marks of the pit vipers, not only the pit between the nostril and eyes of the rattlesnake, copperhead, and water moccasin, but the undivided postanal caudal plate. He explained how this solid plate is necessary for any snake that springs and strikes. They must have a solid grip on the ground with the ventral face of their tails. The nonvenomous do not need this.

At last we heard that a Confederate, General Wheeler, was in Concord instead of the feared Stoneman and that it was safe to return. That night he gave me a lesson out of his old wisdom that has been one of the greatest pleasures of my later years.

He said, "Son, now I will show you the stars. Look at that sky. That great star is Arcturus, to your right is Spica, and to the left is Ursa Major. The time will come when you cannot chase birds and butterflies, or hunt snakes and rabbits. But, if you will learn the stars, you can sit always at the door of your tent, and they will come to you nightly and return at the same time every year, old friends that will never fail."

XIII

STONEMAN'S RAID

CHILD AS I WAS, I knew full well in the spring of 1865 that something disagreeable, or even worse, was approaching; it was in every eye and on every lip, and I felt it without understanding. I heard more and more talk of Stoneman, the Federal general who was as much feared in North Carolina as Sheridan was in Virginia, or Sherman in Georgia. General George Stoneman had six thousand seasoned raiders, and it was their business to destroy all means of communication, transportation, and supplies. They were to live off the land and destroy all food and stores. I heard all this, but I did not know what it meant although I felt the tension. In a way, the matter was cleared up for me by a remark of my patriarchal friend, old Rheinholdt Sutter, who said, "The Yankees will be in Concord soon, and I wouldn't let them catch me riding a pony with U. S. branded on it!" My beloved Rebel-Victor had become a menace! I tied him in the bushes and came back for him after dark.

Soon after this my sister Anna and I paid a visit to Cottage Home. I did not take my pony with me, for there I had General Jackson's favorite horse, Fancy, better known as Little Sorrel, that being the name that Stonewall Jackson's soldiers gave their commander's favorite mount. The horse was known to the family as Fancy because when several horses were submitted for General Jackson's choice, he said, "This is my fancy." I rode him everywhere, often with Anna and our two little cousins, Julia Jackson and Hattie Avery, piled on behind. The overseer who lived in the original plantation house had two boys about my age, so I was over there often, especially when it was time for the mail to come in on the Charlotte to Lincolnton mail coach.

One day, while we were waiting for the stage driver's horn which he always blew half a mile down the road, we heard other sounds from afar—rifle shots and the coming of a rider at full speed. We knew the war had reached us, that Stoneman's raid had come. First a lone Confederate on a magnificent mule came in sight, and as he passed us he threw a heavy object over the garden fence into the shrubbery. There the road curved, putting him again in line with his pursuers. Then came another and much nearer burst of rifle fire, and a dozen bullets whizzed by within fifty feet of us. We ran around the corner of the ginhouse in time to see the fugitive slide off and release his mule with a slap. The mule ran on down the road, followed by some half a dozen or more Yankees. Much later I picked up the object that the man had thrown over the fence and found it to be a canvas encased ham, a novel sight to me as I had never before seen a ham done up in canvas.

That same evening a full regiment of Yankee cavalry passed by, stopping long enough to take all the horses on the place including Fancy and General Jackson's other horse, a stallion, named Superior. In fact, they took all the livestock, mules, cows, sheep, hogs, and chickens, and there was great consternation among the servants over this dastardly affront to their white folks.

Aunt Anna had a sentimental attachment for the two horses, and she knew that General Stoneman and her husband had once been friends; so she wrote him a note asking for the return of the horses and mules. The Federal troops were camped near Doctor Hunter's mill, a mile or so away, and she sent me with the note and old Abram to accompany me. At eight years of age, I was the able-bodied man of the household. Arriving there, I asked for General Stoneman but was told that he was not with the raid. I was directed to the commanding colonel in a certain tent to present the note. Everybody around the camp seemed nervous, no doubt because of the proximity of Confederate General Joseph Wheeler, whose exact whereabouts were unknown. The note was taken to the colonel, and when he came out he was swearing, at whom or what I do not know. He asked me if I would know the horses, and I said of course I would, as I had ridden them many times.

He took us over to a temporary corral, and I saw Fancy at once; when I pointed him out, the colonel told me to go and get him, and he even gave me a United States bridle to put on him. Superior, the stallion, was not there at that time. It is not generally known that General Jackson possessed this horse, which was, I believe, presented to him by a cadet school somewhere in Kentucky. He rode Superior the night he went from Trevilians to Richmond, a distance of fifty-one miles, to interview President Jefferson Davis and on other occasions of great stress when he wanted to save Fancy.

I am sorry that I do not remember this colonel's name for he was certainly most considerate of us. He said, "I am going to return the mules also," and asked Abram to point them out. Abram at once went up to "Ole Kit," who stood out like a large white image amongst the mules, and found one or two others that belonged to us, but he told me, "Marse Paul, I'll never find all our mules. I b'lieve we better jus take us a bunch er good mules." The colonel laughed and told Abram to go and take his pick. So Abram took "Ole Kit" and several others that he knew, and then he made up the dozen or more from choice four- and five-year-olds that he did not recognize, being very careful not to make the mistake of taking any that he knew belonged to our neighbors.

I rode Fancy back to Cottage Home, while Abram rode "Ole Kit" without a bridle, the mules meekly following that curious phantasy of equine life, the leading "white mare." I carried a courteous note of apology from the colonel to Mrs. Jackson, and he sent three troopers to guard the place from further depredations. The next day this extremely gentlemanly colonel returned Superior with more apologies.

The horse, Fancy, I may add, lived to a ripe old age, and at Cottage Home, my uncle, Doctor Robert Hall Morrison, Jr., a practising physician, used him for light work until he was thirty-three years old.

The Confederate Cavalry under General Wheeler arrived in a day or two. They allowed our Federal guards to remain, treating them with unusual courtesy, but as soon as General Wheeler was out of sight, the Federal soldiers departed with our blessing, taking a different road. To tell the plain truth, we at Cottage Home were more afraid of Wheeler than we were of Stoneman, for his men were much more famished.

While our Yankee guard remained with us they would not permit anyone, with the exception of the family and our servants, to go near our well. General Wheeler respected the rights of the guard, so as a result of this situation I launched my first business venture. I filled everybody's canteen—blue and gray alike—flush and full for the price of three cartridges. Business was so brisk that I had a line of pickaninnies passing canteens through the fence while I sat on the top rail, taking in cartridges at the cashier's desk. Somehow I persuaded a youthful Confederate veteran to trade me a carbine that had lost its ramrod, and this weapon I carefully concealed. The Confederates had muzzle loading, fifty-eight caliber carbines with paper cartridges and percussion caps. The ramrod was fastened to the gun, slipped through the holder, and turned over at the muzzle to be inserted. The Yankees had Spencer carbines, breech-loading through an opening in the butt plate; their cartridges were to give me much trouble as I had to open them to get the powder, and they were of that hazardous form known as "rim fire."

The perfect peace that had reigned at Cottage Home while I was there with my sister and two little girl cousins was broken up with the arrival of my cousin, John Irwin, with whom I had visited at Davidson. Although John could not have been quite twelve years old, he was, as we said in those days, "very much of a man"; he could and would fight, he was a good swimmer, and a number of times he had been allowed to shoot a gun. We immediately cut loose from the girls, and I, eager to learn new strokes, went with him each day to the swimming hole. At odd times we worked surreptitiously on making a ramrod for my carbine which was a smooth bore. My swimming improved, and we completed the ramrod, but my iridescent ignorance had left us in sore straits for we did not have a single percussion cap. Then our young uncle, Alfred Morrison, who was fourteen or fifteen years old and going to school at Davidson College, came home on a visit and showed us a new "wrinkle."

We took a bullet out of a cartridge and on a smoothing iron held between our knees hammered it to a thickness of about an eighth of an inch. Then with a case knife we cut this sheet of metal into squares of one-sixteenth of an inch, rolled them until nearly round between two walnut planks, and thus made a squirrel shot. After diligent inquiry we learned that a boy who lived near General Burton's place had a box of musket caps, so we went over there and traded him two or three dozen Spencer carbine cartridges for these essentials. By this time Uncle Alfred had left, so we did not know how much powder to use to shoot squirrels. I had the bright idea that the amount in the paper cartridge must be the exact quantity needed, so we tried our first shot with that load. Unfortunately, John persuaded me to fire first. Although a big boy for my years, I weighed less than one hundred pounds.

I sat down and stuck the gun through a crack in the fence, but John who must have suspected what was going to happen objected, so we tore the fence down almost to the bottom and rested the carbine on the top rail instead of between two rails. My target, a foot square paper, was some thirty yards distant. John was justified in his fears, for when that gun went off, it rose and went back over my head and landed some ten feet away, throwing me on my back with a badly-damaged shoulder. We had rammed the charge too tight, and the war load for a fifty-eight caliber one-ounce ball was too much. Of course, Aunt Anna and my grandfather learned of a concealed carbine in this previously peaceful home and promptly confiscated it with some, but not all, of our ammunition.

All the men having gone to war there was little hunting, and under such conditions it is remarkable how quickly deer and other game return to sections long forsaken. Squirrels were abundant on all plantations devoted now to food production rather than to cotton, so ere long John pleaded for the return of the carbine, so that he might shoot a "sassy" squirrel which persisted in perching on one of the balls of the front gate. Grandfather himself loaded the gun and allowed John to shoot and, strange to say, he got the squirrel. Soon he became a regular provider of squirrel meat for the family, but as he was a poor shot our ammunition was soon exhausted.

John got permission for us to drive down to Charlotte to get some ammunition. It was thirty-five miles in a shaky buggy pulled by a frisky horse. When we got to the Catawba River, the bridge had been burned by the Yankees, so we had to cross in a rowboat which we found tied near by. We took the wheels and shaft from the buggy, put it across the boat, and rowed over. Then back for the wheels and shaft and swam the horse, tied to the back of the boat. Reassembling ourselves, we went on to Charlotte to the Navy Yard. Since Charlotte, North Carolina, is two hundred miles inland and on no body of water whatsoever, this Navy Yard needs a little explanation. When Norfolk was captured, all the Confederate equipment was put in boxcars and moved inland. A stockade was built around it, and an arch over the gate carried the inscription "Confederate Navy Yard." We got four shells about two feet long, with a nose about four inches long. We had no packing, so we put them in the back of the buggy where they rattled around over rocky roads for the thirty-five miles back. When we reached the river, we found a ferryboat waiting and were thankful we didn't have to risk getting our powder wet.

When we reached home, we took out the shells, got a wrench, unscrewed the cap, and poured out a quart each of black powder. It was as large as big hominy, so we pondered how to use it for shells. We decided to grind it in the coffee grinder, which we did with perfect success, loaded our shells, and went squirrel shooting!

XIV

A VISIT FROM "MR. PRESIDENT"

I WAS IN Concord when the news of Lee's surrender came, but it produced little disturbance, doubtless because the news for weeks had been more and more hopeless, and the residents had discounted the impending disaster. I soon realized that this was what they had been fearing, and yet I had never before heard the word "surrender." Now, the trembling tone and halting voice told me that it was the end of all things, but its direct meaning had to be explained to me. The Confederate Army under General Joseph E. Johnston was still operating in North Carolina, however, and this eased the strain for me. Soon there was talk of his "surrender" and later of Kirby Smith's. By this time I accepted the word "surrender" as one more stage in the program of disaster.

Stoneman's raiders had succeeded in destroying the hated Confederate prison and all equipment in Salisbury and had taken at least a thousand prisoners; they had also driven Johnston into the path of Sherman, who was advancing up from Georgia. Lee's surrender was glad news to them, as it seemed to signal the end of their North Carolina campaign; they were starting back to Tennessee and were incensed when they received orders to follow and capture the escaping Jefferson Davis and his cabinet. Davis, after the evacuation of Richmond, fled first to Danville, Virginia, where he established a temporary capital and later moved for a brief period to Greensboro, North Carolina. Finding that location untenable, he became a fugitive whose only hope was to escape to foreign shores.

While the talk of Johnston's surrender was still in the air there occurred one of the most interesting incidents in my life. Throughout the war I had gauged the rank of impending arrivals by the amount of real coffee prepared for them. A lieutenant got a few grains mixed with the homemade substitute, a captain got a few more, and so on up the scale. My astonishment was unmeasured, therefore, when I saw old Ellen go to the coffee grinder which was nailed to a post in the kitchen and proceed to grind up a large amount of *pure* coffee! Frankly, I thought the Almighty was coming, so my disgust may be imagined when, later in the day, I saw a group of bedraggled old wrecks walking up through the garden from the barn.

My appraisal was somewhat changed when Uncle Victor got up on his feet to meet and shake hands with them, but they were a sorry looking lot, dust covered, travel-stained, and none of them very young. The older men wore talmas, long gray woolen capes popular then as a protection against rain. Although the weather was pleasant, they stuck pretty close to the house, and I had almost forgotten them when suppertime came. Then, from my side table, I heard somebody say, "Mr. President," and I saw that it was directed towards, perhaps, the most striking looking man in the party. After supper I found that I had been moved out of my bedroom and was told to go to a neighbor's to spend the night.

I slept soundly without even a dream of them, but when I went home the next morning I knew they were still there, because I received repeated injunctions not to make a noise. So, to ease the strain, I got out the chessboard. Uncle Victor was a great chess player, and Mr. Charles Phifer, Mr. McDonald, or some of his other friends often dropped in for a game. Sometimes they could not come when he wanted to play, so to save the trouble of reaching over and playing the other side, he taught me the game, and I played on command. I learned a number of the opening gambits and grew so fond of the game that I often wanted to play when Uncle Victor was not in the mood; so I taught little Ellen, the cook's eight- or nine-year-old daughter, to play. We used Uncle Victor's chessmen which would be worth a thousand dollars now. The kings and queens were real monarchs, carved from ivory; the bishops stood with mitred caps; the knights were armed cap-a-pie; and the castles put on elephant backs. This, however, did not bother us at the time, and little Ellen and I, with the chessmen between us on the back porch, were having a good time when I heard a voice say, "For God's sake, Mr. President, come here!" Out came the gentleman whom they had addressed as "Mr. President" and with him a Mr. Mallory who was Secretary of the Navy. As they stood watching us, I could see that they were distinguished-looking elderly gentlemen, very unlike the weary riders of the evening before.

After gazing at us for a moment "Mr. President" said, "Do you suppose they can really play?"

To this I replied, "I can beat you," moving the pieces back to position. So "Mr. President" took Ellen's place, and I finished him in three or four moves with a "fool's mate."

By this time the whole crowd had come out, and I was talking to them over the chessboard, explaining how to open the game with the proper gambit for a "fool's mate." When Aunt Maria joined us and told them how it came about that I was a chess player, I was much elated.

She told me to get my copy of *Rasselas*, my recent birthday present, and asked the gentlemen to write their names in it. This they did, as follows:

Jeffer. Davis
19 April, 1865.
F. R. Lubbock
Ex. Gov. of Texas,
Col, and A.D.C. to the President
19 April, 1865.
Wm. Preston Johnston
Co. and A.D.C. to the President
19 April, 1865.
J. Taylor Wood
Ap. 19/'65
Burton H. Harrison.

A VISIT FROM "MR. PRESIDENT"

    C. E. Thorburn
    19th April, 1865,
    Guest of the President
S. R. Mallory
    Sec. Navy.

When I saw "Mr. President" sign "Jeffer. Davis," I understood all, or thought I did, as for the past four years the little Negroes and I had been singing:

> Jeff Davis is a wise man,
>   Abe Lincoln is a fool.
> Jeff Davis rides a big white horse,
>   Abe Lincoln rides a mule.

And here he was. I talked with him for a while after that, but while our guests remained, it was evident to me that I was generally kept away from the talk. Mr. Davis spent most of his time with his secretary, Mr. Burton H. Harrison, father of the scholarly Fairfax Harrison, whom I knew many years later. The others loafed around the house, toying with the library, and particularly with Uncle Victor's old copies of the *London Times*. As there was a price of more than half a million dollars on their collective heads, they were not parading their presence, but I am sure that quite a number of Concord people knew of their stay, and some of the leading men called upon them.

No doubt my uncle knew perfectly well that he might be called upon to pay with his life for harboring these men; certainly he was in danger of imprisonment and destruction of property, for that fate was promised to all who gave comfort or assistance to the "Rebel Chiefs."

I am not sure whether they remained twenty-four or forty-eight hours, but I know that they left one evening; their horses were brought around to the front, where they mounted and rode away. Notice: they had come directly to the barn, but they left by the front. They went to Charlotte, and took with them a letter that my uncle gave them to Colonel William Johnston, whose wife was my cousin, Eliza Ann Graham.

After they left there was a series of mysterious comings and goings, some of which I subsequently cleared up. I learned that Secretaries Breckinridge and Benjamin arrived at our house an hour or more after Mr. Davis left. They stayed a short time, got fresh horses, and followed Mr. Davis's party to Charlotte.

The exhausted family had retired for the night, and we all were sound asleep when there came an imperative knock on the door. This brought Uncle Victor to his feet without the aid of Yankee Jim, and as he came towards the door, he held a Belgian pin-fire six-shooter in his hand. Our one thought was that Stoneman's men had arrived to take vengeance for harboring the refugees. Aunt Maria hovered on the stairs while Yankee Jim slipped to a front window, peered out, and said it was a soldier. He ran back and steadied Uncle Victor. Once more responsible as the able-bodied man of the household, I opened the door. It was a man in Confederate uniform who asked the whereabouts of President Davis. We invited him in, and a long conference with my uncle followed. After this the soldier was given something to eat, a fresh horse, and was sent immediately to Charlotte.

I learned afterwards that this man was a courier sent by General Joseph E. Johnston who was at Durham, facing Sherman in the process of surrender, and his message contained the official notice of Mr. Lincoln's assassination. Rumors were already afloat, but this was official confirmation, and in order that it might not be delayed, I think the courier bore passports from both General Johnston and General Sherman. I can find nothing to verify my statement as to the passports, but it seems to me that I heard my uncle and aunt indicate this.

Before the courier arrived, however, Mr. Davis received a telegram from General Johnston, handed him as he was dismounting at Colonel Johnston's house in Charlotte. For many years, an iron tablet sunk in the street at this point bore the announcement: "Here stood Jefferson Davis, President of the Confederate States of America, when notified of the death of President Abraham Lincoln."

Early the next morning, Uncle Victor ordered his carriage and declared that he was going to drive to Charlotte. My aunt protested that he was not well enough to make this trip, so he took with him a Doctor Logan who was on his way home from Appomattox and had been at our house a good deal. I do not think Aunt Maria would have let him go without a physician. In Charlotte he had a long conference with Mr. Davis on the latter's chances of getting out through Wilmington, North Carolina. Mr. Davis, however, after conferring with all parties, determined to adhere to the plan of going to Florida and thence to Havana. Later we heard of his capture on May tenth in Georgia and all the lying that was published about it.

In a letter written from Alexandria, Egypt, and published in the *Ballot*, November 8, 1886, Uncle Victor described in full the details of Mr. Davis's stay and also the following: "Soon confirmation came of Mr. Lincoln's assassination. Viewing the altered situation which this event was likely to produce, I went immediately to Charlotte, accompanied by Dr. Logan of Charleston, an army surgeon who was staying with me at Concord. We went in a carriage by the country road. I called on Mr. Davis. He was lodging with a Mr. Bates who had, he said, hospitably given him shelter. He was occupying, however, at the time of my call a small room (at Colonel William Johnston's) as a business office, near where the First National Bank now stands. I found Mr. Benjamin and Mr. Breckinridge with him. He was by no means in a melancholy humor, but easy and chatty rather. I fancied that he saw his path clearer—that the end had come and he had made up his mind to face it. This fancy became a settled conviction before I left him. Alluding to Mr. Lincoln's death, the thing uppermost in every mind, he declared it to be an unmeasured calamity from every point of view. He had become convinced that the spirit of the South was broken. Further resistance by armed force would be criminal. He touched delicately on the aloofness of the people in Richmond. But he excused it on the ground of undefined fears in the presence of a probable wreck of the cause. Yet it was proof that resistance was no longer possible. He talked at considerable length, gently towards all, with one exception. He avowed that he had little or no faith in President Johnson."

As I approached manhood, I began to wonder where some of the other members of the cabinet were while President Davis was in Concord. I wrote to Judge John R. Reagan of Texas who had been Postmaster General of the Confederate Government and the substance of his reply was as follows: He and Secretary of War John C. Breckinridge, who, I have heard, once taught military law at West Point, were sent from Greensboro, North Carolina, to Durham to assist General Johnston to surrender to General Sherman. At the same time Secretary of State Judah P. Benjamin was dispatched to Durham to pay off Johnston's army with $20,000 in Mexican silver, which he transported on mules. Benjamin and Breckinridge, as I have already noted, called to see Uncle Victor in Concord on their way to Charlotte, and I think, judging from a photograph of Mr. Reagan, that I also saw him a few days later when he stopped for a conference with my uncle. Mr. Reagan, by the way, was the only member of the cabinet who was with Mr. Davis when he was captured.

I wrote to Mr. Benjamin in London but did not receive a reply. I have, however, an interesting anecdote to confirm the safe arrival of the silver in Durham. As Johnston had about ten thousand men at that time, each man was given about $2 in specie, a thing that none of the men had seen during their years of service, and some of them treasured it carefully. Years later, Miss Ruth Hannah, a kinswoman of my wife, told me that she had one of the two silver dollars which her father had received when Johnston surrendered; it had been pierced and, as a girl, she had worn it hanging around her neck. She said that her father had begged, borrowed, and stolen his food homeward, so determined was he not to deprive his two daughters of a silver dollar each.

At the time of Lee's surrender, General Kirby Smith also had managed to raise $5,000 in gold. He hoped to get Jefferson Davis from Cuba to Texas where it was planned that a new army would be mobilized, either to continue fighting or to force better terms from the enemy. Kirby Smith selected his aide, Captain Ernest Cucullu, to convey this sum to Cuba and to escort Davis. The Cucullus were old citizens of New Orleans; some of them had been Spanish officials when Louisiana was a colony of Spain. After the city was ceded to the French in 1800, they remained in New Orleans and engaged in sugar planting and other commercial and political activities of the city. Captain Cucullu embarked from Galveston on a blockade-runner and was shortly overtaken by another ship bearing the news of Davis's capture. After imperative outlays already made by Kirby Smith, only $3,300 of the original $5,000 remained. Captain Cucullu was given the following order, the last to be given to a Confederate soldier:

> Galveston Harbor, June 3, 1865.
> —Captain when you reach New Orleans you will, after deducting your necessary travelling expenses, turn over to Maj. Gen. Canby, U. S. A. commanding etc., $3,300., being the secret service funds C. S. remaining in your possession.
> Respectfully, your obedient servant,
> E. Kirby Smith, General
>
> Captain Ernest Cucullu

He returned to New Orleans to deliver this sum to the Federal general and arrived on June 6, 1865, two days after Appomattox. As he and an army surgeon, Dr. Yandell, stepped ashore in full Confederate uniform, they were immediately rushed by a dozen infuriated Negro soldiers with drawn bayonets. Captain Cucullu drew his army pistol, and he and Yandell managed to escape in a hack to the Federal Headquarters. There he received a receipt from General Canby for the $3,029 which he delivered ($270 had been given by the General to Dr. Yandell who was destitute, and $1 was given to Captain Cucullu who claimed this, the hack fare, as his travelling expenses). The Captain's parole was obtained the following day, the last known to be issued. Kirby Smith conferred upon him the title of "The Last Confederate." The son of this last Confederate now lives in Lynchburg, Virginia, and my youngest son, John, married Anne Cucullu, his daughter.

XV

OUR RECONSTRUCTION

SHORTLY AFTER THE visit of Mr. Davis, a great catastrophe occurred for me, for the first result of the war was the leaving of almost all our servants. My uncle called all of them in and told them that they were now free and from henceforth could go where they willed, Mr. Lincoln's proclamation having been made good on the field of battle.

Then the astounding thing took place—old Ellen and all her tribe left, and that meant all of my childhood Negro playmates. Ellen was an old family servant whose devotion had been unfailing, but she was half Indian and thoroughly hard-boiled. "Wash," Ellen's husband, did not leave. He forsook wife and family to remain with us, but Uncle Victor robbed this act of all its glory by saying that Wash knew he was so trifling that he could never make a living anywhere else. Yankee Jim also stuck like a leech, and that was surprising, for Uncle Victor had bought him only a few years before, and we had not thought of him as one of the "old family servants." Although Aunt Maria's menage was badly disrupted for a time, things began to adjust themselves in a few weeks when Ellen's oldest daughter, now a better cook than her mother, returned to stay with her father. All over the South, like birds affrighted, the Negroes took flight for an initial sail, but many returned to their starting point.

Now came a change in the atmosphere of Concord, not barometric nor due to manifest humidity, but emanating from the unspoken phrase, "the Yankees are coming." The large prison camp in Salisbury, twenty miles from Concord, was approached from the north, and few people in Cabarrus County had ever seen a Yankee. I, of course, was much better off, having seen them in Lincoln County. When they actually came, I was literally astounded at their quiet entrance. A big Yankee four-horse wagon with men in uniform drove up and dumped out a lot of tent material between our house and the office, and in twenty minutes two tents were up. Then a Federal cavalry band rode through Main Street followed by a battalion of troops. They turned to the left near the McDonald cotton factory and camped in the wide fields near the present mill town of Kannapolis. This was the rank and file. The officers were billeted with us downtown. We drew a young lieutenant whose orderly occupied one of the tents, and a more trying, underbred upstart than that lieutenant was surely never inflicted on a patient, long-suffering family. He was mean; he wanted to make us feel that we were now a conquered people and that the Negroes were now not merely our equals but our superiors. He was the only human being I had ever seen against whom I revolted on sight, and he affected the grown people the same way. They got the full curse of his presence, while I had complete recompense in my friendship with his orderly who was just as much a gentleman as his superior was the reverse. The general turmoil was so great that soon I was sleeping on a cot in his big tent. This man's name was Mike; he was tattooed in red, white, and blue from wrist to breast, and he had the itch, which I promptly caught from him. I also acquired a vocabulary of rich Irish profanity which far transcended my former feeble efforts. For all that, I am glad to have known him.

Doubtless, that lieutenant's commanding officers knew his characteristics as well as we did, and it was not long before a miracle happened. Major McBride walked into the house and told the lieutenant to get out. He took the room, and there began a relationship which lasted for months and was always pleasant and mutually agreeable. It was a trying position to be quartered in a former enemy's home, and Major McBride, feeling this, made every effort by courtesy and consideration to compensate us for the affliction. When he left, he was our friend. Some years later he brought his bride to see us, and they were our honored guests for a week. I am indeed sorry that I cannot recall Major McBride's full name, but I think he was of the Sixth Michigan Cavalry, and because of him I have always had a high estimate of that state.

In those days when Northern troops were quartered with us, Mattie Gibson contributed much to my edification. While the war was still raging, she had visited in Virginia where seemingly Yankees roamed wild. Upon her return to quiet Concord, she showed her friends how to hide their bracelets, breastpins, and watches in the "rats" that they wore on their heads covered by a peculiar arrangement of hair. It was assumed that no simpleton Yankee would ever suspect such a clever place of concealment. And now she continued to run true to form. When the Yankee colonel and his staff first passed her house, she seated herself at the piano and played "Dixie" until they were out of hearing. I think it was a Roosevelt piano which had once been melodious, but it had not been tuned for five years and had suffered considerably under the thumping and fingering of domestic war. After this, against the advice of her friends, she persisted in repeating her performance whenever the officers passed. One afternoon, in retaliation, the Yankee regimental band appeared on her front porch and played "Yankee Doodle" at intervals until sundown.

The act that brought her most fame, however, was the graceful gesture of withdrawing her skirts, as if from a leper, whenever a Yankee officer passed her on the street. This gave me the idea, which immediately became popular with the boys, of walking into the street and making a detour around every Yankee flag that hung across the sidewalk to force us, "a subjugated people," to walk under it. No yoke for us!

However, it must be understood that the relationships between the conquerors and the conquered after the Civil War were not like those after the World War. Our forebears had fought for, lived under, and revered the Stars and Stripes, and in the future we were to do the same. The Northerners were our people and, with the exception of the numerous foreigners in the Federal regiment, we understood each other perfectly for we thought in the same way. There were a number of marriages between the factory girls and the occupation troops; these were frowned upon, of course, but frowns are useless in such cases.

There was, however, one wedding during the Reconstruction period that literally raised Cain. It took place at Chapel Hill, and Uncle Victor, being a member of the Board of Trustees of the University of North Carolina at the time, went to Chapel Hill to a board meeting, taking me with him. We stayed with Professor Charles Phillips and heard the whole story.

Old Governor Swain was greatly beloved and honored both as governor of the state and as president of the state university, but things changed when he announced that his daughter was going to marry an officer in the United States Army, Brigadier General Smith Atkins. With the sense of power inherent in his type, he gave notice and invited precisely what he got. The people, at first astonished and then angry, finally made preparations for insult.

To appreciate fully the ludicrous aspect of this episode, it is necessary to recall that during the war the Confederate Government had called in all the bronze or gun-metal bells in the state. The old church-bell alloy was the very metal needed in making three-inch fieldpieces, the howitzers, and the mortars. Before melting the bells, they took a mould and cast a duplicate of each, using door weights, handleless skillets, broken stove-lids, and such things. These replacements were duly installed in the church towers, but they were rarely used, for the tone, to put it mildly, was terrible. In this case, however, it was a situation made to order for the citizens of Chapel Hill. They determined that, as the bridegroom put his foot in the stirrup to go to his wedding, all the church bells in town would begin to toll. And toll, they did, in this insulting pot-metal tone!

It was expected that he would order his men to fire on the belfries, and elaborate preparations had been made to fortify them with bags and barricades. But the general took it like a man. I am told that at first he hesitated, but being a soldier he mounted and rode with dignity through the ordeal. Although the tolling continued for three long hours, he did not permit his men to interfere.

Everyone connected with that marriage, even the minister who performed the ceremony, was an anathema amongst his home people. Such was the sentiment of the South at the time of Reconstruction. Animosities are transient, however. When the children of that bitterly resented marriage visited their North Carolina kinsfolk, they and the bell-ringers laughed together over the incident.

XVI

A PRISONER OF WAR

NATURALLY AS SOON as I understood the meaning of Lee's surrender, I began to inquire when my father would come home, but as to this there was an ominous uncertainty. Of course, we did not know immediately that he had been captured. This occurred early in April, 1865, within a week of Lee's surrender at Appomattox.

My father wrote me many letters from prison; he gave me a graphic description of how the privates, less well-nourished than the officers, trapped rats and ate them. To our cook's great horror, I proceeded to do this. I must have caught a young one for it was not bad; I can only look back in wonder now that my cooking was sufficient to protect me from a million parasites.

One letter, particularly full of interesting detail, I quote in full:

"Fort Delaware. Del.
June 10, 1865

"My Dear Children:

"I was so happy to receive your sweet little letters again. It has been a long time since I had the pleasure. Ah! how many sad scenes I have gone through since I last wrote you. But, while I have seen and heard of others suffering so much, Our Heavenly Father has been good to me. I have been kindly treated by the

Yankees, have found many friends, and had good health, and have had plenty of plain food to eat. For all these blessings I feel very thankful. I doubt not you have both been good children —that you have studied your lessons—been good to Uncle Victor and Aunt Ria—assisted them to keep house—said your prayers every night. I hope they have been answered in the blessings shown you and me in sparing our lives, preserving our health, and giving us so many comforts.

"I will tell you more what it is to be a prisoner of war. They don't put us in a close prison like a jail. They put us in a large lot, with a great high fence all around it, and one big gate. They have cheap frame houses built all around, inside, called 'Barracks.' In these Barracks they put up shelves, one above the other called 'Bunks' or 'Chibangs'. On these the men sit, sleep, and stay all the time except when they walk about or go to their meals. They have no chairs, no bedding except their blankets & they just lie down & *think, read, talk* or *sleep nearly all the time*. In the center of the lot, there is a large court or open space, where they can walk about & take exercise. Sometimes they run races, jump, pitch quoits, throw each other up in blankets, play marbles, etc., etc. In one corner of the lot is a large, long barn called the dining-room, in which are many high slender tables. When breakfast or dinner is ready, the men march out of the barracks in long rows & go in to these tables, and get their bread, meat and soup; then they march back again, each to his own bunk & eats his 'grub'. They have no knives or forks. They have tin cups or little tin buckets for soup. But if they have money they can buy from the sutlers store (in a corner of the lot) many little things to eat & to fix up with. Some have money, some get it from kind Yankee friends, but most of the poor fellows haven't a cent. They do all sorts of work. Some make and mend clothes, boots, and shoes. Some make all sorts of wire and carved rings, breast-pins, necklaces, bracelets, sets, watch charms, shirt buttons, etc., etc., and sell them to those who have money or to the Yankee soldiers. Some wash clothes. They get the water from the little canals or 'moats', that are cut all through the lot, and the water let in, from the Delaware River, which runs all around the island. The men that get money in any of these ways buy lumber or old planks, and fix up little shelves, tables, stools, chairs, etc., etc., & live right nicely. They buy coffee pots, buckets, wash-pans, cups & saucers, knives & forks, etc., etc. They buy old pieces of wood or coal to make little fires in the yard & boil coffee, boil meat, etc. They get water to drink and cook with from great tubs or cisterns in one corner of the lot, where it is brought in boats from a creek three miles off. The river water ain't good. In winter they have large stoves in the barracks to warm them and cook by. The water in the canals or moats is not very clean but the prisoners have to wash in it; nor is that very good they have to drink. We all have to clean our own boots & shoes, brush out our bunks & sweep out our Barracks. The Barracks are laid off in Divisions, each Division has a chief & all have to attend roll-call once a day. A Yankee sagt. calls the roll. All around the great high fence is a platform or little walk (just on top) along which the Yankee sentinels walk with their loaded guns & if we try to get out, or do any thing they don't allow they holler at us & if we do not stop, they shoot us. Some officers have been in here over two years, & never been out. Some are so ragged, some so dirty (its hard to keep clean) & some look so pale & weak. Many have almost lost their minds. When they get sick, they are taken out to the hospital, outside the big fence. There they have little beds or cots. When they get well, they make them go into the barracks. Many die. Every morning I see them carrying off 5 or 6 to be buried.

"Such is prison-life. When I come home as I hope soon to do, I will tell you much more and will bring you all some rings & other specimens of the work done here by our poor officers. It is a hard sad life. I hope dear little Paulie may never be a prisoner of war. But we must be prepared to meet any fate that awaits us. Live honestly, do our duty, be good and God will notice and sustain us. I hope and pray we may all live to meet again, enjoy many years of peace & happiness & part only to meet in heaven.

"Give much love to Uncle Victor & Aunt Ria. Kind regards to all the friends & accept a Father's blessing from your affectionate

"Papa

"Uncle Robbie [Morrison] is here and will go home in a few days."

All through that summer my sister and I had used our father's office as a haven where we could whoop and howl to our heart's content. Here she brought her girl friends, and here I kept my rapidly growing collection of birds' eggs and snake skins which I cured in accordance with Dr. Bachman's instructions. I had most of the garter snakes, black snakes, king snakes, and one giant bull snake. He had shown me how to open a snake's mouth, cut the backbone and around the tissues with a Barlow knife, and leave the skin untouched. Then, grasping the severed backbone projecting from the mouth, I drew the snake's body from his skin and hung that up to dry. Of course, this collection smelled to high heaven, but in those days so did the butcher shop, so why worry!

Uncle Victor received his clients in his sitting room and never came to the office, one half of which he owned, so I was astounded when Anna and I were notified that the law office was to be "cleaned up." Within a few days the three-room office was ready, with beds, book shelves, and tables, and to all my inquiries there was but one answer, "You wait and see."

The mystery was solved one day when in walked a medium-sized soldierly man in citizen's clothes, with beard all over his pale and thin face. He ran to me, picked me up, and said he was my father. I would not have known him from Adam. This was about the middle of August, and he had been in Federal prison at Fort Delaware on the river below Philadelphia since early April. He did not have a button, a shoulder strap or any insignia of rank, and I who had heard him spoken of as "General Barringer," I thought for years, was grievously disappointed. But as he was not only a man, but a man's man, we soon became fast friends. He rode well, shot well, and swam well. He knew more men in the hundred miles around him than any other two men in that section. He started to practice law in Concord and boarded at Harris's Hotel, and when he did not have strangers in his office I was with him morning, noon, and night. This year of our close association is one of my most treasured memories.

XVII

GENERAL RUFUS BARRINGER, C.S.A.

MUCH OF MY father's war experience I got from his own lips during the years of our intimacy after he returned, but there are records existing of his service from the time when as a boy of four I saw the flag made by the local ladies presented in front of his law office until his unrecognized return when I was eight and a half years of age. He left as a man of thirty-nine, in the prime of life and returned an old man and was never really strong again, though leading an active and able life. Four and a half years of sustained combat had taken their toll.

He had organized the Company F in Cabarrus County, which received its flag just in front of his law office. It was an unusual body of men, each supplying his own horse and other equipment and volunteering for "the war." In order that this distinction may be understood, I will say that there were hundreds of companies, "partisan rangers" and "legions," organized in the South for periods varying from three months to a year, rarely two years, which in the consolidation of an army had to be reorganized and adjusted. Most wisely the Confederate authorities gathered together into the First North Carolina Cavalry Regiment all those who had volunteered for "the War."

This regiment, in which my father was successively Captain, Major, and Lieutenant Colonel, was given to Colonel Robert

Ransom, a West Point graduate, as its first commander. He was succeeded by Colonel Gordon, another West Pointer and, in 1863, by Colonel Cheek when my father was made Lieutenant Colonel. On this occasion, General J. E. B. Stuart, after the Inspection Reports, wrote to my father and expressed his high appreciation of "that ability and devotion to duty, which has enabled you to raise your regiment to such a degree of efficiency, that it should be called, 'a pattern for others.'" This letter closed with the hope that "you may be able to inflict still weightier blows upon our enemy who has so often trembled and fled before the rush of the First North Carolina Cavalry." It was accepted as the model body of cavalry in the Confederate service. When he was promoted from a Lieutenant Colonelcy to Brigadier General and took command of the first four North Carolina Cavalry Regiments, his heart still went out to the old First and Company F.

During the next four years he was in constant action, except when rebuilding his command. He fought around Richmond, then in northern Virginia at Fairfax Court House, next into Maryland, and into Pennsylvania at Chambersburg. From there they recrossed the Potomac, were engaged around Fredericksburg, and moved back to Richmond again.

In all, he was in seventy-six engagements, had two horses killed under him, and was wounded three times. His major engagements in Virginia, were Willis's Church, Brandy Station, Auburn Mills, Buckland Races (where he led the charge), Davis's Farm (where he was the sole commander), and Ream's Station (where he commanded the division of cavalry).

In June, 1863, at Brandy Station, he was severely wounded by a shot in the mouth and did not recover for five months. During this rest period, he was approached as a candidate for Congress, but a letter from Orange Court House, Virginia, October, 1863 declines firmly, saying: "I entered the Army from a sense of duty alone, counting the cost and knowing the sacrifices.... Our great object is not attained... and I think it is better for those in service to stand by their colors... whilst those at home should all unite... in feeding, clothing and otherwise sustaining the gallant men (and their families) who are fighting not only for our rights, but for the safety of our homes and firesides. If croakers, grumblers, and growlers, who torment themselves and all around them with imaginary evils, could only lay aside their fears; if all hoarders, speculators and money makers could only be educated to forget their selfish ends for a season; if conscripts, skulkers and deserters could only be got to their commands and all come up to the work like patriots and men, the Army, by the blessing of God, would soon secure us victory and peace."

In a postwar letter to his brother Victor in January of 1865, he gives a full account of all engagements. The following extracts describe the last days of the war. For brevity and clarity, I have selected only the actions of his command, which could be approximately duplicated for all other Confederate commanders. All were desperately engaged—it was a death struggle.

"We now went into winter quarters at Bellfield, near Sussex C. H. where the command suffered excessively for want of Forage and other supplies. But, so thorough was the organization, and so active and determined the spirit of both officers and men, that the Brigade entered upon the spring campaign with full ranks, and with the confident belief, that it was reserved for them to annihilate Sheridan and his victorious troopers. Whatever may have been the general demoralization of our army and however desperate the hopes of the Southern Confederacy, this brigade did not shrink from the conflict before it.

"Trusting to the justice of their cause, strong in the... confidence of each other, and proud of their past achievements, all went forth, with undaunted spirit, to renew the strife of carnage and death....

"We came to the dreadful conflict at Chamberlain's Run on the 31st of March. Sheridan, with his immense cavalry had seized Dinwiddie C. H. and was gradually extending his lines towards Five Forks.... Early on the morning of the 31st we were ordered to advance and face the enemy.... I put in the 1st, 2nd & 5th Reg'ts—the 3rd not being up. They all attacked with great vigor, broke the enemy & rushed him in confusion and disorder into and across the creek, in high water, quite up to the arm-pits, and filled with brush and floating timber. Not one instant faltering, both officers and men plunged into the water ...under heavy fire and drove the enemy from the opposite bank and started him in full retreat.

"...Seeing my command badly cut up, and completely exhausted, I ordered them to recross the stream, which was without further loss. I found I had lost some 20 officers and not less than 100 men, killed and wounded. At 2 o'clock we were ordered thru Maj. Gen. Lee to renew the attack and to force the Federals from their positions. Considering the exhausted condition of my men I requested a suspension of this order but was not granted.... I was told to select my own plan of attack.... After this decision all were told of the object in view, and exhorted to steadiness and promptitude.... When Col. Cheek gave the command Forward! the 1st moved off with a pride of step and confidence of purpose worthy of its best days. With line unbroken, it bore the whole fire of the enemy from all his works and all along the opposite shore.... My loss was again heavy, 10 officers and over 50 men killed, drowned, and wounded.... Notwithstanding these sad and heavy losses, the entire Brigade was wild and jubilant with excitement and joy. We had defeated Sheridan's Cavalry, and none doubted now but that Lee would whip Grant. But the joy was of short duration, and the victories of this day probably gave Grant the crowning success at Five Forks on the day following.

"Sheridan, seeing his forces driven back at all points by Pickett, Fitz Lee, Rosser, and W. H. F. Lee, called for reenforcements and received the 5th corps, which so moved as to threaten the rear of the Confederate position and necessitated our whole line to fall back early next morning.... During the day Sheridan advanced and threw his whole force against our left and center. Meanwhile his cavalry passed our front in overwhelming numbers, and soon sought to turn my right flank thereby enveloping the entire force engaged. Again and again the 2nd, 3rd & 5th regiments charged this cavalry, impeding their progress and enabling our fleeing army to escape. It was not until dark began to close upon us, that I gave the order to fall back and as rapidly as possible. We barely escaped annihilation. This day sealed the fate of the Confederacy.... The next morning we marched to Namozine Church and halted until all the cavalry had passed, when I was ordered by Mjr. Gen. Lee to hold the position as long as I safely could. I stated the condition of my Brigade, its loss of officers and utter exhaustion, but there was no alternative. ... Soon the enemy appeared in force, with shouts of triumph and trumpets blowing. ... I ordered the whole to fall back and skirmish in retreat. The 5th Regt, which was dismounted, fought with ... obstinacy and seemed slow to give up the contest. Before it retired under further orders, the enemy had gained the main road of retreat. I then moved this reg. by marching through forests and byways, and conducted it safely out to a point six miles above, where I hoped to find Mjr. Gen. Lee and the rest of the Brigade. Nearing this point I found it picketted. While reconnoitering who the pickets were, I was taken prisoner, with Lt. Foard, and three couriers, by a party of Sheridan Scouts, dressed in Confederate uniform. The Reg't learning of my capture, made good its escape."

Captain W. R. Webb, who was in General Barringer's command, was also captured and has left an interesting account. All were taken to General Sheridan's Headquarters at Mrs. Cousins where they had supper with General Sheridan and staff. They slept on the floor and during the night heard a Federal spy giving reports to General Sheridan on the orders issued to different Confederate generals, and they marvelled in whispers at the accuracy of the information. This was gained by Federal men in Confederate uniform posing as lost from their command. (However they must have been expert in a Southern accent as well.) The next morning, since the army supply wagons had come up, there was, to the Confederate eye, an imposing breakfast. All officers were invited except Captain Webb and Major H. I. Foote who had been brought in during the night. Captain Webb declined to go to table unbidden, but Major Foote said firmly he was not going to take the forty-five mile walk to Petersburg without food. They had taken his horse, and he would certainly get breakfast. He went in to breakfast, drew up a chair, engaged General Sheridan in conversation, and plied himself with the abundant food. Then began the long trip to Petersburg in charge of a mounted corporal. General Barringer was allowed to retain his horse, but the rest were dismounted. Since the narrow roads were filled with General Meade's advancing troops, the prisoners had to make their way through ditches, briar, and stumps along the roadside. When General Meade and his staff came into view, Major Foote hailed him loudly until noticed and, facing the guarded attention of General Meade's staff, gave him very welcome news of the safety of his brother-in-law General Wise of the Confederate Army. He then introduced General Barringer. General Meade promptly rode forward to shake hands and offering his purse said, "General Barringer, prison life is bad at best, and I take it you have no currency that will be of service to you on our side of the line. I will esteem it a favor if you will allow me to supply your present wants." General Barringer thanked him but did not accept the favor. He requested the privilege of communicating with his friends who could supply his needs. General Meade then asked who was in charge of him and, when he saw the mounted corporal, called a g neral officer from his staff. He was introduced to General Barringer, and told him to act as escort and to pass the order to the Provost Marshal at City Point that General Barringer was to communicate with whomsoever he wished.

Captain Webb states, "I have always been glad that I was present, to hear this interview between two men of great ability and culture, under circumstances so unique. Though commanders of opposing armies, they were as courteous and obliging, as if they had met as personal friends. It was also interesting to see the difference between General Sheridan and General Meade. The former had showed no courtesy, and had put General Barringer in charge of a corporal, while General Meade showed every possible courtesy, and put General Barringer in charge of an officer of equal rank with himself.

"I do not think I could have survived that forty-five mile walk to Petersburg, without food, and depressed in mind with the humiliation of capture, had not General Barringer, although an older man, often given me a ride, and walked himself amongst the rubbish of the roads."

General Barringer was the first captured Confederate general to arrive at City Point near Richmond where Federal Headquarters were established. There he was courteously received and assigned to one of a row of tents, apparently to await the next arrivals, Generals Ewell and Custis Lee. After them came hundreds, and then thousands, of prisoners of every possible rank and description.

General Barringer requested shaving materials, which were promptly provided, and he had settled down to that long deferred luxury when a voice outside asked, "Mr. President, have you ever seen a live Rebel general in uniform?" Mr. Lincoln said, "No." Then the tent flap was pulled aside, and the first voice said, "Here is one now." There was an instant apology from Mr. Lincoln and a reprimand to the attendant officer who was not the Commandant. At any rate, there was a meeting later, arranged by the Commandant, Major General Charles H. T. Collis; for Mr. Lincoln did want to meet a Confederate general and General Barringer was equally anxious to see what manner of man was the President of the United States. Since he was muddy, tattered, and torn, he felt hardly presentable for such an occasion, but brushing, shoe polish, and the completed shave restored morale.

This meeting has been well described by General Collis in an article appearing many years ago in "Once a Week," now *Collier's Weekly*. He states that one evening he formally presented General Rufus Barringer of North Carolina to the President of the United States in the Adjutant General's tent. Mr. Lincoln extending his hand, warmly welcomed the Confederate general, and bade him be seated. There was only one chair when the President arose, and this the Southerner very politely declined to take; so the two men stood facing in the center of the tent, the tall form of Mr. Lincoln almost reaching the ridgepole. He looked General Barringer over from head to foot and said, "Barringer from North Carolina. General were you ever in Congress?" "No, Mr. Lincoln, I never was." "I thought not," said Mr. Lincoln. "I did not think my memory could be so at fault, but there was a Barringer in Congress with me, and from your state too." "That was my brother, Sir," said the General.

Until then Mr. Lincoln had worn that thoughtful, troubled expression that is known so well, but now the lines relaxed and the whole face laughed. "Well, well," he said, "Your brother was my chum in Congress. Yes sir, we sat at the same desk and ate at the same table. He was a Whig and so was I. He was my chum, and I was very fond of him. Well. Shake again." A few more chairs had been brought in and conversation drifted from Mr. Lincoln's anecdotes of the pleasant hours that he and the Honorable Daniel Moreau Barringer had spent together to the war and then to the merits of the military and civil leaders, both of the North and the South. All of this was illustrated with some appropriate story, entirely new, sometimes full of humor or again pathos.

Several times General Barringer made the move to depart, but each time was told to keep his seat. Mr. Lincoln remarked that they were both prisoners and that he hoped the General would take pity and talk with him about the times when they were both their own masters.

Finally the General arose and was bowing himself out when President Lincoln took him again by the hand and, laying the other hand on his shoulder, said with great seriousness and simplicity, "Do you think I could be of any service to you?" All laughed and General Barringer replied with difficulty, "If anyone could be of service to a poor devil in my situation, I presume you are the man." Mr. Lincoln drew a card from his pocket, adjusted his glasses, and turned up the wick of the lamp. Then, seating himself at the desk, he wrote with all the seriousness with which he might have signed the Emancipation Proclamation. While writing, he kept up a running conversation to this effect: "I suppose they will send you to Washington and there I have no doubt, they will put you in the old Capitol prison. I am told it isn't a nice sort of place and I am afraid you won't find it a very comfortable tavern; but I have a friend in Washington,—he's the biggest man in the country—and I believe I have some influence with him when I don't ask too much. Now I want you to send this card of introduction to him and if he takes the notion, he may put you on parole, or let up on you that way or some other way. Any way it's worth trying."

Then very deliberately drying the card with the blotter, he held it up to the light and read:

This is General Barringer, of the Southern Army. He is the brother of a very dear friend of mine. Can you do anything to make his detention in Washington as comfortable as possible under the circumstances?

A. Lincoln

To Hon. Edwin M. Stanton,
Secretary of War.

General Barringer could not utter a word. He made some effort to say "Thank you" or "God bless you" but was speechless. Following the Commandant, he wheeled and left the tent.

Outside, the Commandant found him completely overcome. General Barringer had won his stars in a score of battles, but the reaction from kindness after the gruelling strain of these last days of defeat was too much for control. He took the Commandant's arm and, making his way back to the tent, was at last able to express his profound appreciation for such thoughtfulness and generosity. General Collis met General Barringer later in Philadelphia many years after the war and says that in discussing this meeting with Lincoln the Confederate general's eyes filled "at the deep damnation of his taking off."

Nevertheless this priceless card proved anything but the assistance it was intended to be. The Confederate generals were shortly after sent to Washington and to the Capitol Prison, which was about the present site of the Supreme Court building. Shortly after their arrival, President Lincoln was assassinated. The prison was attacked by a mob, in a fury of resentment and suspicion against the Confederacy, and General Barringer said afterwards that the only time he was ever glad to see a Yankee soldier in uniform was when Federal troops came to their rescue. A week later the presentation of President Lincoln's card to Secretary Stanton was received with obvious amazement. In view of the very recent date of General Barringer's meeting with Mr. Lincoln, his rank and connections rendered him suspect. He was interrogated thoroughly as to time, event, the Colonel in charge, et cetera. So although General Barringer was sent to Fort Delaware as requested, he was held until the end of July, long after many others had been paroled or returned home.

In the latter part of this prison stay he was given parole twice a week and allowed to spend some hours in Philadelphia, passing each time by that island on which his grandfather, John Paul Barringer, had landed September 30, 1743.

Although delayed until August in reaching home, he was still investigated by the Federal authorities at intervals—even after the death of Booth and the execution of the unfortunate Mrs. Surratt and all suspected accomplices.

XVIII

HARBINGERS OF PEACE

AS A HARBINGER of peace there was now an invasion from the North very different from the military conquest that we had just witnessed. Posters were put up in Concord for the first time in my life. Don Castello's Circus was coming! It was not as good as Barnum's and totally unlike the first-class circuses of today, but it *was a circus,* and no ten-year-old in the South could remember ever having seen one. We stood around for hours before those preposterous and highly-colored posters with their wild beasts and "wild men from Borneo." Right behind us, watching the ecstasy of the children, were gathered most of the adult population of the town in their own unashamed enjoyment.

I was given a fifty-dollar Bechtler native gold piece to take downtown and change into "shin plasters," the new paper money issued by the United States Government, and I brought back a tremendous roll. I would say that the five-cent sheet was about three and one-half by two inches, the ten perhaps half an inch larger, the twenty-five cent issue still larger, and the fifty-cent sheet almost as large as our present bank notes. I had enough of it changed into five- and ten-cent currency to enable me to see every side show, and I walked Uncle Victor nearly to death for I was the "circus" for him. Aunt Maria scorned to be caught in such rabble. Frankly, I had long since come to the conclusion that elephants, lions, tigers, camels, and such exotic beasts were mere myths, like ghosts, jinns, and "hants," and now to see them in the flesh was a revelation and an inspiration.

I could ride bareback anything that stepped in horse-flesh, so the riding of the short-skirted girls had no appeal for me. The features that interested me most were the acrobats on the trapeze and especially the Japanese jugglers, for these were new and remarkable. I had heard of tumbling but had seen nothing of it during the war, and now to see a nice little brown man walking a wire, and for his amusement keeping two or three oranges in the air, was a revelation.

For the grown people an unexpected feature of the show was the reunion of old friends who had not met for years, and in many instances even their survival was uncertain. People came from miles and miles around in all directions, and so hungry were they for diversion that they would gladly pledge their souls for the wherewithal to get in. It was a great day in my youthful experiences.

As soon as the circus was gone, all the boys of the village felt an overwhelming desire to duplicate it, and each one of us began looking for a stunt. Wade Harris, afterwards editor of the *Charlotte Observer,* was our best tumbler although Hiram Foard ran him a close second. Will Hall was the strong man, and Clauselle Black won great acclaim when he climbed the pole and practised contortions on top. I was the juggler, and somehow I managed to keep three oak balls up at a time with perfect ease.

Of course, we needed a circus tent, so we provided ourselves with a large number of guano sacks which could be had for the ripping up. We wisely decided that we could dispense with a top for the tent, a decision readily understood by those today who remember the odor of guano under brilliant July sunshine. It was a fertilizer recently introduced into the South, imported from Peru and the coastal islands of South America, consisting of the maritime bird-dung of ages. No amount of washing could remove the odor from the bags, and our circus tent smelled like the devil before breakfast. Everybody came, even Aunt Maria. They held their noses but they enjoyed the show.

Tickets were sold for a ten-dollar Confederate note with "Uncle

Jackson's" picture on it. Everybody had quantities of this money, now worthless as currency, and they were glad to be rid of it. We also accepted Confederate stamps for circus tickets, and after the show we threw away a quart measure of these stamps as not worth the trouble of counting; now they would bring thousands from a modern stamp collector.

So great was the general social depression during the whole war that youth had few games. Everybody from fifteen years old and upward was in the army, and these boys when they came back, either sound or wounded, did not turn to athletics. Now came a renaissance, and the boys who less than a year ago had been defending trenches at Petersburg were now turning "ball bats" and sewing pigskin. Baseball was coming.

Locke Phifer, a great player, once told me that in a way it had begun before the war. Its origin, of course, was the old English game of cricket but this American version was played without wickets under the name of "cat." Probably it was a process of colonial slurring speech from cricket to cat, as the first and last letters are the same. Soon "two-hole cat" was corrupted into "two old cat."

To play two-hole cat, four boys, two bases, a ball, and two bats were needed. These bats were sometimes called paddles. Bases were marked by shallow holes (where wickets would have been) and the game was played in a straight line. The "outs" alternated as pitcher and catcher as needed; for if the ball was not hit by the first batsman the "out" behind him threw it in turn to the other batsman, the first pitcher now becoming backstop behind the second batter. The two "ins," or batters, when they hit a ball long or short, ran and exchanged bases, repeating this several times if the hit was long. Those familiar with the game will naturally see that there was no fun in this for a full crowd of players. Thus, if there were more than four would-be participants, the result was that whenever a runner made a successful run he stepped out and somebody else on his side took his place. This gave the game in some localities the incongruous name of "rotation." I have often played rotation.

This rotation seems to have been the germ from which the new game developed, in North Carolina as well as New York and New England. The next thing I remember, it was called three-hole cat, a triangular infield replacing the straight line. The pitcher was in the middle, one hole being at the home plate where the batsman was placed, one hole at first base, and another at what is now third base. The batsman if not fully successful in striking the ball, stopped at the first corner (or base); if a little better ball, at the second corner, now third base; and if it was a long drive, he came home, completing, so to speak, an isosceles triangle. Then some other of the "ins" stepped up in "rotation" to carry on. The fact that he had to run past the pitcher to go from first to second base led to confusion, and the addition of a base behind the pitcher, now second base, gave the present diamond-shaped field. When this circuit was completed and rotation was an accepted procedure, "town ball" came into being.

There were certain conventions and phrases now in the limbo of forgotten things. The order of rotation was against the clock, why I do not know. The catcher when calling for a high or low ball chanted, "high buck or low doe, above (or below) the elbow." Some member of the "ins" shouted the names of three teammates as "at bat, on deck and in hole," to indicate the batting order, just as is still the custom with sand-lot players.

Town ball ultimately became organized with a captain and eight men, four bases, and a pitcher and his line. New rules appeared; the pitcher could hit the runner with the ball and the first bounce of a hit ball was out for fouls. With a few minor developments the approximation of modern American baseball was an established game, and soon all were playing only that. The "Lone Nine" in Concord in the early 1870's could outplay almost anything in the state.

And now I have to confess to a bit of youthful pilfering which marks a step in the evolution of this game. The new railroad passenger cars on the North Carolina railroad had under each end of the transverse beam of the truck a big India-rubber "spring." It looked like an eight-inch ball of solid rubber pressed down to about four inches, and finding that India rubber made the best "core" on which to wind the wool for a ball, we would lie in wait at the North Carolina depot. With a razor borrowed from my uncle's bathroom shelf, we would shave these great "cheeks" of rubber down flush with the sill and get a mass which made one little rubber core an inch and a half in diameter. This frenzy of mutilation spread along the railroad from end to end, and I think it was Uncle Victor's subsequent attempts at shaving with this razor that revealed the course of the widespread injury to rolling stock. At all events, a new "Thou shalt not" was added to my theology, and I found it the same almost everywhere. Very shortly India-rubber balls of this size, to make baseballs, were on the market.

About this time there was a weird arrival in our town, a new and freakish device for locomotion called a velocipede. If I had not seen it, I would not have believed such a thing possible. The velocipede man rented the public hall for a talk and demonstration. He claimed a speed of twelve miles an hour, which he probably exceeded for he went as fast as a good pony in a tournament. Then he removed the seats from the hall, devised an oval track, and for five cents he permitted anyone to ride round and round until utterly exhausted.

The velocipede consisted of two thirty-inch wheels, the front wheel being yoked so that the rider could turn it either right or left, and as he rode he had to kick backwards against the ground, using the right and left foot alternately. An expert, by a rhythmic waving from side to side with his stroke, could attain a speed of ten to twelve miles an hour on a smooth road, and I know of no motion in which the personal equation of balance between skill and muscular power counts for more. For the month or more that the velocipede man remained, I literally lived in the gallery and saw it all. But I was merely a spectator as there was no machine small enough for me. When he moved on to some other town he left half a dozen wheels which he had sold to the most proficient propellers, and after that travel on the street was hazardous. The proud owners went to work on the city fathers and finally got them to smooth down about three blocks of one of the streets. In order to do that they rigged up a new device, the "split-log-drag" of modern days, the plan of which I am sure was furnished by the velocipede people. However, the "hands" and mules for the work were donated by the new velocipedists. After a rain they would all get to work with the "drag," and as a result some half mile of street surface was made reasonably level.

A couple of years later the high-wheel bike, with a big wheel in front and a little one behind, appeared, the operator working directly on the crank shaft of the big wheel. This type was followed by the "safety"—the contemptuous name applied to the early bicycle with chain gear which was certainly safe as compared with the big-wheel type which preceded it. The safeties grew multiple, and the "bicycle built for two" was not the end for five and six seats became common. All had solid tires until a dentist in Ireland thought of coupling up an air distended garden hose around the wheel on a concave rim. That was the first pneumatic tire, and the rest was easy; the motorcycle and the automobile came to stay.

Uncle Victor was a wise man, and Doctor Scott, who had been in the Navy, a man of world-wide travel. There were some half a dozen college graduates of distinction around us, and yet I heard no single word to indicate that any of them thought that the velocipede was the forerunner of a great transformation in human locomotion. The old sawed-out wooden wheel of the early Orient had seen its last legitimate offspring. Henceforth wood was gone, and steel was on the way—then lighter and lighter steel, until there came the alloys of aluminum, magnesium, and beryllium.

XIX

GATE-BOY

AGES AGO, in that fog-infested area of ocean lying between Cape Hatteras and Cape Fear on the North Carolina coast, roamed and ranged a mysterious maritime monster. The American Indian called it "The Abductor"; the sixteenth-century English explorers called it a "Demi-gorgon"; Matthew Fontaine Maury made it clear to us as the "Gulf Stream"; but its results were that colonial North Carolina had none of that intimate maritime relationship with the mother country that Virginia and South Carolina had. This forced her to become a manufacturer of even the necessities of industrial life from the very beginning. No ship from London or Plymouth came up her streams to welcoming wharves as in the states before mentioned, and as a result, in North Carolina the rivers were settled from their headwaters downward to the sea rather than from the sea upward.

In central North Carolina during the eighteenth century this demand for local industry reached its height—the state was growing rapidly and every local supply of raw material was sought and sampled. Many primitive industries were started which practically died with the advent of railroads and yet were easily revived during the Civil War. Many of these were to pass under my eye and then pass into oblivion for the last time—unless some not impossible racial catastrophe befalls. Of these extra-plantation industries, the one most closely associated with my locality was ironmaking.

My uncle, Joseph Morrison, who left the Virginia Military Institute to go to war at the age of sixteen and served as courier for his brother-in-law, General Stonewall Jackson, came home near the end of the war with part of his foot shot off. When I went to Cottage Home, in the summer of 1866, he had reached the recovery stage of one crutch, and one day he said he was going over to Bolinger's Forge and would take me along as gate-boy. I did not know what that meant, but I was always glad to go with him anywhere.

With a mule and carryall we drove along the Brevard Station road a mile or so, turned to the right, and were suddenly confronted by a closed gate. When he grunted, "Hop out and open it," it immediately dawned upon me what "gate-boy" meant. I scrambled out and tiptoed up to lift the latch, but it would not budge. He calmly remarked, "It's the wind that's holding you. Wait a minute and when this breeze dies down you can open it." This was true, and while it was years before I understood the physics of this, his knowledge of magic went up greatly in my estimation. He drove through and then I found I could not close the gate against the wind. Again it was, "Wait and take your time," and so, at the royal pace of three miles an hour we moved on through a half dozen gates, and I was almost weary when we suddenly rounded a corner and arrived at a scene of industry down on the banks of a creek.

This was Bolinger's Forge, one of the old Forney-Davidson-Graham-Brevard Iron Works drawing from the great Lincoln County ore bank. With the death of my great-grandfather, General Graham, it had passed into other hands and practically died, but it had been revived by the war. It was too far from the scene of war to make munitions but it had a "finery" and a cupola furnace, and using pig iron from the neighboring furnaces, it made both castings and blooms. I had frequently seen these blooms, arrowhead-shaped masses of iron a half inch thick and about two feet long by a foot wide at the center, in our plantation blacksmith shop and had wondered whence they came. They constituted the source of all wrought iron used on the plantation. The castings made here were of every kind from three-legged pots to sorghum-mill cylinders used in extracting the juice. These castings were a new departure as for several years we had ground sorghum between eighteen-inch wooden cylinders with inserted white oak teeth. The cast rolls were much more efficient.

Wandering around over the place with my uncle, we came to old Peter Forney's tomb, a large slab of marble on a low brick-work support. The Forneys were Alsatian in origin, Protestants who had fled to America under religious persecution and finally settled in western North Carolina. They were important people in the building up of Lincoln County, and General Peter Forney was the outstanding character of the family. It was from him that my great-grandfather, Joseph Graham, bought the iron-ore land on which he built Vesuvius Furnace. I have read the inscription on this old marble slab many times, and I quote from memory:

> HERE LIETH THE MORTAL REMAINS OF
> PETER FORNEY
> WHO PROVED HIMSELF A PATRIOT AND A GENTLEMAN,
> BY VOTING IN SUCCESSION AS PRESIDENTIAL ELECTOR,
> FOR THE FOLLOWING DEMOCRATS:
> JEFFERSON, MADISON, MONROE, AND JACKSON.

He did not put on his tomb that he had lived for nearly a century; that he had been an incomparable Indian fighter, a notable soldier in the Revolution, a landowner and industrialist of no small measure; that he had literally made his section, and was many times a member of the North Carolina General Assembly. He merely stated that he was "a patriot and a gentleman."

The reader of today will wonder at the gates previously mentioned, but he must remember that North Carolina was then in the transition state that came to almost all American sections. Man was originally a forager, then a hunter, then a herdsman, and then a farmer, all these merging one into the other. We in Lincoln County, North Carolina, were at that time, like most America, mixed herdsmen-farmers, with the result that we fenced our crops as every first settler had to do, and let the stock, cattle, hogs, and sheep range at will. Since that time a new order has come, and the stock are now fenced and agricultural products stand in the open fields. It is impossible now to conceive the bitterness manifested, neighbor against neighbor, years back during this transition. At the time of which I speak each plantation marked its cattle, its hogs, and even its sheep by a peculiar slit in the ear and they ranged the woodlands for acorns and the canebrakes for buds for miles and miles. The horned Dorset in which both sexes carried fighting horns could alone exist amongst the sheep and the razorbacks (Tamworths) amongst hogs.

The next day Uncle Joe called on me to go with him as "gate-boy" up to the old family burying ground at Machpelah Church. I was not so anxious as before but took my place beside him in the carryall and found to my joy that it was a route of no gates. Machpelah Church was near the road from Cottage Home to Lincolnton, and near by had been a burying ground for the Grahams and Brevards since 1801. The later church building was of brick, and at the time of which I speak my grandfather, Doctor Morrison, even then preached there once a month. There I saw the tomb of General Joseph Graham who died in 1836, age seventy-seven years. Quite a eulogy was carved beneath this statement, and he had indeed played no small part in the history of North Carolina. There my grandmother, Mary Graham Morrison, was buried, and the place has always been to me a hallowed spot.

From there we went to Vesuvius Furnace, then in action, and I saw the making of pig iron from the ore. I saw the machinery for the pumping of the air that kept it in blast, and its feeding and general care and attention. But the drawing-off took place only in the evening, and we could not wait; so my first view of a furnace was rather disappointing, but mentally I was able to connect the pigs still lying on the floor of the casting shed with the output at Bolinger's Forge. One little incident on these excursions survives as if of yesterday. A small water wheel revolved a cam which lifted a lever and dropped a big wooden pestle into a huge wooden mortar that cracked corn and other grains for the horses. Corn on the cob was placed in the mortar and the pestle fell every six or eight seconds. In spite of the movement I saw a guinea fowl jump into that mortar, grab a grain of corn, and hop out safely a dozen or more times in succession. It was literally uncanny, the certitude with which he made his seizure and escaped the falling weight. No other fowl known to me has such powers of quick and certain movement.

I judge it was in 1866 that Uncle Joe took me once more as gate-boy to the Rock Spring Camp Meeting. Such evangelical gatherings deserve some explanation in these modern high-pressure days. In order to fight Martin Luther, Ignatius de Loyola had obtained from the Pope, in the sixteenth century, permission to preach in unconsecrated buildings. About a century later John Wesley, who was a great student of Loyola's life and organization, adopted the same proceeding at Bristol, England. Little could he dream that his Methodist followers in America would find in the outdoor "camp meeting" the real hormone for the building of that sect. At the end of the summer, when the crop was laid by and before fall planting began, was "camp-meeting time."

We cannot imagine today the tremendous influence of these congregations. This was, I am sure, the first one after the War, a real gathering of long-scattered families. As I remember, there were nearly six thousand people assembled that day at Great Rock Spring, not very far from Lincolnton, which was an ideal place for this meeting. They came from as far south as Georgia and as far west as Tennessee, for it was the one place in which separated families could meet under an outside stimulus. Counting at least three persons to a wagon (and usually more), many of whom had driven over most primitive roads for as long as two weeks, there would be at least two thousand covered wagons and four thousand horses or mules. The dust and smells created an indescribable aura extending far into the countryside. You can imagine what a profitable thing it was for farmers from twenty miles around to bring their corn or "roughness" to sell at such a market.

The Great Rock Spring did not belie its name and was the living center of this vast assemblage, but the spiritual center was "The Arbor" which, as its name implies, was a covered, open-air pulpit where the preaching took place and the seekers of redemption found salvation. Around this were the hundreds of split-log seats for the congregation and choir. Then a circle of cottages, for the habitual attendants, and beyond this, a wide zone of shacks and covered wagons where the transient families lived and visited, definitely a domestic zone; then the open air stables, horse troughs, and tents, a more masculine zone; and beyond this, the horse swapping zone, with a fringe of "trade and barter."

Circumscribing the whole congregation, however, were the "zones of Sin." First, the hard liquor zone; a little further, to avoid interruption, the cockfighting and gambling zone; and still further, in the outer darkness, was the "bawdy" zone, for even a camp meeting would have its camp followers; and, not all sinners who came desired to be saved.

XX

A TRIP TO "YANKEEDOM"

IN 1867, when I was ten years old, I made my first trip above the Mason and Dixon line and went into "Yankeedom" all the way to Boston. Aunt Maria was famous far and wide as a housewife; her manuscript cookbook was much in demand, and she conceived the idea of putting her art into print, hoping that she might thus retrieve to some extent our fast failing finances. She was a woman of rare social instinct as well as an excellent cook, so when the Lorings, who were Boston publishers, heard of the existence of *Dixie Cookery* they urged her to bring it on. She at once began getting ready, and as ladies did not travel alone in those days and Uncle Victor was not well enough to stand prolonged travel, I was to go with her. Bully! I was ready. At the last minute Father decided to go with us as far as Philadelphia where he had some business.

First we went to Richmond on the North Carolina Railroad, and I learned for the first time that third class on that road had been abolished although second class continued until my early manhood. In Richmond we stopped at the Ballard and Exchange Hotel; the buildings were on opposite sides of Main Street and connected by a second-story bridge over the street, an arrangement that gave a child a magnificent view of city traffic. I was much impressed. For the next fifty miles we traveled on the Richmond, Fredericksburg and Potomac to Aquia Creek, where the train ran out on a pier and we were transferred to a paddle-wheel steamboat which took us to Alexandria. Thence we went by bus to the old Sixth Street station of the Pennsylvania Railroad in Washington and took the train for Baltimore. I remember only the grandeur of my distant view of the Capitol and the insignificant Washington Monument then in process of building, a truncated obelisk with a derrick on top. When we reached the city limits of Baltimore I had a novel experience. The train slowed up and the rear coach was detached; the engine proceeded for another hundred feet or so, and another coach was detached. This singular manoeuvre was continued until all the coaches were detached at regularly spaced intervals; then the engine switched over, backed out, and chugged away. In a few moments a team of four Conestoga wagon-horses were hitched tandem to each coach. In this manner, by horse power but still on the rails, we trotted through the city, the brakeman standing by his brake to regulate the speed of each coach. Years later I learned that the "ground rent" deeds of Baltimore contained a clause forbidding the passage of those new demons, steam engines, through the sacred streets of the inner city. Later they overcame this inconvenience by tunnelling and building the central station down in a valley inside the city. When we reached the other side of Baltimore, an engine picked up the train and we continued on our journey to Philadelphia in the usual fashion.

My father pointed out to me the evidence of the recent straightening of the track we were on. Everywhere we saw the remains of a previous roadbed now abandoned for a less curved route, an improvement probably due to the exigencies of the late war.

Arriving in Philadelphia, we took a cab to 1022 Arch Street, the home of Aunt Maria's kinsfolk, the Masseys. I recall the address because, after great solicitation and struggle, I was allowed to wander around the city pretty much at will so long as I carried a tag stating that I came from 1022 Arch. Father devoted a day to showing me Independence Hall and other Revolutionary reminders. He also took me to the river front and pointed out the large island (now vanished) where my pioneer ancestor landed when he came to America more than one hundred years earlier.

Just before Father left I had an experience that I will never forget. Armed with my tag and a pocketful of five-cent "shin plasters," I rode the streetcars of Philadelphia east and west, north and south, at will. I went back and forth as far as the cars went and enjoyed myself hugely. One morning a streetcar vendor went through and laid a long stick of candy, well wrapped up, on the lap of each passenger. When he came through again to collect, I saw several people pay him ten cents and put the candy in their pockets, so I did likewise. Having one of these large reservoirs of happiness—as I thought—in my pocket, I became hungry rather early in the afternoon. I rolled back the wrapper and broke off an inch or two. It tasted peculiar, but not bad, so I continued until it was gone. I turned up at 1022 Arch Street, after a mule-team ride of some twenty miles, feeling far from well.

As soon as we sat down to supper someone said, "That child looks sick," and in another moment I proceeded to demonstrate that I was sick, with a vengeance. After I had rendered unto Caesar the things that were Caesar's, and then some, they got a doctor, but he was baffled. Father was scared to death. He had bought his return ticket, but he stayed with me. As for me, I just wanted to die and be done with it. I was never as sick in my life before or since, and it was almost morning before the doctor left.

After breakfast I felt much better and slipped out of bed to get my handkerchief, and there was the long wrapper of my candy. Inside was a circular stating that it was a cough candy containing tartar emetic and ipecac, that two inches was a full dose for an adult, and that one should "never take more than three inches." At the age of ten, I had eaten twelve inches and had quite a party. The General was furious, but I was too feeble to flail, so he went home disgusted.

The next day my aunt and I started to Boston. I remember little of New York as we left the train in Jersey City, then a small place, and took the boat around the city to the pier of the Boston line, and I slept in the upper berth of my aunt's stateroom most of the way. I found it rather rough around Cape Cod, but I was a good sailor, a gift for which I have ever been thankful.

In Boston I saw little except the hotel, which seemed much like other hotels. I was confined there because Aunt Maria was with her publishers almost all the time, and she thought that the streets of Boston were too irregular to allow me the freedom which I had enjoyed in Philadelphia. One evening a member of the firm came to call, and he seemed to know of my existence for he brought me a book about birds and birds' eggs. There in my room, with Boston's Fanueil Hall and the famous Commons unseen, I spent my time reading this volume, *The Boys of Chaquassett*. Years later I revisited Boston with a friend, going on the old steamboat, *Priscilla*. Seemingly the city had not changed a particle, but of course I was a poor judge. In fact Boston is still the only major city of the United States of which I personally know so little.

We returned by the same route, stopped in Richmond for a couple of days, and I saw the old Capitol as originally built at Jefferson's suggestion without the side wings. I also saw and admired the statue of Washington and even then heard the old joke, "He is looking at the State House and pointing to the penitentiary."

Thinking over my trip, I was surprised and gratified at the general sameness of the people, north and south, for I had found the same courtesy and general civility in all relationships. The only real difference that I noticed was that of accent, and at that time this difference was more pronounced in Philadelphia than in Boston. It was a trip, the memories of which I have always treasured, and a most enlightening episode in the life of a Southern boy.

At this time my father was living in Charlotte and had formed a partnership with Judge James W. Osborne of that city. My father, a graduate of the University of North Carolina, was an extremely well-educated man and well fitted for his chosen profession, but he was always a "counselor" rather than "a power before a jury." He was one of the directors of the North Carolina Railroad and the legal representative of most of the others in Charlotte, but I never knew him to take a criminal case. Judge

Osborne, on the other hand, was then perhaps the greatest jury lawyer in the state, and his gifts were inherited by his sons, the forceful Judge Frank Osborne of North Carolina and James Osborne, at one time assistant district attorney for the city of New York.

The relationship between my father and Judge Osborne was always pleasant, but a few years later the partnership ended, and my father became strictly a bank and railroad lawyer, practising largely by brief and seldom before a jury. Meanwhile he reopened his office in Concord, coming over from Charlotte once a week. I think he left Concord in the first place because he did not want to compete with his invalid brother whose acquaintance was more or less limited to Cabarrus County, while General Barringer, because of his four years in the army, knew practically everybody within a radius of one hundred and fifty miles. The timing of his return to Concord confirmed my idea of the reason for his leaving. Uncle Victor was then one of a committee codifying the laws of North Carolina, a task which left him little or no time for private practice.

My father was eminently fitted for political life, but as an old-time Whig, he would have none of the Democratic party or its 1872 candidate, Horace Greeley, whom he regarded as a sectional incendiary and old-time abolitionist. He entered politics only once, as a nonpartisan delegate to the State Constitutional Convention 1875. He was a member of the Judiciary Committee, and the present distinctive judicial system of North Carolina was largely his work.

During my early school days my teacher was Miss Margaret Long who came from Hillsboro, North Carolina, and taught as governess in the home of Mr. Foard and later in her own private school which I attended. Naturally I was delighted when General James Henry Lane, a former distinguished officer in the Confederate Army, came to Concord to open a school for boys, and I was transferred from the ladies to the soldier. My classes, however, which would now be called "the grades," were taught by the assistant, Hodijah Meade, as the general taught only the older boys. There was great sorrow in Concord when General Lane closed his school and went to Blacksburg, Virginia, as

Commandant of Cadets at what is now the Virginia Polytechnic Institute, where forty years later I was president.

My father became very well acquainted with my former teacher, Miss Margaret Long, and saw her frequently when he returned to Concord from Charlotte. I think it was about the time of our visit to Mount Pleasant that he told me I was to have a new stepmother, and they were married in 1870.

In 1871 Uncle Victor had finished his work on the North Carolina Code Commission and was called to Washington where he and Aunt Maria established residence. Their home in Concord was now lost to me and since my father's plans for building in Charlotte were not completed, we were once more living temporarily at a hotel.

XXI

MOUNT PLEASANT

YEARS PASSED (which means to a child eighteen months or two years) and then, with that instinct for timeliness that made all of his plans work so smoothly, Father told me to "get ready to go to Mount Pleasant." He said I would need old clothes as we would be crawling through undergrowth. This was interesting, and I dug up what seemed suitable and also, under his direction, provided myself with a notebook and pencil, the purpose of which I did not at the time understand.

For the twelve- or fourteen-mile drive from Concord to the village of Mount Pleasant which was to be our headquarters, my father got a pair of high-stepping horses hitched to a buckboard, the most serviceable vehicle for rough roads of that day ever invented.

Father talked as he drove. He told me I was going to see the site of the two homes built by my great-grandfather, John Paul Barringer, on Dutch Buffalo Creek; I was going to see his tomb in the churchyard of Saint John's Lutheran Church, in which the congregation had built a special pew for him; I was going to see the lands that Tryon, the royal governor of North Carolina, said produced such "excellent hay." He told me how John Paul Barringer, who often signed his name Paulus Behringer, came from South Württemberg, on the slopes of the Franconian Alps, now called Franconia, and crossing to the French side of the border, walked down the Rhine to Hanover, stayed there for some time, and then took ship at Rotterdam for Philadelphia, via Cowes.

He said that the young immigrant came up the Delaware in a small sailing ship of three hundred tons and passed by the island on which the Federal Government later built Fort Delaware, in which he had been confined for nearly six months after the war. During his imprisonment, he had often thought of that voyage. Watching the difficulties that the tramp steamers frequently encountered in breasting the current of the Delaware, he fully appreciated the long fight that a sailing vessel must make while progressing up this stream. And so, my father, the most unromantic man I have ever known, built up for me a dramatic picture.

He drove through Mount Pleasant, stopping a few miles beyond in what looked to me like the center of a howling wilderness, and said, "The old home place was somewhere about here." Immediately my bearcat came to life, and remembering old Rheinholdt Sutter's description, I expected to see such an animal come tearing out of the woods. We got out of the buckboard, and the little Negro from the livery stable dropped down from behind to take the horses while we climbed a scrub covered half-hill. Below us lay Dutch Buffalo Creek with its wide fertile bottoms, our road crossing it about a hundred yards farther downstream. Pointing to the ford, my father said, "Down yonder is the mill which he built." I could see the base of the dam and an aged structure. When he knew that his wife's failing health made a permanent settlement necessary, John Paul Barringer had begun his mill, quarrying and cutting his first millstones from the native Cabarrus granite. Of course it was not Cabarrus County then; it was first Anson County and then Mecklenburg before he arranged for the formation of Cabarrus. About where we stood he had built his first house which he called Mount Pleasant. Here he lived with his first wife, Elizabeth Eisemann, and here she died and was buried.

She was a strong, handsome pioneer woman who could shoot a gun as well as rock a cradle, a woman of extremely high character and intelligence although she spoke and wrote the English language very poorly. She had come from Europe to the Pennsylvania wilderness when but a child of eight or ten.

In this early home, which was a cluster of high-class log cabins, old Paulus Behringer lived a baronial life, operating his mill, trading, and farming his rich lands. Although he spoke scant English, he was a captain in the Colonial militia, and for twenty years a magistrate of the Crown. He was visited by Lord Tryon, the royal governor, as is noted in that gentleman's journal:

> Wed. Aug. 31, 1768.
> The Governor waited on Captain Barringer; a beautiful plantation, skillfully managed, particularly the meadow land, which produced *excellent hay.*

Bernheim, in his *History of the Lutheran Church in the Carolinas,* states that the governor drank too freely of the captain's rich wines and then, borrowing a scythe from a field hand, made a personal attack on the captain's hay. Certainly something must have called his attention to its excellence, or he would not have underscored it. Tradition says that Captain Barringer exchanged a hogshead of his sauerkraut with the Italian Rivafinoli for a cask of his imported wines.

Note that this visit of the royal governor was in 1768, and soon after that Squire Barringer's house at Mount Pleasant became a rallying place for the friends of American freedom. Too old to fight himself, the squire, a member of the local Committee of Safety, gave his wholehearted support to the American cause and outfitted his eldest son, John, who became a captain in the Continental Army. Like many other North Carolina magistrates appointed by the Crown, he did not comply with the royal order of 1776 to raise the King's standard, "to put down this horrid and unnatural rebellion." He was promptly appointed Justice of the Peace by unanimous consent of the Provincial Congress assembled at Halifax, North Carolina. With many others, he was captured by the Scovillite Tories (David Fanning's gang) in 1779 and sent to Camden, South Carolina. He, alone among the captured magistrates, survived his prison sentence, but he contracted smallpox and gave it to his family when he returned in 1780.

Two years before his capture, he had married his second wife, my great-grandmother, Catherine Blackwelder (the name was originally Schwartzwalder, meaning, "Black Forester"). She was a woman of unusual type, and his marriage brought a marked change into his life for he built a new house for her which was unlike any other house in that part of the country.

We crossed the creek to the rounded knoll on which it had stood, a landmark for fifty years. They named it Poplar Grove, and Catherine Blackwelder must have had a hand in designing it, a "half-residence, half-castle" like those described in Baedeker as the typical fireproof residences of the Black Forest. The first story was of stone with barred windows, and the second, overhanging the first by four feet, of heavy wood. I do not think it stood on a higher site than the first house, but here the curve of the river gave a view of broad bottom lands forming the famous meadows which could not be seen from the other side. The house was gone, but the barn and some outbuildings were intact, and I have never seen such superb timbers as those in the barn. One hewn beam was fully thirty feet long and sixteen inches square.

We walked over to see the old millsite. There was another mill a short distance on the other side of the creek which had been built by the pioneer's eldest son, John. When I asked why the two mills were so close together on the same stream, my father replied that being on opposite sides of the stream, they made the entire community independent of high water. Most of the early Barringers built mills, and several are shown on the military map of the Mecklenburg section made by my maternal great-grandfather, Joseph Graham, during the Revolution.

My father drove back to Mount Pleasant where we put up at the local hotel. Word was spread around that "the old general" (Father was then only fifty-two) was there, and a large number of the men formerly under his command came to see him. It made me more than proud to see the high regard, amounting almost to reverence, with which the General was treated by his old comrades, officers and men alike.

I was to have still another memorable experience that day for after supper Father took me to call on an old man who, as a child, had seen and talked with old Pioneer Paul. He remembered him and my great-grandmother well and had known their family intimately. This old man's repeated encomiums on the early members of the Barringer family whom he had known gave me my first realization that a name is simply a trust committed to our keeping for life, and that as time passes the obligation to keep it clean and up to standard grows stronger and stronger. This in reality is the only value there is, or that should be, attached to any old and honored family name. Henceforth you are not simply a participant in the race—you are a tagged and marked participant. If there is any greater stimulus to gentle and honorable conduct and unstinted effort, I, now an old man, have not seen it.

PART II
The World and the Man

XXII

BINGHAM'S SCHOOL

MY FATHER WAS now established in Charlotte and frequently I stayed with him at the Central Hotel. Amongst the other assets of that hotel was a billiard and a pool table. I could barely see over the table but I found that by holding my right arm horizontal, I could reach over the top and handle a cue, and soon I was diverting all my spare cash into playing pool. One day my father, who rarely condescended to visit that section of the hotel, chanced upon me being trained by the adjacent barkeep, and as he looked on for a moment quietly but sternly, I knew that something was coming. So I was not greatly surprised when a few days later I was informed that I was to attend Bingham's School, in Mebanesville (now Mebane), North Carolina, and I began to make fervent inquiry about this land of Canaan. All that I could learn was that it was the one place left in the country where they "whupped by mule power," that it was a distinguished place, and that it gave the best preparation for the University of North Carolina at Chapel Hill, to which educational institution I was of course predestined. In brief, on August 24, 1871, my father and I got off the train at Mebanesville and drove to Bingham's School a mile or more away. This school, started in 1793, was conducted by two generations of Binghams at Oaks and later moved to this location by the then presiding genius, Colonel William Bingham, a schoolmaster *facile princeps*. Education was a matter of serious application there, mental and physical. He discussed my preparation with my father and indicated that I was a little short on what were later to become primary Carnegie units, but he said he would try me out. Before he left my father emphasized the Colonel's consideration and told me that, under the circumstances, I was obliged to make good. So the Colonel and I started out with very pleasant relations which were never really disturbed, no matter what transpired. I found he was a dignified and gentle man who, when necessary, could be very stern but had those qualities of integrity and justice which win the heart of youth.

Of course, I didn't know anything about high schools and I suppose that Bingham's School, if looked at today, would be considered very primitive, yet it had everything that a youth needed. It was in effect a small fort arranged in a "hollow square" two hundred by one hundred yards and composed of a continuous row of one story log cabins. These cabins held over a hundred boys, four to a room, and each room had a great big cast-iron stove; cast by North, Chase, and North, as I remember, because a friend fell against a hot stove and bore the brand, "North, Chase, and" to his dying day. When these stoves were fully going, we were warm; and there was no trouble about ventilation, because the twelve-inch floor boards, without tongue and groove, had shrunk until you could see the ground below. The entrance or "sally port" was the Colonel's headquarters, and there my father and I conferred with him.

Colonel Bingham's brother, Major Robert Bingham, was his assistant and second in command, always a difficult position in a family organization and probably the reason we were not so friendly. His wife, Belle Worth, daughter of the late governor, was always my friend and lives as a saint in my memory. They had two charming daughters and one son, born while I was at school there. This son, Robert Worth Bingham, was afterwards a law student at the University of Virginia during my administration and was later well known to the world as Ambassador to the Court of St. James. Colonel William Bingham had a son, unfortunately a deaf-mute, who was about my age. It was from him that I learned the deaf-mute alphabet which has been of untold value throughout my life as a medical practitioner. I have found it the same in Scotland, Austria, and Bosnia and have written out speeches in a foreign tongue which I did not understand.

The next few days at old Bingham's will be long remembered. As I was only fourteen, which was younger than most of the pupils, I was placed in a room with three of the oldest men in school. In fact, one of these had served for six months under Lee. He was from North Carolina, but the other two were from Arkansas and Texas. The reason I was so assigned was that, while wood was supplied in unlimited quantities for fuel, each room had to cut and split its own supply, and these big bucks were supposed to balance my inefficiency. This was a military school, and as the muskets we drilled with weighed over twelve pounds, I was detached from the line and became a "marker," a cadet who bore a small folded flag and was sent dashing ahead of the company to mark the point, on the street or elsewhere, where they should turn right or left. I did not get my gun until the next year, but a description is not amiss. It was a fifty-eight caliber smoothbore that had once been a "flint and steel" remodelled with a percussion-cap tube. They were, of course, muzzle-loaders, and the cartridge consisted of an oilpaper holder for the powder, one end of which was bitten off to pour the powder in the muzzle of the gun. After the paper was empty, a fifty-eight caliber, one ounce bullet was pushed into the muzzle and driven down with a ramrod. The bullet was deeply cupped behind, and when the explosion took place, it instantly expanded and hugged the bore, giving weapons of great accuracy. Shooting at a moving plank target of a man (hung from a sloping wire) required real skill for success. So proud were they of their skill that many of the students bought extra ammunition for practice.

I was surprised to learn that these students were from all over the South and that a fair number had been in the Confederate Army. Texas ranked next to North Carolina in numbers. The Cook brothers from Dogtown, Texas, held my disregard until I learned that their home occupied an enormous acreage once possessed by thousands of prairie dogs. The Robinson brothers were from Waco. From the cities of North Carolina there were the Sprunts and McDairmeds of Wilmington, Hugheses from New Bern, Battles, Moores, and Lacys from Raleigh, Bordens from Goldsborough, Battles from Tarborough, Parkers from Salisbury, the Tates and Vances from Charlotte. These made up a corps of nearly one hundred and fifty men.

Drilling an hour or more each day, rain or shine, we did not need sports for health, and there were no athletic scholarships in those days. Baseball was coming, and many students had balls which were thrown and caught as usual. But "three old cat" was the game of my day. In the long evenings, half a dozen groups who would make three holes in the ground were often seen playing, but there was never any organized institutional team. Strangely the best players that I can remember, were the Phifers, Means, and Allisons of Concord, and years later a team from my little native village held the championship of the state.

As I have said, this was a military school. A bugle call, or short roll on the kettle drum, called us for all essential gatherings, and striking steel called us to all classes. A "steel" consisted of a bar of steel bent into a four-inch ring at one end, shaped into an isosceles triangle which did not unite at the terminals. Hit that with eighteen inches of gas pipe and you have a sound that is not loud but can be heard two miles. A gentle tap marked the end of classes and a lusty thump, the call for dinner. We fell in, parallel with the long side of the quadrangle, counted off by fours, and marched to dinner. We sat down, ten men at each table, and got unusually good food but, of course, without much variety. Even in those days, Colonel Bingham seemed to know that fresh meat was the food for a growing body, and we had pork, beef, and mutton galore.

Aside from chicken pox, mumps, and such epidemics of youth, there was almost no sickness. I had some trouble with my old friend "malaria," but nearly every one in the South then had his occasional "chills and fever" and took it in his stride. One current malady which was never mentioned was "sinus" though a few boys had catarrh. In my later medical practice which ranged all over a county in this same state, I never had a single case of sinus trouble, except in the steam room of the local cotton mill where it was very prevalent. Dr. Mebane was most attentive and in the matter of sanitation was far in advance of his time. In fact, there was growing, without any clear knowledge of the sources of typhoid, a fashion in the construction of houses that favored health.

Twenty years later, I drove by Mebanesville and went in to look at the old site. There was the well and the pump in the center of the quadrangle, and I could see that they had not carted off a yard of earth but spread it evenly around the well, making it twelve or fourteen inches higher than any other part of the quadrangle and sloping outward. The well platform was laid shingle-wise and a large hewn trough-like spout carried the drippings of this magnificent well far from the platform. The sanitary provisions for the latrine were at least fifteen or twenty feet below the level of the well and one hundred yards away, on stiff clay soil. It was, of course, merely a large, open privy but well cared for. At this later visit, I was a member of the Virginia State Board of Health, and I was simply astounded how natural conditions could conspire against the dangers of unsanitary crowding. The route to the backhouse passed between rooms numbered six and seven and was therefore called by the singular title of "six and a half." Everything was primitive but effective.

In each room at night there were two bunks standing on legs four to six inches high and consisting of a quadrangular frame of eight- or ten-inch dressed pine sideboards with a solid bottom nailed firmly on. In each of these bunks was a corn shuck mattress, two pillows, sheets, and blankets. In the daytime these bunks were out of the way, turned up against the wall, and at night they were let down, already made up and ready for service except for the placing of the pillows. Out of the way in the morning, they were still available for inspection. Each one of us had a week of orderly service per month, and I have always been grateful that I was trained to sweep, arrange a room, and make up a bed ready for critical inspection in my early youth. This was a daily ordeal.

The long roll was beaten about half past six or seven o'clock, varying with the season. It rolled from three to five minutes; and there you stood in line, ready when the Captain called "Attention" and moved down the line, seeing that your cap was on the square, that your hair was not tousled, and that every one of your something like two dozen buttons was buttoned to the chin. Any announcements for the day were read and you were dismissed. It was then that the orderly of the day got busy. He made up the beds and swept the floor carefully, for inspection meant inspection there. In one corner of the room, he had a wood rack which had to hold at least enough wood for the day, brought in from the woodyard some hundred yards away. At intervals he had to go to the commissary to get stove polish enough to keep his stove from that ferruginous yellow ash color which constantly heated stoves tend to take. At all times your room and attire had to be ready for military inspection.

The class rooms at Bingham's were not large. Each boy had a split-bottom chair at his place behind a long, twelve-inch wide, well-finished, unpainted pine desk. This unusual arrangement was born of Colonel Bingham's desire to hold classes out of doors whenever possible. All one had to do was to take up his chair, holding the seat over his head, and march in military formation to any point chosen. In the matter of instruction, I might say it was assigned lessons followed by a quiz, but with Colonel Bingham it was more than that. At the close of each lecture, he gave, in less than fifty words, the skeleton on which we were to hang the next day's assignment.

We had whippings at Bingham's in the freshman and sophomore classes whenever the Colonel thought it necessary. The statement of his enemies that he "whupped by mule power" was a libel. He whipped all right, for he flogged me something like a dozen times, but never without reason nor when in a rage. This punishment consisted of ten or twelve strokes on the right hand with a well-trimmed hickory switch about the size of a lead pencil, and if you think such an implement impelled by duty driven motives did not hurt, you are mistaken.

The Colonel's code covering whippings was very peculiar. It was unwritten but perfectly understood. I will give an example. Charles S., a son of a well-to-do cotton mill owner who was making a fortune, had bought, instead of the regular prescribed Caesar an interlinear text with the English translation printed in small type between the lines of Latin. Not a week after his purchase he was called on to translate and he just rolled it off. The Colonel looked at him a moment and instead of stopping him at the end of a paragraph, told him to go on, and on he went. It was Caesar and Areovistus, and Charles grew dramatic. When he finally stopped, again the Colonel said "go on." Once more he took it and ran through to the mark in his book which ended the forty or fifty lines assigned. He looked quite proud as he ended. And then the Colonel said: "Charles, you read quite well, but I think that if you come up near the window and take my book with big type, you may read better." When he came up, the Colonel handed him his volume and said, "Now start at the beginning." It was pitiable! Charles was completely stalled, making one or two stabs at words he knew. The Colonel said, "Go to your seat." The Colonel then got up, walked across the room to a little corner shelf he had, picked out an unusually large hickory switch and said, "Carolus, ad lignum veni." He gave Charles an unusual dressing down and ended with his usual "Satis." You see, not a word was spoken relative to his crime nor did the Colonel attempt to capture his book. I really believe he would have been glad if every boy there had had an interlinear; he recommended Anthon's Caesar, because when you got through with it, he would know that you knew every definition, declension, and conjugation.

My first year, I started with Aesop's Fables and remember "Haec fabula docet" to this day. I had no love for Latin, and my three years of Aesop, Caesar, and Virgil were years of labor and not love. As for Colonel Bingham, Latin seemed to be his mother tongue; it was to him a living language which we learned to understand and feebly apply. He spoke only Latin to the boys in class and administered punishment in the same language. I can hear him now, "Paulus, et Davidicus et Carolus, ad lignum venite," and "come to the wood" we did until he declared "Satis." Davidicus was my friend, David Vance, son of the old governor; Carolus was Charlie Tate of Mountain Island; and no three musketeers ever lived that had a better time.

Latin exercises were no textbook drill but taken from varied sources. Rendering "Sing a song of six-pence" from Mother Goose into Latin, with conformity to the meter, was tricky exercise. I can remember the first verse only, which goes like this:

> Cane carmen, oboli.
> Pochia seccalis.
> Vier und zwanzig merulae.
> Pastarte pastatis.

The third line is obviously German, because no amount of ingenuity could make "four and twenty" in Latin take its place in the line, so this solution was accepted as a tribute to inventiveness and poetic licence.

The instructor in English was Major Lynch, who lived several miles from the school, and who was a good teacher and charming gentleman, although I happen to know that at that time he was also the head of the Ku Klux Klan for the county. I am glad to say that he was always a very good friend of mine. We studied Bingham's *English Grammar*, written by the Colonel's grandfather who must have been in the first graduating class at Chapel Hill! This grammar had for the English tongue the nominative, genitive, accusative, and other cases of the Latin. All of this was a great help as an approach to the Latin but made English a dead language. But Major Lynch covered all of this and more. His classroom was a salon of recitation, and I have never known its like. Our study of Poe was followed by memorizing "The Raven"; Macaulay gave us the first twenty or thirty verses, to be memorized and recited, of his "Lays of Ancient Rome"; and Scott, page after page of the "Lady of the Lake." The cannibalistic "Wreck of the Nancy Bell," stray bits from Byron, carefully selected, and such rare bits of prose as Johnson's "Rasselas" filled in the session. At the end of three years of this work, an assignment of six or eight verses, was considered nothing! I could get it straight, ready to write on the blackboard, in thirty minutes, and in those days when the cells were in the sap, I would remember it for ever. No other English grammar was used; only this rare product (now a museum piece) and it made no reference to literature. It was purely the anatomy of language without the physiology.

The other teacher, Captain Norwood, who had the chair of

Mathematics, was somewhat alien. His presentation of mathematics did not jibe with my receptivity even though some of his problems are still to be remembered. "If Yankee soldiers are running for their lives at ––– miles per hour, how long will it take Confederate soldiers pursuing at ––– miles per hour to capture?" This was a theme of infinite variations, involving pride of state or beloved heroes, and so popular that we were betrayed into mathematical calculation outside of the class room—which has always been contrary to union rules.

Our uniforms were furnished by the school and were made about a mile away under the supervision of the wife of Colonel Cheek, the former Commander of the First North Carolina Cavalry. You must remember that these uniforms were made for growing boys and were turned up inside about four inches at the ankle. There was a terrible overlap in the middle of the jacket, in the back, and you could go over to Mrs. Cheek's and have your uniform let out while you waited. For my own part, I had to be extended in both directions twice in one year, my fourteenth.

In the light of today's equipment, our extra-curricular activities were ludicrous. We had the drill ground where we could run races; near the sally port were two young white oak trees, with a three-inch gas pipe between them as a "horizontal bar." There was an adjustable white pine hurdle for high jumping, but it started at three feet, and in my first year I seldom tried it. The hurdle could be levered up to nearly five feet, and there were many who took that with ease. There was no gymnasium and no field day.

Holiday on Saturdays was given from dinnertime (two o'clock) until supper (seven o'clock), and I really believe that in the warm months the most interesting occupation of the entire corps was collecting bird eggs. Numbers of students had found, blown, and preserved eggs of nearly all the birds of the immense woodland around the school. When I got to Bingham's the bird-egg season was past and I simply enjoyed the various collections of my friends, having none of my own as Dr. Bachman had said nothing about eggs. But on birds and snakes I was definitely "it." Since Dr. Bachman's tutelage when we were hiding out from

Federal troops, I had thought and worked on snakes and birds, far beyond my years. One of our neighbors in Concord, Dr. Lilly, had a glorious volume on snakes by the famous herpetologist, Davenport (a friend of Bachman's from Charleston). Working with Dr. Lilly, who had no fear of snakes, I had acquired some of his *savoir-faire;* so when in September, 1871, I walked into the quadrangle, carrying a corn snake in my hand, I was regarded as an exponent of magic. Like Indians, there were no good snakes except dead snakes in those days.

The perpetual sport, however, was foraging for food. We were well fed but collective cooking cannot easily be varied, so we were always hungry for outside things; Bar B. Q.'s and snack bars were undreamed of. During the summer, on Saturdays and Sundays, we raided the country for miles around. Experience had taught us that purloining was dangerous, so we bought what we wanted. Eggs at ten cents a dozen were considered high, frying-size chickens were two for a quarter, and this in great big "shin plaster" money in which fifty cents was the size of the present dollar.

The school very sensibly allowed us to cook on our stoves if we were careful, and each stove had an eight-inch eye on top for which a proper size frying pan for each room was purchased. But eggs and chickens cost money, so we turned to a more plentiful source of succor, rabbits and sometimes birds. Guns and ammunition not being available, the birds were caught with snares and the rabbits with a "rabbit gum." This is a term of colonial origin, going back to the first settlers' discovery that the black gum tree, in spite of its healthy appearance, was always hollow inside. The larger cuts were sawed into two and a half foot lengths for "bee gums" and the smaller lengths for "rabbit gums." Br'er Rabbit knows that when pursued by an enemy, he must have some refuge, preferably a hollow log, into which he can crawl. Narrow spaces which obstruct his accustomed path are gnawed to facilitate quick exit, so by studying "gnaws" in a rail fence and placing a "gum" a few feet away, we kept our larder replenished. A pile of rusted pipe discarded from our stoves furnished us with excellent substitutes for wooden "gums" and seemed as acceptable to the rabbit. The sheet-iron "rabbit gum" was closed by a shingle-size oak plank at one end and a similar piece, suspended by a sixteen-inch stick as a balanced lever and guided by four small stakes, over the other end. With a hole in the pipe one-third of the distance from the end in which was inserted a notched eight-inch twig for a trigger, the figure "4" trap was ready.

The half hour before breakfast was usually devoted to looking at our "rabbit gums" and bringing in our catch in burlap bags, though when hard pressed we did not hesitate to use a pillow slip. Tularemia had not entered this world, so skinning and cleaning presented no dangers. We learned to fry these rabbits with salt, pepper, and lard which we kept in a little cabinet in our room, and nothing ever tasted better. Our surplus catch could be swapped for the twice-a-week dessert or "boss." One rabbit, one "boss," was the usual exchange.

Almost of necessity we lived in the woods. One day I saw a singular mass of lichen projecting from the dead limb of a "black-jack" oak. There was a peculiar hole in it, and as I watched a bird darted out and flew away. I recall that it was blue and yellow, an entirely unknown bird to me. With great care, I broke off the dead limb and took the nest with its four eggs home. None of my confreres could place them, so I wrote to my old friend, Dr. Bachman, for help. He was too old or ill to answer, but some bird-minded member of his family advised writing to Dr. Spencer F. Baird, later of the Smithsonian Institute in Washington. He gladly replied and told me to send the nest and eggs, which I carefully boxed and sent. He identified them as the blue yellow-backed warbler (Parula Americana), and named a number of unusual birds and eggs that we might find in that locality. Thus began a relationship which lasted for many years. It was Dr. Baird who advised me to get the then new *Birds of North America* by Elliott Coues. By sending his letter to my father, I was soon the proud owner, and what a companion it has always been!

Looking back at it now, seventy years later, I can but wonder what a modern educator and his corollary, the educatee, would think on visiting Bingham's Classical School at Mebanesville, in the year 1871. I suppose it would compare with a crude C. C. C.

Camp of today or a big lumberman's barracks, but even there the plumbing and entertainment would be more luxurious. In a way, there was nothing else to do but study. We read to the very last item the newspapers that our families sent. But under proper guidance it was a broad comprehension of life, such as I have rarely seen, and I am grateful for the experience.

XXIII

THE FOUR MUSKETEERS

JUST BEFORE Christmas in 1871, I received the appalling news that I was to remain at school for the holidays. My new stepmother was ill, and my father felt that with my accomplishments at the pool table, the hotel would not be an advisable place of sojourn. When a school friend, Sam Morgan, gave an invitation to visit at his home not far away it was heartily accepted.

An old Negro driver arrived in a buggy to take us home, and all three of us piled in on the front seat. It was a cold and rainy trip, and even sitting huddled together our young carcasses gradually congealed, so it was a great relief when the old man suggested that we stop at Mr. "Wash" Duke's to thaw out. It was a simple house, two frame buildings of two stories each, joined by an open covered way (known as a "dog-trot" porch). We were hospitably taken into a room with a large open fireplace, where Sam and I warmed ourselves against the further journey while the old Negro went into the kitchen.

A young woman, I think Mr. Duke's daughter, sat at a table where, by the light of a lamp, she was filling little cotton bags from a pile of finely-shredded tobacco before her. These little bags, stuffed to bursting, were drawn up with a sturdy string run through the top and tied in a bow knot. From time to time she took a pen and wrote in ink "Pro Bono Publico" on an oblong yellow label which she pasted on the filled bag of tobacco.

The lamplight on this table and her quiet deftness and complete absorption in the transition from the aromatic pile of finely-cut tobacco into filled and labelled bags held our fascinated attention. At last we were thawed and departed.

When we drove away, the old Negro said, "The Dukes is sure hard working, industrious folk. Did you see what that young lady was doing? She was filling little bags of smoking tobacco. After the war they sold some of their tobacco to the Yankee soldiers, and now they are writing back from all over the United States for some more of that Duke's mixture."

I learned later that Mr. Washington Duke, who had fought valiantly in the war, had been captured shortly before the surrender and confined in prison in Richmond, Virginia. On his release, he had journeyed on foot the one hundred and thirty-five miles to his home. There he found the home place stripped of all produce and equipment except a pair of blind mules and a broken-down wagon. Under the roof of an outhouse he found some cured tobacco which had escaped depredation. With this equipment and what other produce industry could make available, he started peddling on a barter system. The best cash customers were necessarily the Yankee soldiers.

I had grown up with the sight and smell of tobacco from plant to produce all around me, and every gentleman I knew had his special preference in twist or blend for pipe, but beyond its general value as a salable crop, there was little interest.

We did not know that we had been witnessing the creation of an industry, an industry which under the Dukes' capable management was to become an empire of finance and wise philanthropy, benefiting thousands with utilities, education, and medical care—a monument to a family.

The next year I was no longer with my old and seasoned comrades. Returning as a veteran, I went in with a group of boys about my own age, and my entire relationship with the student body expanded. I, of course, had my special friends, Dave Vance and Charlie Tate; added to this group was my cousin, young Daniel Moreau Barringer of Raleigh, who called himself "Dick" to avoid any jeering mention of "Daniel in the lions' den" which for some reason always called for a fight, and "Dick" he remained to his intimates.

In those days, certain epithets applied in wrath meant a fight and nothing else. If the offender was too large for the boy insulted, it was the custom for him to ask some friend of his of appropriate size to take it up; and in that way it was settled, sometimes by a ten or more round "fist and skull" fight. This made one careful in speech. There was not a pair of boxing gloves in the school. The boys practiced boxing gently with their bare fists, but there was a substitute, which I have never known of elsewhere, which developed unusual skill in defense. Two boys of about the same size and arm length were put toe-to-toe with their caps on, and the trick was to knock the other fellow's cap off with your bare hand. It will readily be seen that the defense used is really a boxer's defense and that some boy's caps, in spite of all attack, were practically untouchable. I know that the skill that I attained in this defense was often of value during my early years.

Between old Bill Bingham and my group there was open warfare, all above board, chivalrous, and according to the code, but warfare in the form of free enterprise versus the established order. It started in this wise. Dave Vance and I were called up for a flogging, and we had previously challenged each other to a proposed ordeal which nearly resulted in our downfall. We had agreed that when I was being flogged, Dave would howl, and when Dave was the recipient, I would perform; and we carried it out. Fortunately he started on Dave, and when I thought it was time for him to give way, I began to roar, "Ouch! Ouch! Oh, Lordy." Instantly the old man, forgetting himself, turned on me. Dave's pent up emotion broke forth, and he made the welcome welkin ring. We wore the old man to a frazzle. He could not even speak Latin, and we parted like three deaf mutes, but after that the gauntlet was in the ring. We were suspect and agreeably tried to live up to expectations.

The final episode that broke the camel's back came about from my fondness for snakes. Old Bill had us on the run for a couple of months, plainly the victor, when I killed a large black snake in my log cabin room at the barracks. After skinning it, I wondered what to do with the body. A brilliant idea occurred. Avoiding the sentries that night, I slipped into old Bill's lecture room and there after immense labor I worked this decorticated snake's body, already aromatic, between the two layers of old Bill's split-bottom chair. It was about the third day when we began to get our reward. We had played selfish and safe; not a human being knew except the four of us; and to see the old man stop when he came to the door, throw his head back, sniff, and irresistibly snort was a thing to remember. He searched the room from top to bottom. He had the books taken from the book shelves and looked behind them, but nevertheless it was still there. At last, things got to a point that when he sat down on the chair, the products of decomposition dropped to the floor; and finding these, he discovered what young sappers and miners could do. He made the punishment fit the crime, and for several weeks there was a state of armed truce. Then came the great calamity. Death to a boy is an irrational and overwhelming tragedy, so when some friend whom you look upon as stable as the rock of Gibraltar suddenly is no more, you are overwhelmed. We could not believe that Colonel William Bingham, headmaster of the school, had ceased to be. All explanation of "a stroke" and "in his sleep" was the superficial dressing of an incredible fact. It was with tears in my eyes, in the selected guard of honor, that I fired a last salute over his grave.

Colonel Bingham's death produced an almost immediate change in the school. It was re-whitewashed for the first time in years, and the student body began to go places. This brought, of course, a pickup in the military side of the institution, and new uniforms of coats with tails were issued in addition to our previous Eton-like jackets. A large detachment attended the funeral of William A. Graham at Hillsboro, ten miles away. He was my great-uncle to whom I have referred before, but I was prouder to attend this funeral as a cadet than as a relative.

This turn of affairs in school, as all new moves must do, produced factions in the student body, and I sided with the old guard, possibly out of a fancied loyalty to my old friend. Anyway, my father received a letter from Major Robert Bingham suggest-

THE FOUR MUSKETEERS 167

ing that it would be better if I breathed a more congenial atmosphere the following year.

Since the future was problematical, it was decided that our crowd would go out of this our world in a blaze of glory. The only opportunity for a big thing lay in the visit of the cadet corps to Raleigh for the big Indian ball game and the embryonic State Fair. These were the same Cherokee Indians I had seen in Asheville who lived in Cherokee County, which was practically an Indian reservation. Here they lived an almost tribal life, and continued their old games and religious rites undisturbed. This ball game, which somewhat resembled lacrosse, is played with a long narrow type of tennis racket in which the net is slack and cupped. The ball is caught in flight and returned with equal swiftness. In principle it is somewhat like hockey in the air. It has a very crowded field, is very fast, very dangerous, and frequently fatal; an interesting and exciting game.

The State Fair always had this Cherokee ball game as a major attraction since fine livestock had not yet come into the South after the war; but the main show for us was a dress parade and march past the Governor's reviewing stand. At school we marched with a drum only, but here we were to have a brass band, and all looked forward to it with the utmost interest. Our carefully perfected plan was that when we marched past the Governor, the cadet flag was to bear instead of three stars on a blue field a black "Jolly Roger," that we knew would "rile the in'nards" of old Bob sitting in state with the Governor.

Fortune favored us. Rain threatened, and the flag, on which we had pasted the cheesecloth scarehead, was kept in its case until the last moment. When taken out it hung limp until we started to move, but when the band struck up and we moved into a quick step, it floated in the breeze, briskly enough for the Governor and his staff to enjoy Major Robert Bingham's discomfiture. We called it square and quit.

While we were pleased with our so-called victory, the leave-takings of the four at the end of the year were most lugubrious. Dick went to Princeton, Dave to West Point, and Charles into business soon after. Only I was left with an uncertain future.

XXIV

THE SPORTS OF THE GENTRY

NEAR THE BANKS of the Catawba River where it flowed south about twelve miles west of Charlotte, my uncle, General D. H. Hill, had a small country home called Hard Scrabble. It was near the Rozzel Ferry which we had to cross when we went to Cottage Home. One summer after our return from a visit to one of the Virginia springs, I was visiting there and chanced to meet my old friend Charlie Tate, who promptly invited me to come over to the Mountain Island Cotton Factory where he lived, adding as a further inducement that in about ten days there would be a "big cocking main." In the fashion of the day he invited me to stay "a month," but I decided to pay a visit of a fortnight and arrived shortly before the date set for the main.

Mountain Island Cotton Factory had been one of the largest cotton mills in this section of the state, but it was almost worked to pieces during the Civil War; and the Tates, too poor to replace worn out machinery, had staggered along getting what they could out of the old mill. It was a typical cotton mill of those days. Each employee lived on his own four- or five-acre tract anywhere within half a mile of the mill with his cow, pen of hogs, and garden. Money for work at the mill was almost incidental; these laboring people were illiterate but intelligent.

The Tates, several brothers, lived on an eminence overlooking the river which was divided here by a cliff-faced island that gave the factory its name. Everything was destroyed by fire long ago, and now a six million dollar electric power plant stands near the old site, and the backwater of the dam floods the old Rozzel Ferry area.

The cocking main was to take place in a large abandoned dyehouse. The next morning after my arrival I went over to the dyehouse and saw for the first time the preliminaries of a great cocking main in full swing. Shelves were put around the walls of the dyehouse about three feet from the ground. On these shelves empty guano bags four or five layers thick were tacked down, and on these the twenty-five or thirty cocks which might be engaged were being "ordered." The hand was run under the breast and the cock tossed up three or four feet to drop back on the bags. But for the bags, the soles of his feet might be made sore, and they were very careful to keep him on a soft place. After ten or fifteen minutes of severe exercise of this kind he was put in his crate and another was taken out. Three or four men were at work tossing when I came in. I went around and looked at all the cocks and saw my first large number of fine birds trimmed and sawn for fighting.

When a young fighting cock is about six months old or more his high, natural, thin comb is trimmed with a razor, and this must be done properly. Starting in front, almost level with the skull, this cut is made backward and upward until at the rear the comb is left about a quarter to a third of an inch high. This leaves a good buffer to protect the brain from injury and concussion, and yet not enough remains to allow the opposing cock to seize hold of it. When taken up from the "walks" to be used, these cocks are carefully examined, weighed, and tested to see that they are not blind in one eye. If found suitable, they are "trimmed"; the ends of the wing feathers are cut obliquely to leave on each quill a stiff barb which it was hoped might hurt the other cock's eyes in a flutter. The long tail feathers are trimmed off and the body of the tail trimmed a little from below upward giving a sharp fan-like appearance. The hackle is trimmed fairly short and stepped up, to give less chance for a deadly beak hold during which a fowl strikes with accuracy. The spurs are then sawn off with a small fine saw and left as truncated cones about a half an inch or three-quarters of an inch long. Then the bird is ready.

In our section of country at that time, the birds used were White Pyles, Shawl-necks, Irish Grays, Flaery Eyes, and Warhorses. They ranged in fighting weight from four pounds eight ounces to six pounds and a half, and in matching you could give or take two ounces. In other words, a four pound fourteen ounce bird could be matched to fight a four pound sixteen ounce or a four pound twelve ounce foe. The average fighting weight was about five pounds and a half for the breeds mentioned although the Warhorse type usually ran higher.

In this old dyehouse, I saw for the first time cocks being "sparred." This meant that about five minutes each day the cocks were taken out and a pair of kid or buckskin boxing gloves fitted on their spurs. Two were then placed in the pit and allowed to spar and fight without any chance of serious injury. On a thin metal base, which fitted tightly over the spur, were fastened buckskin boxing gloves stuffed with cotton and about an inch to an inch and a quarter in diameter. Great care was taken that these sparring pads were about the same weight as the gaffs to be used in the coming fight.

The gaffs were usually of two types. The inch and a half gaffs called "Singleton gaffs" after old Governor Singleton of South Carolina, were intended for the quick, agile cock, while the heavy two and a half to three-inch, drop-socket gaffs were used for heavier birds. Much attention was paid to how a cock stood on his feet and the angle at which the natural spur came off from his leg. In short, cocks were classed as narrow- or wide-heeled. If gaffs too long were placed on a narrow-heeled cock, he might drive the gaff into his own brain when he drew his legs up high and struck a blow. In other words, cocking at that time was a highly developed art as would be expected from a sport in which from a hundred to five hundred dollars was wagered on each contest.

Needless to say, I took in every part of this industry during my week there. Nearly every one of the hands in the mill had on his little place a "stag" for the Boss. When young Tate took one up to fight, he put another in its place to roam with half a dozen to a dozen hens as a new cock of the walk. This system of training is known as "on the walk." As Tate felt a little uncertain as to some of his weights, we drove three or four miles all around the country, picking up other cocks and examining them as substitutes, if necessary, for those already chosen. It must be understood that this was an easy task. We simply carried an old gamecock in a bag under the buggy seat, and when we arrived we took him out, carried him in crowing loudly, and held him out to the local cock of the walk who charged him blindly regardless of the fact that his opponent was held in a man's hand. All you had to do was to reach out and pick the local cock up and replace him with a newcomer waiting in a basket.

The evening of the main a crowd of about two hundred gathered, a dozen or more of whom came from contiguous states, and they brought with them an experienced judgment and a large wad. Quite frequently they carried away much less. In general terms this fight was between North and South Carolina. The opposing fowls were brought up from Edgefield County in South Carolina with an ex-Confederate general as their main backer, although he had a number of compatriots to wager on their success. The main was to consist of seven battles between five and six pounders, and the scales on which they were weighed were by the ringside. Let us say North Carolina would bring out a cock and put him on the scales and an impartial weigher would call his weight, and then the opposing wisemen would go into a huddle to decide which one of their cocks would match him. Here good judgment was really required, and old Ned Clavin and Mart Lyrbrand were our wisemen. To make a long story short, they won five out of seven.

The side bets and "spur of the moment" bets added no little to the excitement. For instance, I recall when a Dominique Muff at the first pass received a gaff through his windpipe and when the blood poured out of his mouth, a man in the crowd hollered, "Fifty to one on the Red." His opponent, one of the mill hands standing near, cried, "Taken," and laid down a dollar. Within five minutes the hand received from a discomforted South Carolinian fifty dollars in good greenbacks; for the old Dominique, coughing and gurgling, went at the Red like a demon and on the third pass sank an inch and a half gaff through his brain until the point showed through the skin below. This sounds like a cruel and bloody sport, but we must remember that no cock in the history of the world was ever "made to fight." They fought because they loved it. It was a part of life's long story of love in which, through the ages, the victor carried off as his own the mate for whom he fought a rival to the death. This long evolution gave an unbroken succession of winners and victors, and true-bred gamecocks never falter or show the white feather, a term related to the fact that the hack feathers at the back of the neck are light colored at the base and show white when raised in fear. Our word "hacked" comes from the pit.

The original jungle fowl of India, *Gallus Bankiva*, was as small as our present bantam and his weight has been increased to its present standard by selection and careful nurture. Where heavier weights were needed a black fowl known as the Malay has been used to bring the weight up. The feather-legged fowls like the Cochin, Langshan, and Brahma, in spite of their size, could not be used in increasing the frame of the cock as they will not "stand the gaff."

There are tricks in this trade. Every old-timer knows that the twelve-foot ring has been beset with dishonorable methods. Capsicum (red pepper) powder has been blown in the eyes of the opposing cock, although handlers are ordered to keep well back during the fight and are not allowed to touch their bird unless he hangs himself on the ground or the canvas of the ring when fighting. In the days of which I speak the code duello was still in vogue in the South, and for one backer to charge another with dishonorable conduct would have brought a battle of another kind. Looking back at it, I may say I never attended a more enjoyable occasion. Courtesy to an extreme degree reigned and not a vulgar or harsh word was spoken during the main.

A "main royal" did not succeed our ordinary main, although quite common in that locality. In a main royal the pit is surrounded by a canvas boundary about four feet high and each side brings, let us say, seven cocks which are all placed in the

THE SPORTS OF THE GENTRY 173

pit together, and there they are allowed to fight until one cock alone survives. The really barbaric "Welsh main" I have never seen in the United States except in Louisiana. In the Welsh main eight pairs are matched, the eight victors again being paired, then four, and finally the last surviving pair. Of course, this barbarity has its compensations. A cock who survives a Welsh main is never fought again, but with half a dozen or more carefully-chosen hens is used for breeding purposes for the rest of his life.

At various other times in my life after Mountain Island I dropped in on cock pits, but this was the first time that I had the opportunity of seeing cocks from various sections. In my opinion for beauty and style the White Pyles of Georgia and the Shawl-necks of South Carolina are the most beautiful game birds in existence, but for pit valor some of the Black Malays, bred by the long departed Old Arrington of central North Carolina, were the most effective birds in this whole *mêlée*.

Of course, there was a law against cockfighting. I never saw the law, but I have always heard that it was treated as a misdemeanor. Personally, I never knew it to be enforced, and I have often wondered at this, so as a boy I worked it out on about this basis. The constable of my youth had to be handy with a gun, in fact, he was himself a "bold, bad man" and as such naturally appreciated the qualities with which the gamecock was endowed. It must be remembered that these were also duelling days and the solicitor or commonwealth's attorney to a certain extent lived the life of a target. This was then also a fighting man's job, but this legal office seemed to me a necessary steppingstone for ultimate judicial preferment which young lawyers had to pass through to attain their goal. Another thing I recall is that nearly all the judges and referees at cocking mains in the seventies were old soldiers of rank—generals, colonels, but perhaps the community might get low enough to use a major or a captain occasionally.

Looking back at it after fifty odd years, it is not a bad sport, legal or illegal. At a time like this when the "inferiority complex" is stalking around loose seeking whom it may devour, to see a bird, stuck and stabbed until almost bloodless, rise in his might and make one more supreme final effort that finishes his enemy is a useful life's lesson.

There was another sport very common in the South in which I attained some skill. This was riding in a tournament, a test of skill almost unknown now. It seemed to be the last manifestation of the surviving love of the old arts and sports of chivalry. It is a strange fact that in recent years in reading of this art in England and on the western continent, I came across exactly the phrases and titles used in the South around 1870 and perhaps to a later day. The old lists in the South knew nothing less than "queen," "marshal," and "squire."

My own opportunities were unusual. I received a good pony at five years of age. I could ride him anywhere at six and jump him over anything up to thirty inches at seven. I must have been nearly ten years old when I saw my first tournament run at some down-at-the-heels place in Lincoln County, and to hear these benighted barbarians using "marshal" and "squire" interested me very much. I took full note of all details. As soon as I returned to Concord I rasped down a long hoe handle, and out behind the Methodist Church I put up a "course." This consisted of a level, straightway path about a hundred and fifty yards long over which was suspended from the arms of growing saplings three brass two-inch rings. These were usually obtained from some old martingale and were so hung on bent wire hooks (we used girl's hairpins) that when they were engaged by the rider's lance they came off the hook with ease. These rings were twenty-five yards apart, and in the real tournaments the time between the first and last ring, seventy-five yards, took a good horse; my little pony could in no wise approach it, but ere long at his best speed, eight seconds, I was riding with a 90 per cent record, and for style, at the end of the course, I always presented my lance with its three rings to an imaginary marshal. Later on I learned how this became a necessary part of the performance. It was very easy to start with three rings on the lance and take off the others at which you rode on a finger, (although the blow was quite severe with a heavy brass ring). Ordinary wooden lances about nine feet long were pierced at the junction of the front two-thirds and rear one-third by a metal pin that took this blow when the engaged ring ran down to this guard. For my own part, I always preferred a lance with the weight well forward, having them sandpapered down until the ring would gradually become tight some slight distance in front of the guard. This gave very little jar, and going at the speed necessary for the rules any jar was detrimental. In later years I learned that the best horses were under-sized thoroughbreds; they threw their very souls into it, made the time, and seemed to take a joy in the sport.

My first experience in a tournament came my last year at Bingham School. Some kinsman of Major Lynch was riding at his home course in preparation for a tournament at Company Shops. I was standing there, a simple observer, when one of my friends remarked to Major Lynch, "This boy says that he has ridden a good deal at rings himself," and the Major, perhaps thinking that the horses needed more riding on the course than they were getting, told me to get up on the horse hitched there and try it. The horse was of fitting size and an unusually steady runner, and my success surprised them. I walked back to the campus highly gratified that my childhood training had not been lost.

A week later I was surprised to receive a note from Major Lynch asking me to come out every evening and ride the ponies on the course to get them steadied. After a day or so of this he suggested that if his nephew could not ride he would like to see me go down and ride as a squire, a sort of second-grade contestant whose opportunity came after the knights. To this end he gave me a set of smaller rings, about one inch, which were always used in the tournaments if the contestants tied with the two-inch rings. At first the small rings utterly upset me, but by the end of the week I was going with what I judged to be a 50 per cent record when I noticed that I almost never failed with the third ring if I had gotten over the first two. This gave me the idea that it was the weight of the rings, taut on the lance point, some twelve inches back, that improved my last stroke. The rings were rather heavy for their diameter.

In conformity with this idea I took a gimlet and bored four holes through the lance neck about twelve inches back from the point and poured them full of lead. This improved my skill immensely, and I painted my shaft dove color to keep others from learning the same manoeuvre. To make a long story short, I went up to Company Shops (now Burlington), and rode, and made the queen of love and beauty feel like thirty cents by seeing a squire's record far surpass that of the knight who crowned her. All I got was a new lance that wasn't very much until I had leaded it.

Naturally, a boy riding as I did over several years constantly imagined the old jousts from which his sport came. I read everything that I could find on the subject. I once had a wide-horn Texas saddle with a cap on the pommel nearly six inches wide. I dug out a small depression on the right hand side of the front of this and sometimes tried riding with the lance in that position. I could do nothing with this pose, and I am convinced that the old stories of lances so held must be more or less mythical. The real sport must have been riding for the apertures in the helm or headpiece. Any fool could hit a breastplate, and this must have been the target for those who put the butt of the lance against some part of the saddle.

Chivalry was dying in my youth. The Mordecai and McCarthy duel was fought just about the time I was riding. The last one in the South that I know of, the Cash and Shannon duel, came later. The Puritanism of the North was venting its spleen on a defeated chivalry, so the tournament, which was a survival of this cult, gradually passed into the discard. I was sorry to see it go for it was a test of seat, sight, and stamina second to none. To ride for ten rounds at one-inch rings, riding off a tie after a regular tournament, took steady nerves. Perhaps it was too great a trial, but one never felt that at the time.

XXV

KENMORE UNIVERSITY SCHOOL

IN VIRGINIA there were many thermal and therapeutic springs whose healthful properties were well-exploited all through the South before, and long after, the Civil War. It was an early and distinctive racket to spread the delusion that no gentleman could live through the Southern summer unless he spent the hottest months at one of the various baths. An overseer might manage to live, and the proletariat could languish through, but a gentleman and his family would certainly die of malaria if they stayed at home. At the Blue, Red, Pink, and Spotted Sulphurs they gathered. At the Rockbridge Alum and the Jordan Alum they overflowed. They came from far and wide, and long rows of cabins were named the Mississippi Row, the Louisiana Row, and the Georgia Row. They were great places for courting and equally delightful for the children. I dare say the Virginia springs did more good than all the institutions of learning in the South; for there the great intellectual minds were brought into contact for weeks or months each year during the rest period.

One summer we were booked for the Rockbridge Baths near Lexington, Virginia. To get there we went by rail through Richmond to Goshen, whence a stage coach deposited us safely at the springs. For some reason I was left behind to follow the family alone a week or two later, and when I reached Richmond I learned that I could not take the Chesapeake and Ohio to Goshen. A recent forest fire had destroyed a quarter of a mile of timber trestle on that road. This was not an unusual occurrence for forest fires menaced more than forests in those days. The proprietor of the old Exchange and Ballard Hotel suggested that I go on the Richmond, Fredericksburg and Potomac Railroad and the Potomac steamboat to Alexandria, then come down by the Orange and Alexandria to Charlottesville, and from there take the Chesapeake and Ohio to Goshen as that was on the other side of the broken unit. I counted my cash and found that I was able to do this.

At Aquia Creek, the passengers got off the train and took the steamboat up the river. Shortly before the end of the trip, the captain rang the bell and announced that anyone who wished to stop over at Mount Vernon could do so without additional cost and take the next boat up.

I was one of those who got off, and I spent a most interesting two hours during this, my first visit to Mount Vernon. The view of that old mansion from the river shows one of the most impressive pieces of American architecture that I know, and the details of the hilltop grouping of house and gardens impressed me profoundly; the result was that when I reached Charlottesville and found that I could visit another home of a president, Monticello, in a two-horse hack for seventy-five cents, I decided to see it.

Thomas Jefferson's home was then in chancery, poorly-kept, and shown by an old colored caretaker, but no lack of care could destroy the beauty of its setting and outlook. Of the two, as an architectural unit I preferred Monticello, and I pondered the story of Jefferson with a new interest. So, when I returned to the old Central Hotel, which stood near the present Chesapeake and Ohio Station, and learned that for an additional twenty-five cents I could drive up to see the University of Virginia which he founded, I also took that in. To say that it was a revelation is to put it mildly. The road passed then at the foot of the Lawn, and I got out of the hack.

For at least twenty minutes I stood there viewing the Rotunda with its deep perspective of grass-grown Lawn and made up my mind, then and there, that I was going to live in that atmosphere.

I knew that my great-grandfather, Joseph Graham, had been one of the organizers of the University of North Carolina in 1780; that my grandfather, Robert Morrison, had graduated there in 1817; also my father in 1842, and his uncles and brothers as well. I was practically born to Chapel Hill, but I knew that recently the newspapers and general talk indicated that all was not well there. Reconstruction, the Ku Klux Klan, and Solomon Pool bade fair to make the University of North Carolina of that day very different from the institution of the earlier generations. I saw no reason to sacrifice my education for a sentiment, so when I saw my father at the springs I gently broached the subject. I could see that he was pleased that I had been attracted to the University of Virginia, and he said in his direct, brusque way, "All right; I will begin to make preparations for you to go there."

Immediately he began making inquiries among his friends at the springs regarding the merits of the preparatory schools in Virginia, with the result that I was entered for the fall session at the new Kenmore University School at Amherst. He gave me a catalogue and told me that I was to stay at the springs until the middle of September and go from there directly to school. I have always been grateful to my father for his way of doing such things. He gave me money, not a lavish amount but enough, and told me to go to it.

Although I was in Rockbridge County which adjoins Amherst, I had to go to Charlottesville by the Chesapeake and Ohio and from there take the uncompleted Virginia Midland to Amherst Court House, which seemed to me a sort of falling-off place. I knew that the headmaster's name was H. A. Strode, a "math medalist" of the University of Virginia, and I had pictured him as a grave and reverend senior and a cold-blooded disciplinarian. When a young man who seemed only slightly older than I spoke to me at the station, I told him that I had written to his father and supposed he had come to meet me. He laughed and said, "I am Mr. Strode, the headmaster, and I received your letter." As we drove over to the school, he astonished me by saying that

Kenmore was almost without rules; that it had two ends in view, health and scholarship; and that each student was free to get either in his own way, provided—and this was to be clearly understood—that *drunk or sober one must always be a gentleman*. When I digested this, I knew that I was entirely free to be concerned with the interesting things presented in the classroom.

When we reached the school I saw a nice old brick country homestead, extended in the rear for a dining room, lecture halls, and laboratory, with brick dormitories in the yard. "Tell it not in Gath," but I had never seen a laboratory, and I went wild! The apparatus was simple, almost crude, but effective. By the end of my first year I could make a qualitative analysis of almost any alloy and even give an approximate estimate of quantity.

The boys were from everywhere; many came from North Carolina for the same reason that I had come and some were from the deep South; Delaware and New Jersey were represented, and there were two English boys—some fifty students in all.

Kenmore was *in esse* what would now be called a junior college, and the atmosphere was scientific not classical. Dr. Brock, who had the classical subjects, hardly got a fair showing, and my Latin and Greek of Bingham days faded. One of the things new to me at Kenmore, and a recent development anywhere at that time, was the mandate of parallel reading. For example, when I studied Cicero and Virgil I had to read up on their lives from books in the library. There was also a combined astronomy, navigation, and land surveying book by Courtney, I believe, and similar cognates.

Mr. Strode's job, like that of every other headmaster of a classical school of that day, was difficult. He was preparing boys for college, and as there were no Carnegie units, he had to know the ultimate school towards which each student tended so that he could more readily prepare each one. He studied the drift of Harvard, Yale, Princeton, the University of Virginia, and others in order to do this. There was little to indicate where they began and where they ended such subjects as Latin, Greek, and mathematics; the textbook used was usually known, but

KENMORE UNIVERSITY SCHOOL 181

little more. Such preparatory schools represented something of a cycle in educational evolution, and I can but think of the relatively short-lived service given by most of their headmasters. Major Horace Jones of Charlottesville, Virginia, alone amongst the group that I knew personally, continued to a really ripe old age.

Mr. Strode's methods were unique, absolutely original, and perfectly suited to the needs of his students. He picked out about a dozen of us who had neglected our mathematics, and in order to foster a mathematical spirit in our group, he stated that he was going to build a swimming pool. The pool could be used for ice in winter, and therefore must be perfectly drained, and the drainage area insured.

One afternoon he took us down, drove two stakes representing the ends of the dam, inserted a pole in the middle to give the height of the dam, and divided us into two groups—one to take care of the drainage area and the other to build the dam. I was assigned to the former group, and I never in my life worked harder than I did surveying with a compass the twenty-five or thirty acres in this area, the boundaries of which I was myself to be the judge. Another group would follow to determine where they thought the flow would begin towards the ice pond. I even walked over to the village and ordered a copy of a certain Euclid, the very same work that I had ostentatiously burned upon leaving Bingham's. I believe Strode put all the plane geometry ever written into that drainage area, and the boys down at the dam had solid geometry to the point of exhaustion. This merely gives an idea of Strode's pedagogic method which varied with every one of his pupils. Unfortunately for him, his administrative methods for the farm and dining room were not at all equal to his talents as a teacher.

In addition to the honor system and "acting like a gentleman" there was one other fixed rule at Kenmore. You went to church every Sunday—anywhere you liked, but you went—and only if you were sick and unable to go did you report to Mr. Strode. I sampled all four of the denominations within reach and decided to continue sampling. Our contact with the town of Amherst brought into my life for the first time a more or less adult participation in social life. There were half a dozen young ladies on whom the boys called, and several of them became my good friends.

Life was entirely different. We did not have to cut or carry wood, for the cutting to fireplace length was done by two Percheron horses running the saw on a treadmill. Even our sports were different. Baseball was organized; it had come to stay, and we got up two "nines" which gave good competition. After a time I played at shortstop. Strangely enough, wrestling was also one of our sports. A couple of young fellows in the village were trained wrestlers, and the boys who were interested learned most of the tricks and holds.

There was a quiet, consistent love of sport that I found most congenial. We had the run of the neighboring plantations because "the Kenmore boys were gentlemen."

On the place and adjacent property were several famous night hunters. It was the first time I had known this sport and it had a great appeal. First opossum hunting and finally, in the graduate school, coon hunting. We had a couple of hounds kept for us by an old colored man on the place because Mrs. Strode loved a bird dog but hated a hound. While I had no ownership or equity in a hound, I often joined the night hunters. One young countryman near us had three coon dogs that were literally incomparable; and while they would not ignore an opossum, if a coon track crossed the trail, they would instantly be diverted. It was in this pleasant winter sport that I heard the philosophic axiom, which is true, "the smaller the tree, the bigger the 'possum."

One incident is indelible, or I surely thought it was at the time. The dogs were running an opossum and when we found them, they were not barking or treeing but standing around a hollow log, growling and showing irritation. We thought there was an oversize opossum in the log, so Jim Bayard of Delaware took his hatchet and cut down a pine pole. Finding it too large and too long, he cut off the butt, which I picked up and went to the other end of the log while he shoved the slender end in. I had never seen a skunk, but I had once or twice smelt the odor; so when a very angry animal trotted out from the log, I hesitated a second too long, and the delay was fatal! For a few days I was marooned in the "office" and my meals were sent in to me. Thoughtlessly I had soaked my clothes in the ice pond and it had to be drained and refilled, all of which created some commotion. Since that time the skunk has remained for me an active figure of imagination and terror.

Amongst our other hunters were rabbit-trapping artists, and they held long discussions of the two cults, the "baited trap" versus the "empty trap." Most of the boys from Delaware, West Virginia, and Ohio believed that a piece of apple, peach, or pear tempted the rabbit to go into the trap, but the Southern boys scorned the use of bait. They claimed it to be positively detrimental, and they had good reason for it told the rabbit that someone had been around very recently. The empty trap apostles believed with good cause that a rabbit explores every possible recess on his range so that he will know where to seek safety from dogs, and his age-old instinct tempts him into the hollow gum tree. We used sawed-off "gums" as we did at Bingham's, and our records with the empty trap were better than those of the baiters, especially when we bored a one-inch hole in the plank covering the rear of the "gum." Apparently the rabbit went in and looked out of this hole.

My old friend, Dr. Bachman, and that wonderful book, *Birds of North America*, recommended by Dr. Spencer Baird of the Smithsonian Institute, had made me an ardent student of birds and their habits. I was accepted as the bird crank of the community.

With no rules or limitations in the school, except the relationship of old gentlemen and young gentlemen, we went anywhere and everywhere. I had a bird dog and a good but cheap pin-fire, breech-loading shotgun. I ranged the country for miles around, but nevertheless I moved steadily ahead in my classes. It was, I think, in the spring of 1874 that a great event occurred at Kenmore.

One may imagine my excitement and fervid interest when the wild pigeons of the eastern Atlantic decided to make a great nesting place on the slopes of the Nelson County mountains only a short distance away. Technically, these were passenger pigeons, much larger than our doves, but with a similar flight. They had habits, however, utterly alien to the American mourning dove and, I think, entirely unlike any of the European wood doves, habits born of an American environment.

First we would see flocks of several dozens, then flocks of hundreds, and ere long, flocks of thousands, all heading for the Three Ridge Mountain some miles off. We did not get up early enough in the morning, even with early rising, to see their morning flight, but of course we saw the evening flight, and when I state that the sun would oft times be literally darkened, I am not exceeding the truth. A flock of hundreds of thousands, a mile long and half a mile deep, passing between you and the setting sun, leaves little light for vision. At times, their passing overhead concealed the whole heavens.

They fed everywhere; one favorite place was fifty or a hundred acres of woodland right behind the school and a little higher on the mountain. By going up there and sitting about three or four o'clock in the afternoon, sometimes with our guns, I observed closely their method of action.

A flock of a few thousand would sweep slowly through the oak woodland, those in front seeming to hover over the ground with a violent flapping of wings but never alighting. This violent agitation of the air blew the leaves into windrow-like piles and stretches, uncovering the acorns, grubs, and insects. The central mass of this flying flock scampered over the ground and gathered everything in sight; then the rear end of the flock passed over to take the place of the exhausted front end who in turn descended. I saw this performance many times in all kinds of forests.

Mr. Strode took a couple of two-horse wagons and those who wished to go drove over eight or ten miles to the heart of the hatchery. I limited myself to one side of the ridge and therefore cannot speak as to the real size of the area on the other side. There must have been seventy-five or a hundred acres on this side of the ridge in which primitive nests and young covered every inch of available space on the trees. I am told that a neighboring peak, the Priest, also had miles and miles of area devoted to these same hatcheries.

Even then I recall wondering about the problem of nesting material for so great a host. I had seen them gathering sticks and straw around Kenmore ten or more miles away, and I have often wondered how many twenty-mile journeys they had to make for each bit. This was the scientific side of it. The other was far more boy-like and juvenile.

Only three of us had shotguns, and I alone had a breech-loader. We used to stand on the high hill behind Kenmore, and using BB shot, we fired until the guns were dangerously hot. We ate the pigeons until we were nauseated and gave the surplus to the kitchen, and the Negroes reported that they thought the hogs were sick of them too. But ere long, by mild suggestions that the young were hatched and the death of each pigeon would result in useless suffering for the young, Mr. Strode broke up the wanton shooting. Nevertheless, it was the accepted custom for farmers to drive out and club to death whole wagonloads to be fed to their swine until they were glutted.

This was in the early seventies, and if any one had told me that in less than fifty years, or ever, every passenger pigeon in America would be dead and gone, it would have seemed an impossibility. About 1900, nearly all were gone, and I saw at a zoological garden in Cincinnati half a dozen or more survivors of these countless hosts that once roamed America. They refused to breed in captivity and in 1913, the last one, a female, died.

Many surmises have been brought to bear upon this subject; some said chicken cholera and some said an unknown plague was to blame. But philosophers, with biological history behind them, have given a broader theory. It is summed up in Deperet's "Les Transformations du Monde Animal": Just when a species has reached the height of its power, either in bodily size or in weapons, offensive or defensive, and thus seems safe against all enemies, that species is invariably on the verge of disappearance." To this theory, Sheldon of the Biological Survey added the suggestion that seemingly the females of harried types suddenly become sterile. This seems to have been borne out by the reported fact that passenger pigeons have bred in captivity but that those in Cincinnati absolutely refused. At all events, I had early the great philosophic impress of seeing a departing type.

XXVI

A VISIT TO MY FUTURE ALMA MATER

MY RETURN HOME that summer was clouded by the tragic death of my sister Anna from typhoid fever, an infection which was peculiarly fatal to the Morrison family. She had been a student at the Augusta Female Seminary in Staunton, Virginia, conducted by Miss Mary Baldwin and now a well-known college which bears her name. It is obvious from the exchange of letters at that time that her illness was regarded as some sort of bilious attack since she was nursed by her roommates with a Negro girl for extra service. Possibly it was the type known then as "walking typhoid" in which the patient is a walking menace. Whatever the diagnosis, when the school closed in June, she was obliged to be brought home to Charlotte. The rigors of travel made this a fatal ordeal. My later interest in preventive medicine and hospital facilities for all was demanded by the recollection of this unnecessary and untimely death.

When I returned to Kenmore for my second year I found my paradise poisoned at the font. A few of the boys were complaining of the sameness of the fare; they harped on it and even bet on it. In turn they bet on what we would have for dinner, then for supper, and when emotions were energized to the blowing off point, every one of us signed a round robin of protest. The food was good and abundant so we did not refer to that—only to the sameness—and the note was not otherwise offensive. We did not know the meaning of the round robin form, but we rolled the words as a sweet and forbidden morsel on our tongues and wrote our names alphabetically in a circle, Adger of South Carolina preceding my name which was followed by Bayard of Delaware, and around the circle ending with Waugh.

If action was what we wanted, we got it—that note raised Cain. H. A. Strode, the peaceful, philosophic, and paternal, became a wild man. He rang the high-mounted pot-metal bell to call an assembly and stated that although he regretted it exceedingly we must all leave; there could be no preference in punishment as all of us had signed the round robin. "Go, pack your trunks," he said. "In half an hour the wagon will be at the door to take you to the station. If you haven't the money to get home, I will furnish it."

Amongst the boys there was one older than most of us, Uvalde Burns of Texas, a philosopher and a seasoned sinner of his own type. He went to Mr. Brock who predicted that Strode's steam would blow off in a few days and advised us to go to near-by hotels to await the subsidence of a sensitive soul. The hotel in Amherst was soon full, and I, having the money in hand, went to Lynchburg and put up at the Norvell House. I found that the Lynchburg Fair was in full swing, perhaps the first fair after the war, and it was a great show. I lost on every running race and on every trotting race except one. Being much struck with the name of a horse called "Orange Blossom," I won a "French pool" on this nag which restored my finances to the exact amount with which I had arrived a week earlier. During my stay in Lynchburg, a Doctor Owen, whom I had met before, was very kind to me and so was a druggist, Mr. Strother, whose son William was a student at Kenmore. Through Mr. Strother's influence I was able to trade in my pin-fire gun for my first centre-fire. I had enough money to buy a cartridge belt, and no Indian brave ever wore his scalp belt with more pride than I wore this latest "wrinkle" filled with a man's load of shells.

Soon we each got word from school that if we joined in a note of apology to Mrs. Strode, whom her husband thought we had insulted, we could return. The document that Burns drew up for us to sign would have drawn tears from a cabbage; and as a proof of the character and intrinsic good will of Mr. Strode, I can say truthfully that for the rest of the session, I do not think any boy detected any change in his relationship with us.

During this year at Kenmore I received an invitation from an old friend of Bingham School days to visit him at the University of Virginia, where he was rooming with another old friend from Charlotte. When I spoke of this to Mr. Strode, more for advice than permission, he advanced me the price of the railroad fare, told me of an accommodation train that left shortly after my last class on Friday, and said he was glad that I was going up to see the life at the University. Fortunately I was at Amherst Station a good half hour before train time for the train puffed brazenly in twenty minutes ahead of time.

An "accommodation" train in the South was a local freight with one compound and complex passenger coach at the rear. The front end of this car carried express, baggage, and small freight, and the rest of it was bare accommodation for passengers. There were often one or two bunks where the brakemen who rode the top could catch a nap during the frequent long delays. The conductor, always called "Cap'n," was an all-round railroader, and from this position came many high officers of the eastern railroad system. They were friendly men, and this "Cap'n" and I discussed hunting and railroading during my journey.

On reaching Charlottesville, I took my carpetbag which had little or nothing in it to Mr. Parrot at the Central Hotel, and he got me a hack in which I drove to the University. As I expected to enter that institution later I now had an appraising eye; so I was interested to learn that after passing through Main Street we went up Vinegar Hill, with the stage yard on the right and a large and dignified residence at the top. This mansion was later torn down when the old Midway Public School was built. Between that and the University lay a tortuous red road on the north side of which a planked pathway was perched on spaced uprights about a foot high. It consisted of three six-inch planks fully six inches apart which made it necessary to concentrate one's gaze on the pathway throughout all journeys. It was a saying amongst the students that if you found an unidentified dead man, you could turn up his pants, and if his shins were barked you would know that he was a student. I remember seeing the Delavan Negro Church, often called the Mudwall, near the entrance to the present Southern Railway station. A brick cottage faced that and farther up was Judge Cochran's home, now the Dolly Madison Inn, and the McKenney house was opposite. There may have been other houses, but I do not recall them.

The driver knew the address my friend had given me, House E in Dawson's Row, so we made our way directly there, and I paid the customary "two-bits." The house was a two-story brick building with four rooms to a floor, and it stood on the road to the cemetery at the "edge of the wilderness," the present site of the Clark Memorial law building. I asked a young man who, I thought afterwards, wore a quizzical smile where "P. D." and "T. B." lived, but he simply said, "Upstairs, first on the left," and up I went.

I knocked at the door and no response. Thinking they were having an afternoon nap, I knocked with vigor and still no response; and yet there were certain metallic sounds of uncertain origin coming from the room that led me to believe it was occupied. I was just about to knock again when I heard a violent stamping and jingling in a remote part of the room and this tempted me to call the nickname of my old friend quite loudly, "Pig! Pig! This is the Seasoned Sinner!" Then I heard a mumbling and a walking of some animal; and a key was turned on the inside, the door opened a crack, and out came the head of the hairiest donkey I had ever seen in my life. He burst right into my face, literally pushing me backward, and then the door caught on his neck and shoulders holding him fast. I could dimly see my friend in a night shirt mounted on his back and drawing violently on the reins while he punctuated time alternately with interjections of woe and profanity.

In explanation of this unusual scene I will have to say that in the early seventies alcohol was everywhere in the South, and cut glass decanters stood on every sideboard. Barrooms kept it, groceries kept it, and everybody had it. Beer was just coming, unless we except "persimmon beer" and "locust beer" made on every plantation and in many village homes. Nevertheless, while drinking was almost universal, there was one unvarying rule—that "a gentleman had to carry his liquor." Tom, Dick, and Harry might get drunk and stagger and swear, but such noise and disturbances they were afterwards ashamed of. The rule held as the Negroes put it, "A gemman must tote his liquor like a gemman."

Now these two friends of mine were not only good students but one of them was a brilliant student, and they determined on this Saturday to have a little more liquor than they were sure they could carry, so they rigged up this dramatic presentation of a week-end drunk. On the mantelpiece they had bottles of old Henning, Old Bumgardner, and probably old Monarch, then three highly-prized liquors in Albemarle. With great effort they brought up this donkey, which must have weighed between three and four hundred pounds, by carrying him up two men to each leg, and then they hitched him to the bed post. They lay in bed and read and smoked, and when one proposed that they take a drink, they would both mount "Billy Mahone," ride over to the mantelpiece, each take his favorite liquor straight from the bottle, and return. It was a seance of this kind that I had broken in upon, but my friend "Pig" was still adequate, and when he heard my name he did not forget his dignity. He mounted and rode to the door.

I spent a day and a half with these congenial friends and went back to Kenmore quite well initiated into the mysteries of my future Alma Mater. "P. D." boarded with Mrs. Ross and "T. B." boarded at the Massies home. They told me to appear at these respective dining rooms, walk up to the lady in charge, and say that I was a guest, giving their names. I did this and it worked, but the fare, although abundant, was hardly notable. I wandered around the University a good deal, from the Rotunda to "stiff hall," picked up a few other friends whom I had known at various places, and went back to Kenmore thoroughly satisfied with the outlook for my approaching sojourn at the University.

The next time I went home I did not have to make the long detour by Richmond for the Virginia Midland Railway from

Charlottesville to Danville was open, and I went down on one of the very first trains over that route. A most interesting experience awaited me for at Danville there was "a change of gauge" from four feet eight and a half inches to five feet. This difficulty was overcome by a very cumbersome but effective device. Each coach was lifted by hydraulic press at the four corners until it was several feet above the rails; the truck chains were unhooked, the 56.5-inch trucks rolled out from underneath, and 60-inch trucks were substituted. The coaches were then lowered, chains hooked up, a new wide engine attached, and away we went after spending from one to two hours over this laborious performance.

Fifty years previous to the date of this incident, Stephenson of England was experimenting with the first practical locomotive. During this interval, flat rails, "U" rails, and "L" rails were evolved leading up to the "T" rail. In this country the distance between the rails also varied from the six feet of the Old Colony Railroad of Massachusetts to the three feet of the Narrow Gauge, but the time came when the United States had to fix a common gauge. The width of the old stagecoach, four feet eight and one half inches, was agreed upon as this was the width already used by fully 75 per cent of the roads. Unfortunately between Danville, Virginia, and New Orleans, Louisiana, there was a five-foot gauge. This was safer for speed and large freight cars than the standard gauge, but of course it had to be changed to conform.

I had seen thousands of Chinese laborers passing Amherst Station. Liberated by the completion of the Southern Pacific, they were shipped east to change the gauge of the Southern roads which they, with truckmen drawn from neighboring roads, were able to accomplish in a few days. Working on one hundred and fifty mile sections, they removed spikes on the inner side of the rail until very few remained, and the trains had to run very slowly. On a given Sunday, *mirabile dictu,* the remaining inner spikes were drawn, the rail shoved over, and this vast body of workmen drove new spikes on the outside. It was all done in a day. Cars with suitable trucks under them had been made ready; the car wheels were slipped over the proper distance on the axle and frozen against new collars. It was different with the engines, but a bright mechanic suggested a solution that saved much money. He devised a circular gas jet that rapidly heated the outer steel tire of the engine wheel while ice water was poured on the hub. It was possible then to push the tires in one and three-quarter inches on either side. In cases where this method could not be used the old engines were shipped to benighted lands where they had never heard of the old English wagon-gauge of four feet eight and a half inches, which probably came from the Greek javelin of similar dimensions.

I have often wondered what would have been the result on our civilization had the six-foot gauge been sufficiently widespread to have become adopted as the standard. I can but think that it would fit modern conditions much better than the present gauge. Of course it would require a tremendous outlay for long crossties.

XXVII

THE UNIVERSITY OF VIRGINIA

WHEN I WAS ready to enter the University of Virginia in 1875, I was definitely committed to turn from the traditional classical education of the South to the modern scientific. My natural bent in this direction, first awakened by Doctor Bachman, was tremendously stimulated by my two years at Strode's school. My father was deeply disappointed, but being a man of unusual common sense, he knew that forced favoritism in study yielded small returns, so he accepted my decision. I was eighteen years old and well-developed.

En route to Charlottesville, I stopped at Kenmore to go over the new University of Virginia catalogue with Mr. Strode and decide on my courses. As Mr. Strode considered me "unusually well-prepared," he advised me to take six courses, or "tickets," although three were the usual rule. I was to take general, industrial, analytical, and agricultural chemistry; natural history, covering both botany and zoology; and as I wished some training in drawing, applied mathematics.

Arriving at the University and knowing the lay of the land, I at once went up to the office of the chairman of the faculty, Doctor James P. Harrison. Although the number of matriculants was small—363 for the year—one would have expected a queue outside of the chairman's office, but there was none, for it was not good form then to form queues around a dignitary's official residence. Three or four students stood and lounged around while others formed a larger group on the steps of the Rotunda. The smaller group was augmented from time to time, and the larger group, sitting on the Rotunda steps, was entirely unrestrained; the "old men" were talking, and I was so much interested in getting a review of the past session and a preview of the coming one that I was quite late in matriculating.

When I entered Doctor Harrison's office, I found a fine, erect man who had been a surgeon in the United States Navy until the Civil War and who, strangely, had been brought to the University to teach obstetrics. When I gave him my name he asked if I were related to General Rufus Barringer. I told him that I was his son, and he said, "I want to tell you that he had the best brigade of cavalry amongst all the Confederate forces, and I hope you will live up to the name." I outlined the formidable group of studies that I was going to undertake, and he asked who had advised me to take all of that. When I told him that I had studied under Mr. Strode at Kenmore, he replied that it was all right—"Strode knows," he added. Then he directed me how to find the proctor's office down on East Range and, shaking my hand, wished me a pleasant and profitable year. He was an ideal executive to make easy and straight the path for a bashful boy.

Major Green Peyton, the proctor, was of another kind. "Guardian of the Treasury," he bristled like a bull dog, but it was all outside. He examined all checks with meticulous care and vouchsafed nothing. He too spoke of General Barringer and said he knew the brigade, and these references to my father's record made me feel pretty proud. He assigned me to a room in House E on Dawson's Row, and with one parting shot on general economy and the fearful state of the country, the deed was done.

I went over to see my room, and then walked on the narrow plank pathway down to Charlottesville to rent my furniture: a bed, table, rocking chair, straight-backed chair, and washstand, and the man threw in a heavy metal bootjack. For my books I went to the University Book Store, established in 1825, and then my layout was complete.

I already knew the plan of the university that Thomas Jefferson had founded in his old age, the famous "academic village" which he had designed and constructed. The focal point was the library, the Rotunda, an adapted copy of the Pantheon in Rome but flanked by two one-story wings and surrounded in the rear with a sweeping terrace. It faced north and south and was approached from the south by wide steps from the terraced, tree-bordered lawn, two hundred feet broad and five hundred and fifty feet long. On either side, regularly spaced, stood five two-story red-brick houses occupied by professors, each with its classic columned façade, and between the houses, and connecting with them by a low arcade of smaller columns, were one-story student dormitories. These were known respectively as East and West Lawn. To the rear some two hundred feet distant on each side ran a parallel row of simpler houses, dormitories, and connecting arcades called East and West Range. Such was the grouping of the "academic village," and in 1825 it was sufficiently large to accommodate the seven professors chosen by Mr. Jefferson, five of whom were brought from England and the Continent, and about two hundred students.

The founder foresaw growth, of course, and provided acreage sufficient for many additional buildings, but he did not foresee the utter deterioration of taste which, some twenty-five years later, permitted the building of the "Annex" adjoining the north front of the Rotunda and sticking out from it like an enlarged boxcar. That monstrosity, happily destroyed by fire in 1895 and never rebuilt, still marred the landscape in my student days. There were also a few other utilitarian box-like structures to the east and west; a few dormitories on Carr's Hill, where the president's house now stands; and beyond, in a southerly direction, lay Dawson's Row which consisted of two-story, detached brick dormitories, designated by the first six letters of the alphabet.

My roommate was Tom Marshall of Mississippi. I had met him at Rockbridge Baths, and he had written in for a room on Dawson's Row about the time I wrote; so the businesslike proctor assigned us both to the southwest corner of House E. He was an agreeable fellow, but he had none of the same classes and was not interested in a single subject that interested me. A descendant of Chief Justice John Marshall, he bore the stigmata of that family, but one joint in his little finger. It was unnoticeable in general contact, but this boy and his brother were very proud of it and claimed that the Chief Justice had it on both hands.

I was pleased with my large room with its view of the Ragged Mountains and Carter's Mountain. Originally it had a four-foot fireplace, but that had been bricked in to an eighteen-inch grate, with an iron hook, poker, and coal scuttle on one side, and a sheet-iron blower which fitted over the grate and made a strong draft, on the other. I was soon to discover that the blower and poker were the armamentarium of indignant students. When for some reason they decided to "take the town," all they had to do was to don nightshirts over their clothes, provide themselves with pine torches, a blower in one hand and a poker in the other. Then they would swarm down Vinegar Hill on a "callithump," as these raids on Charlottesville were called. Sometimes it was thought necessary to capture one of the two guardians of law and order, the village policeman known as "Old Moose." Once the coalbox back of House D on Dawson's Row had the distinction of holding him caged until he was rescued by "Old Harris," the mayor, accompanied by a detachment of the Monticello Guard, the local military company. On the rare occasion when a student was arrested, the others with callithump equipment charged through the town, singing "Who'll Drive the Chariot when the Bridegroom Comes?" When they made their way to the jail, they were confronted by the chairman of the faculty and the mayor and balked of their prey. Once, before the chairman went on his bond, I talked through the bars to a young man who later became "chief-of-counsel" for the Norfolk and Western Railway.

For these dormitory rooms there were Negro janitors, mostly old men, many of whom had been in that service for nearly half a century. Each had his hero, and when he came in at dawn to light the fire, he would tell tales of ancient days. The coal was kept in large wooden boxes, six feet high by four in width, with lock and key which stood outside each door. The janitor brought basin and drinking water in a pitcher, and water for a bath was placed in a tin bucket close against the coals. The water supply came from wells dotted around the grounds; there were two near Dawson's Row. Toilet arrangements were of the simplest. The cold, outdoor backhouses were occasionally flushed by means of water drawn from a reservoir on the side of the mountain below the present observatory. This water was fed into an iron reservoir in the walls of the northwest corner of the Rotunda and was utterly inadequate for any other purpose than an occasional flushing. As fire protection it was negligible.

I engaged board with Mrs. Ross at the southern tip of West Range at a cost of $19 a month, and there, as well as in my classrooms, I became acquainted with the general appearance of the student body. I was profoundly impressed. They were the pick of the land, but more than that, they showed what I have since learned to call a hereditary intelligence stimulated by adversity. Ten years after the Civil War they were still wearing anything they had, for in dress they were utterly regardless, but the Western men were conspicuous by their wide hatbrims. One custom, as singular as it was universal—and many men carried it to their graves unchanged—was the cult of the partly buttoned vest. The two bottom buttons were usually fastened, and then only the top one. The average age of the students was a little above my own, but every one of them that could do so sported a coming mustache.

A freshman was in no way regarded as different from other students—in fact, the word was unknown, "new man" being almost universally used. Later he was called a first-year man. There was only one custom which marked the difference between "new" and "old" men. During the first week or two of each session, a new man coming into a dining room was greeted by frenzied tapping on the edge of each man's plate, which resulted in a terrific racket and was sometimes quite disturbing to the new arrival, but I am told that it started merely as a genial greeting. The present titular noun "Cavalier" was never applied to a University student, and seldom to the residents of eastern Virginia. Men seemed to know in those days that the word had adjectival and adverbial cognates.

The relationship amongst the students was marked by a somewhat unique dignity and restraint. Only your most intimate friends were called by their first names; others were addressed by their surnames and new acquaintances as Mister. Between student and professor, the relationship was covered by the general term "old gentleman" and "young gentleman." There still prevailed the dignity of speech of an older generation. The professors, both in class and outside, addressed the students as *Mister*, and only those professors who had medical degrees were called doctor; others were addressed as Mister, whatever their degree. If you called Mr. Minor, the great law teacher, "Professor Minor," he would correct you without heat *the first time*.

In contrast to all this seeming formality, the students gave nicknames to all the professors. They also employed the utmost ingenuity to find suitable nicknames for repugnant personalities amongst their own group. The first time I heard someone remark, "There goes Old Monument," I did not know that the man referred to was from Baltimore and that his full title amongst the elect was, "the Monumental Ass from the Monumental City." A certain hopeless dullard was openly called "Necessity," which to everyone except himself meant "Necessity knows no law, neither does...." Such were some of the outlets for humor.

There were a few Greek-letter fraternities but no fraternity houses, and membership was never paraded, nor was breaking into a fraternity with a golden axe tolerated. Ten years after the war, the average parent was hard pressed to send his son to college, and the average son recognized that fact and conducted himself accordingly.

Whenever the son of a war-made *nouveau riche* boasted that he could "get in anywhere," he was duly invited to join a certain mythical organization called the Sons of Confucius. It was skillfully and artfully done by one or two older students who called upon him, but if they found him worthwhile they would "lay off." If, however, the man persisted as a braying and blatant ass, a time was set for his initiation, and a runner passed around the grounds whispering, "Sons of Confucius tonight, under the Rotunda at twelve o'clock!" The bulk of the student body had quietly assembled by the time the committee brought in the blindfolded victim. After a long seance of rite and ritual, during

THE UNIVERSITY OF VIRGINIA

which the spectators sat silent as death, the bandage was removed, and the candidate found himself surrounded by some twenty-five men holding lighted candles while he sat between a great stuffed jackass whose hide was considerably the worse for wear and a *pot de chambre* holding the contents of a bottle of foaming beer. This was the end of the chapter. The only initiate I ever knew personally left college, and he was a good riddance, but the jackass was carefully preserved in storage for gate-crashers were about as common then as now.

The University of Virginia Magazine was widely subscribed to and eagerly read by the students, and the best minds in college contributed both prose and poetry. The two debating societies, officially named for Washington and Jefferson but always called "Wash" and "Jeff," played a part in student life that is not readily understood today. Bitter debates were held which in the absence of organized sports provided virtually the only vent for youth's natural tendency to voice emotions. More than half of the student body belonged to one society or the other, and to be elected to the presidency of either was to win the public seal of approval. On election, the winner of that and other honorary positions was expected to give a *soirée* either on Carr's Hill, where there were few dormitories, or in the grove behind Dawson's Row. In order to make hospitality superlatively manifest, a dozen kegs of beer were provided to be opened as needed, but unopened kegs were returned for credit. At these *soirées* the men often sang in chorus the songs that we now call "spirituals," led by Luke Matthews, a popular brawny-chested baritone.

During my two years at the University there were never more than about four hundred students, and they came from everywhere, North Carolina and Texas leading the out-of-state registration. Other North Carolinians came for the same reason that I had come, but for Texas it was the "return of the native" for seemingly every Texan who hailed from Virginia returned his son to the state university. One of the early Mavericks was here; at my dining table sat two future United States senators, and a great actor-to-be, although at that time he was basking in the glory of a world record on the racing track, "2:30" made by his father's trotting horse, Dexter. I knew as fellow students three future university presidents, Frank Venable of the University of North Carolina, Charles Dabney of the University of Cincinnati, and Lyon Gardiner Tyler of William and Mary. I was surrounded by latent power, concealed behind laughing eyes and a languid air.

I, an alien and an outsider, had a dormitory room, but most of the sons of "old timers" lived in the private boardinghouses of their fathers' day. The boardinghouse people were an unusual group; many of them were widows with one or more sons in college, and the simple social life of these homes contributed no little to the making of a man. Another factor which made for the greatness of the University was the personal responsibility fostered in the boy who made his own arrangements for board, lodging, and laundry, paying his accounts weekly or monthly. Steering his own boat and watching the weather, he had entered already upon the real sea of life. He gave serious thought to his studies that I have rarely seen elsewhere, and his classroom record really measured his standing with the better element among his fellows. In such an atmosphere a man entering college accompanied by his father to make arrangements for him looked and felt like a pup in leash.

We literally wore out the library books passing them around for much parallel reading was required and few books available outside. Mr. William Wertenbaker, "Old Wert" to the students, was the librarian. He had been appointed some fifty years earlier by Mr. Jefferson himself. When he could be induced to tell them, he had interesting stories of the famous founder and of Edgar Allan Poe with whom he had been a student. He used to tell us that Poe, although a small man, could out-jump and out-fight any man in college; that he had many acquaintances but few intimates. An omnivorous reader, he was a silent, secluded man whose habitual exercise was a solitary evening walk, often of many miles. "Old Wert" always called you by name and remembered what volumes you had taken out without referring to the official record. Having seen the library grow from the beginning, he had a complete knowledge of its range and placement.

THE UNIVERSITY OF VIRGINIA

In those days there was no president of the University of Virginia, the functions of such an office being assumed by a member of the faculty who was chosen by that body as "Chairman of the Faculty." This was in accordance with Thomas Jefferson's plan, and it prevailed for nearly eighty years after his death. He also designated the outside governing body as "the Rector and the Board of Visitors," and so it remains to this day.

When I was a student there were no entrance examinations; the text books were announced in the catalogue, and each student, after conferring with his preceptor, was expected to know what he could do with the selected course. Many were mistaken, and it was not unusual to find in a class along with new men one or more others taking the course for the third time. The sole requirement for graduation was to pass the final examination, usually about eight hours, at the end of a given course. Everyone left the University of Virginia trained in standing examinations and with profound respect for the system. Instruction was largely lecture and quiz. One half hour of persistent quiz on the preceding lecture or any preceding part of the course was followed by a solid hour of vocal instruction, a sinister seance which in every course came three times a week.

One of the distinctive features here was the custom of striving to graduate in "schools," as for instance, the School of Mathematics or the School of Physics. This meant that a student concentrated on junior, intermediate, and senior physics, and as much more as they gave, and then received a distinctive diploma declaring him a "Graduate of the School of Physics." Some cognates were taken, as, let us say, mathematics and astronomy; and these graduates of schools of the University of Virginia once did the best teaching all over the South. The modern Doctor of Philosophy degree is the same thing under a different name and is of much more variable quality.

I have already referred to Mr. Strode as a math-medalist, or a graduate of the School of Mathematics of the University of Virginia. My chemistry studies resulted in a diploma in the School of Agriculture, an endowed Miller school, which had an interesting history. Old Samuel Miller, a native of Albemarle County, was a tobacco merchant in Lynchburg when the war broke out.

He managed to save the tobacco he bought during that four-year struggle, and at the close of the war he made a great "killing" and became a wealthy man. Always friendly to the University of Virginia, he gave several hundred thousand dollars to endow a school of agriculture. Colonel Charles Venable, then Chairman of the Faculty, in his broad wisdom foresaw that the land grant, or agricultural and scientific, colleges would usurp the major functions in the teaching of agriculture, so he went to see Mr. Miller, and persuaded him to change the deed of gift from "the art of agriculture" to "the sciences which underlie the art of agriculture." Across the railroad we graded and leveled our experimental fields where Lambeth Field, years later, subserved athletic sports.

One of the things that impressed me very strongly and almost at once was that here Jefferson was more honored as an educator than as a statesman or political prophet. At the University which he founded he was appreciated as a great pioneer in educational thought; for it was recognized that he had designed a university rather than a college. All courses, fortified by the free elective system, were directed towards the university viewpoint. The one academic degree devoutly desired was the Master of Arts of the University of Virginia. The Bachelor of Arts was simply a consolation stake for those who could not attain the greater honor.

Practically every boy educated in one of the fine classical schools in the South knew all about the honor system of student self-government. That system was widespread because the best educated teachers of that day were University of Virginia graduates of schools who carried this ideal with them. I knew all about the code at Bingham's and we lived under it at Strode's. Coming to the University I simply passed under a new phase. During my student days we had no honor committee or any kind of organization, but if the code were violated the entire body of students rose in their wrath. I recall no violation during the years 1875-1877, but every man knew exactly what would happen if one occurred.

XXVIII

FACULTY AND FRACAS

I SOON GOT into my stride as a student and took the measure of my professors. Doctor John W. Mallet, professor of chemistry, was one of the few men I ever knew who became bigger and bigger the nearer you approached him. An Englishman of Irish training, later a Fellow of the Royal Society, and always a gentleman, he exerted a profound influence on my college career. With the rank of colonel he had been chief chemist and powder maker in the Confederate Ordnance Department. It was he, when the nitre supply of the South was exhausted, who turned to human urine, the leachings from under old houses, bat manure, and other far-flung sources of supply.

Under Doctor Mallet I took General and Industrial Chemistry; with his supervision, under Instructor Francis P. Dunnington, I took Analytical Chemistry, both qualitative and quantitative, and under the latter alone I took Agricultural Chemistry. The great drama of Organic Chemistry was then unfolding, and many of us fully realized the impending eminence of chemistry. Traces of that interest were shown in many bits of student doggerel like the following:

> Shades of potassium
> Lie white on the hill;
> The Song of the Silicate
> Never is still—

> Come, love, come,
> Tumpty, tum, tum,
> Peroxide of Soda
> And Uranium!

My classroom for lectures under Dr. John R. Page was under the old Annex which then stood adjoining the north front of the Rotunda. The auditorium occupied the main floor of this building, with the engineering drawing rooms above, and the law lecture rooms and the old Lewis and Clark Museum below. Here among the stuffed animals brought back by the explorers, Dr. Page held forth to two students on botany, zoology, astronomy, geology, and varied agricultural additions. He was the worst lecturer and yet one of the best teachers that I have ever known; for the hungry student he was a teacher by suggestion, and for any other he was overwhelming. My sole partner in class soon quit, but I ate the old man alive with great, and I hope, mutual enjoyment. He had been educated abroad, and at that time the teacher with European background was vastly better than any American. Dr. Page's discourses covered "the earth and the fulness thereof" and bore no relation whatsoever to the prescribed subject. I learned as much Geology as Botany and as much Astronomy as Geology in this course. It seemed to me that I read the entire library trying to keep up with him.

Professor William M. Thornton, head of the School of Engineering, then a "new hand at the bellows," was a young man of such scholarly attainments that he had recently been professor of Greek at Davidson College, North Carolina. At the University of Virginia he succeeded a singular genius, Leopold C. Boeck, who had just resigned to serve the Centennial Exposition in Philadelphia in an engineering capacity. When that work was done he remained at the exposition as interpreter-general, taking anything that came, Oriental or otherwise. He had done construction work in most parts of Europe, including Russia and Turkey. He met with trouble, however, at Thomas Jefferson's university by holding an occasional lecture on the Sabbath. When reproved for that he responded, "I do not pelieve in dat Mosaic Narrative, but I will use it to answer your complaints. You vill remember dat Christ commended de man who pulled his ass out of de mire on de Sabbath day. I have under my care here fifteen asses, and I feel de same responsipility." According to tradition, at his first lecture he tapped himself on the breast and delivered this brief monologue: "Voici! You see here de greatest engineer in de vorld. Now go and tink about dat, and meet me here tomorrow." He was indeed a great engineer and a great linguist, but his eccentricities made him well-nigh impossible.

Following such a man, Mr. Thornton was superbly fitted to teach engineering and was gladly welcomed. But as I was taking his course only for the drawing I was undistinguished as one of his students, and even now any mention of "the moment of a particle" or an "infinity sign" will recall that class and give me the cold shivers.

Most of my work in this course was done under the instructor in drawing, Julio Romano Santos, a Peruvian gentleman with whom I became quite intimate. The subsequent career of "Santy," as we called him, was interesting. Years later when I was chairman of the Faculty at the University of Virginia, I received a telegram from the United States Department of State advising me that Santos, in rebellion against the Peruvian Government, had been captured and threatened with execution. He claimed American citizenship, so the commandant of the American gunboat in the harbor demanded a stay of execution and threatened to shell the town if not granted. The State Department wanted to know if he had acquired citizenship while living at the University.

Knowing that Colonel Charles Venable had been Chairman in "Santy's" early days, I took the telegram to him. He read it twice and then said, "Barringer, you cannot possibly appreciate the situation in those reconstruction days. No ex-soldier could vote. We came near to having a colored Mayor and Aldermen for a University town. Yes, we voted Santos, many times, as we needed every white vote." Then, in a tone of apology, "The only oath they had to take was, 'I have never borne arms against the United States.'" My reply to Washington was, "Claim justified, living witnesses can testify, Santos took the oath and voted Democratic ticket many times. Unquestionably American citizen." The gunboat threatened the town, and "Santy" was saved. He wrote gratefully and later sent two nephews to me when I was president at the Virginia Polytechnic Institute.

As the months passed I came to know a number of the fourteen full professors on the staff: "Old Ven," Colonel Charles Venable, who had served several years on General Lee's staff; "Daddy Holmes," George L. Holmes, one-eyed and myopic, who had read more history in Greek than most historians had read in English; M. Schele De Vere, a Swede, with the diploma of J.U.D. (Juris Utriusque Doctor) from the University of Paris, the third one ever conferred, he claimed; old "John B." Minor, who taught "the law and the reason thereof," and several others. Since each wore a different variety of beard, collectively the faculty was dubbed by the students "The Buccaneers of the Spanish Main."

While I was in college, Professor Basil Gildersleeve left for Johns Hopkins where, as professor of Greek, he shone gloriously for many years, but "Old Gill" was brought back to be buried in the University Cemetery. Tradition has it that when the old man's doctor told his wife that the end was near, she went to his bedside and said, "Basil, we have talked over almost everything, but you have never told me where you wanted to be buried should anything happen." "Is it as bad as that?" "Old Gill" asked, and on being assured that his physician gave little hope of recovery, he said, "I made up my mind long ago. I want to be buried in the cemetery at the University of Virginia." His wife was surprised, but he reassured her by saying, "I know what I am talking about. I was buried down there for twenty years, and I liked it like hell!"

A year or more before I came, Doctor McGuffey, of McGuffey Readers fame and professor of moral philosophy at the University, had died; but the students who were under him never tired of perpetuating "Old Guff's" memory, and his anecdotes were still common college talk.

During my first spring season I had a bad attack of malarial fever, and because of this I came to know another member of the faculty who was to become another guiding influence on my life. That was the Nestor of the Medical School, Doctor James Lawrence Cabell, who visited me as the doctor in charge of student health. When I told him that I had suffered malarial paroxysms during the four years of the war, he was justly indignant, knowing that the Federal Government had made quinine "contraband of war." He told me that he had often seen cases like mine for "coming to the mountains seemed to bring malaria out." We had many talks; I told him of my early friendship with Doctor John Bachman, and because of my increasing veneration for Doctor Cabell, I determined to take medicine the next year, fearing that he might not be there if I waited. I never dreamed that he would live for fifteen years and upon his retirement nominate me as his successor in the chair of physiology.

Soon after recovering from this fever I, with several other students, volunteered to help the Monticello Guard out of a difficulty. They were to be inspected and were unable to muster a sufficient number of members to pass, so as I had been drilled as a cadet at Bingham's and happened to fit a spare uniform, I was selected among others. The inspector was well pleased, and we were allowed to carry our "Spencer rifles" up to the University, subject to call. Securing a little ammunition, we took potshots from an upper room in House E, thus breaking the usual academic calm. Our favorite target was the clockface on the Rotunda which was well peppered before the guns were recalled. By standing far back in the room no telltale smoke came forth, and we risked only one or two shots a day, but soon "Old Harry" the Chairman, was tearing his hair. Twenty-odd years later when the University was presented with a new clock, I, as chairman, ordered a bullet-proof face, a unique order at that time.

Little sins, such as this, were all I could indulge in for I had no time, with my six courses, for anything else. I literally lived, day and night, in the laboratories and drawing rooms and even had to call off "calico adoration" to which I was urged by my fraternity brothers, the Zeta Psi's. I did take one hour a day for soccer, which we played on the site of the present Brooks Museum. Ten years after the Civil War we were expected to work, and work we did. During the ten months of the session there was not a single holiday except Christmas, and we had that only when it did not fall on Sunday. It was an orgy of effort, but the best part of it was that everyone wanted it and was proud to be able to stand up under it.

Hard as he worked, the student of that day was not without amusement. Those who "took calico as a ticket" were not referred to as "lounge lizards," but those with marked interest in femininity were characterized as "dikes." Such a young fellow would be watched, and when seen "diking up," his disgusted roommate sent out runners to call, "Dike!" He would be met at the door by a number of boys in callithump equipment and might then give up his intention of calling on the girls—in which case he would have to make a speech from the Rotunda steps. If he persisted in following the feminine trail, however, the "dikers" would form in line behind him singing softly. On reaching the house they opened out into a double rank through which he advanced, not running the gauntlet but approaching to the attack thoroughly advertised. Some of the girls liked it and counted their "dikes" as trophies, but others did not. One stern parent, an old Civil War veteran, met a mob fifty yards away and ordered them back, expressing his contempt for any young man who would approach a private residence so accompanied. This dampened the ardor for "dikes" and there was a manifest decline in the custom during that session.

The student body did not limit itself to such unusual forms of amusement. In season there was baseball and soccer; and in season and out, stud poker, whist, euchre, seven-up, and casino were popular and, to break the routine, pitching horseshoes. The card playing was for fun, and the "tippling" was not noisy. If a first-year man made a noise when drunk it was recognized that he was either unfamiliar with traditions or else one of those psychological unfortunates who could not stand any alcohol. A second- or third-year man making a disturbance when drunk was looked upon as one devoid of background and decency.

Surprising though it may be, it is nevertheless true that the Temperance Society was one of the most popular institutions at the University of Virginia in those days. A young fellow who found himself drinking too much for his general good sent in his name and, in the presence of his fellow reprobates, took the pledge for the rest of the session or for some other designated period and kept it. This was no insignificant institution but a "center," occupying a two-story brick building with the post office, express office, and book store underneath. It held debates on the liquor question, some serious and some satirical, but they drew and held the interest of the student body. It was a great institution, notable for its sensible handling of a difficult problem, and great was the indignation when a new temperance movement began to profess a holy horror of our local society with its short term pledges. That new movement accomplished nothing except to make the students mad.

For many, drinking was a Saturday night indulgence, and while I was at the University a law was passed providing that no barroom should be nearer than a mile of the University grounds. That meant that old Ambroselli, son of a marble cutter brought from Italy by Mr. Jefferson to carve the marble capitals of the Rotunda, had to move. After due measurement, he located his saloon on the "Main Road" about opposite the Delavan Church. A recent state law had doubled the price of drinks sold in a bar and these were recorded for taxation by a "Moffit punch-bell," the handle of which had to be revolved each time a drink was sold. We grew accustomed to the one, two, or three tintinnabulations of the bell, but one night Z. B., always heretofore a rather quiet, well-behaved student, came in inventively drunk, grabbed the handle, and began playing a tune. Ambroselli made for him, but Z. B. pulled a six-shooter from his pocket and pumped lead into the floor right at the barkeeper's feet, at the same time changing the tune from "Home Sweet Home" to "Turkey in the Straw." This was ten dollars a minute. Ambroselli couldn't stand it, and he charged again as soon as he thought the gun was empty, but the boy dropped the empty gun, drew a derringer from his vest pocket, and threatened to kill Ambroselli in a tone that meant business. After playing the Doxology, this wild man let go of the handle and went somewhere else to try the same manoeuvre. It was said in college that he blew in one hundred dollars of other peoples' money (a vast sum to us) that night. Twenty years later I saw the bell-ringing artist transformed, marching in priestly robes in a holy procession, but the spiritual change did not come until some years after he left the University. Ambroselli did not lose in the long run for he was paid back a goodly sum, and in defense of student honor the men patronized him freely.

There was another new law in Virginia at that time which at last had public opinion behind it, namely the law against duelling. The men who drew that law knew their business. It was ordained that when any elected man applied for the oath of any public office, the prior question had to be asked him under oath, "Have you ever sent or accepted a challenge for a duel?" If the answer was in the affirmative he was debarred from office-holding, high or low. This struck right at the root of the evil as the duelling class was the usual office-holding class.

Now if I were asked to answer retrospectively concerning the chief source of emotion and excitement in the student body in those days, I would say without hesitation, cockfighting. The rear room in House D on Dawson's Row was our pit. We built a strong eighteen-inch-wide shelf, three feet high all around the room, on which tightly-packed spectators stood; another row stood in front of them, and others sat on benches placed around the rather diminutive pit. We kept some of our cocks in the coal-boxes, and the way they greeted Old Sol every morning would lead anyone to believe that he was living on a chicken farm. Shawlnecks, Warhorses, and Fleary Eyes were among the most successful types. When stags were sent from home, almost any Negro farmer for the sum of one dollar would kill and eat his own cock. He would then accept one of our stags for six or eight months, to be replaced with another when that one was withdrawn.

The vogue then was the full drop-socket gaff, and many students knew how to gaff the cocks with the best. It was remarkable to watch the meticulous care with which they worked the hind toe up and down to see how the tendons ran and then observe the cock standing to see if his spurs stuck close or spreading. The janitors made no little money by tossing each cock twenty-five or thirty times in the mornings to prepare them for the fight.

We began with local cock fights between Dawson's Row and Carr's Hill, but we finally worked up to interstate contests, first between the states of Virginia and Maryland, and then they boxed the compass—Virginia-Kentucky, Virginia-North Carolina, North Carolina-Georgia, et cetera. The cocking jealousy of Virginia and Maryland is, I hear, today still unabated. We had students from all over the country, and while the art was new to the New England men, they were crazy about it but always acted as though they were engaged in a felony. Men from the far South never seemed to think of the legal aspect. Of course, the faculty knew what was going on, but those gentlemen seemed to feel that if they drove the cocks off the grounds, the amateur status of the craft would disappear, leaving only the professional pits. By that time it was against the law in Virginia, classed, I believe, as a misdemeanor, but the spirit remained, and the sheriff was kind. If he felt that he must make a raid (I never saw one) he would send word, and when he arrived he might find two or three languishing cocks. On the whole the sport did little harm; there was betting of course, but it was of necessity moderate.

When Finals approached we were interested to learn that Ralph Waldo Emerson had been invited by the presidents of the "Jeff" and "Wash" societies to make the principal address. This was to counteract the impression by the orator of the previous year who was a fire-eating, unreconstructed gentleman from the Deep South. We were even more interested to learn that the distinguished philosopher was bringing his daughter with him, but naturally this interest languished when we were told that she was somewhat beyond student age.

I think I heard as much of the address as anyone in the audience for I sat well forward to receive my five certificates of graduation, and I agree with the student who summed it up concisely as being "two hours long and fifty feet short." Certainly those in the back of the hall never knew he was speaking; those twenty feet away heard a voice, but not the words, and he continued interminably. For a reasonable time the audience paid him the tribute due a visitor and a man of eminence, and then human nature began to work. The boys began talking to the girls, and a low hum of conversation ran through the audience until the end of the chapter. "Old Harry" and "Old Ven," both holy terrors, glowered and frowned, but they could aim at no one in particular. Mr. Emerson himself did not seem to notice it, and although his daughter did, I think she was more concerned for her father's feeble condition than the conduct of the audience.

He never published the address, but an abstract of it appeared in the *Virginia Magazine,* and in addition the editor lambasted the audience for lack of courtesy. The boy who prepared the abstract was sitting some fifteen or twenty feet farther back in the hall than I was, and he had no better ears. It was simply a student's idea of what Emerson might have said. As a philosopher he was good to look at, but a rostrum view was all we got.

XXIX

THE PHILADELPHIA CENTENNIAL

WHEN I WENT home that summer with my five diplomas in my pocket, my father was so much pleased with my good work that he gave me a season ticket to the Centennial Exposition in Fairmount Park in Philadelphia. There had been no exposition for some time, and the world was on the *qui vive*. Of course, I was filled with summer enthusiasm at the time, but looking back on it now from the vantage point of maturity, I believe that it was the best exposition I ever saw, including the English and Continental as well as American exhibitions. Undoubtedly the results were splendid.

First I stopped to visit with some friends at the Healing Springs of Virginia and then proceeded to Philadelphia, where I roomed with a family from Charlotte, North Carolina. As they lived on Independence Square, my morning trip over to the Reading Railroad station was good preliminary exercise for my daily walk of ten or fifteen miles through the exposition grounds and buildings. I had not been there three days before I met Doctor Mallet of the University of Virginia and William Barton Rogers of Boston. I had once met the latter when he was visiting the University laboratories. Both these gentlemen were judges of award in the great fair and gave me excellent advice on what to observe. Incidentally, "Old Jack" Mallet's industrial chemistry lectures were almost perfectly portrayed there.

Having already pretty well decided to study medicine, I took an active interest in the medical exhibits. I became well acquainted with the man in charge of Tiemann's exhibit, and he showed me a new device convenient for taking the temperature of the sick. It was an ordinary eight- or ten-inch thermometer, bent at right angles into an "L" shaped figure. The mercurial bulb was on the short end, which was placed in the armpit of the patient lying down, with the long arm projecting in front.

One could sit beside the patient, and in the course of five minutes watch the mercury column creep up to the "dead line"—98.6, or beyond. When the doctor made his record and took the thermometer out of the armpit, the mercurial color customarily retreated to the bulb or nearabout. Few people know that the modern clinical thermometer was made possible when some one first gave a thermometer shaft a right-angled turn. One day by mere chance, a doctor noticed that his mercury column did not return to the bulb as usual after use. It was odd. He did not understand it, but naturally he swung it down, and the mercury moved; and so the idea occurred to him that some compression on a straight shaft would give a self-recording thermometer, which is our present instrument.

It was the old "L-armed" thermometer that I saw at the Centennial, and as a new venture in the field of quantitative medicine it was of great interest. I bought one and took it with me to the University, and we used it on the poor devil who fell off the ice chute, with various and divers typhoids, post-partum septicaemia, and with the normal patient.

At the Centennial I looked longingly at a gold-plated hypodermic syringe. No other seemed to have the same refulgence or style. I fell in love with it and ultimately acquired it, with the result that before I studied Materia Medica I was giving hypodermics of water to gain the technical touch. Before the end of the session I was able to measure an eighth to a quarter of a grain of morphine and administer it with safety. I achieved this by constantly returning to the chemical laboratory weighing room; after estimating a blade-poised portion and compressing it under the knife to assure compactness, we weighed it. These days it would astonish the medical profession, now fed on machine-made hypo tablets, to see how accurate the human eye and hand can become after a week of training. As a student and later as a practitioner, I used this method of estimating the morphine for solution in the spoon from which it was transferred to the cylinder of the syringe.

All of my interest, however, was not medical. I had an amusing introduction to one of the great wonders of the Centennial, and it came about in this wise. One hot afternoon I came upon a nice cushioned chair in front of a little building that looked like an office. Being in the state to take it regardless of ownership, I sat down and enjoyed myself for a few minutes. Then I saw a marvellous parade coming towards me, headed by a large and well-dressed man of Mexican coloring who seemed to be a person of importance. Walking with him was a lady of extraordinary charm, a blonde, I believe she was, for they were a decided contrast, and behind them, irregularly spaced, came three or four other couples obviously in attendance. They were headed straight for me, and just before they reached me, a young man came out of the office and with a most deferential and gracious air marched to greet them. Needless to say, I got up from the chair and walked a short distance away, pretending to be absorbed in something else. After a few moments of conversation, the leading lady went into the office, remained for a short time, and came back, looking most excited and enthusiastic. Soon they left, and upon making inquiries I discovered that my Mexican friend was none other than Dom Pedro, the Emperor of Brazil, who had been an assiduous visitor to the scientific exhibits, and the lady was an American friend whom he had brought to see Bell's first telephone, which he had already visited. The others were members of his entourage who were likewise interested.

I found that I was talking to Alexander Graham Bell himself, and together we went in and looked at his machine. It looked rather like a small toy four-inch megaphone, placed horizontally, with some telegraphic-looking device behind it and a few wires. Bell told me to ask a question into the mouthpiece, which I did and received a reply, as he said I would; so it was manifest that there was some intelligence at the other end of the line. Then Bell told me to repeat some sentence into it and ask that it be repeated back to me. I said, "Now is the winter of our discontent made glorious summer by this sun of York," and the repetition came back changed to "this son of *New York.*" That perturbed Bell. He failed to remember that the Hayes-Tilden presidential campaign was on, with Tilden of New York, the Democratic ideal, having every prospect of victory, and that this Shakespearean quotation was a campaign slogan. It seemed that Bell, although an American citizen, was not interested in politics and could not understand why a politically-conscious man at the other end of the line thought of New York rather than of Shakespeare. I was impressed, however, by getting any response at all, and by 1883 I was using the telephone regularly in Charlotte, North Carolina.

I did not stay out the summer in Philadelphia for I was utterly worn out by my hard work of the previous session at the University, and I went down to Baltimore and spent some time with friends from Kenmore before returning to Charlottesville to take up my medical course.

When I returned to the University of Virginia in September, 1876, things were different. I knew most of the men in college, certainly those taking scientific courses, and I knew my measure. Mathematics was my *bête noir*, but "math" with a figure on the blackboard, either geometrical or trigonometrical, I could get some idea of. Even after one year of abstinence my Greek and Latin were fading. When the catalogue of the preceding session finally came out (times have changed!) each man's record was carefully pondered, and his scholastic social standing advanced or lowered, as the case might be. I had done well and received the benefit. This tattered old pamphlet is before me, and it is interesting to note that out of the 363 students, 105 took one of the three modern languages taught, 107 took Latin, and 72 had Greek. Chemistry, under the greatest chemist then in America, Doctor Mallet, had only 105 students; physics, then called natural philosophy, had but 55; and I have already stated that in botany and zoology there were only two. Surely the times have changed!

During the previous year, there was another young instructor in engineering besides Romano Santos, and I came to know him

THE PHILADELPHIA CENTENNIAL 217

intimately. This young man was taking Dr. Mallet's industrial chemistry, and we sat together in class. His name was Henry Rose Carter, and that name, like Walter Reed's, was to fill the whole world of Epidemiological Medicine. Even had Reed failed in his yellow fever researches, Carter would have been famous for his studies of quarantine for he brought the organization of an engineering mind to the problem of preventive medicine.

It was because Carter had clearly demonstrated an "extrinsic period of incubation" that Walter Reed was able to link up yellow fever with malaria. That the micro-organism of malaria spent this incubation period in an insect was proven—why not an insect with yellow fever? Years afterwards Carter told me of his talk on this subject with Reed, who was not only receptive but enthusiastically grateful for the idea. Long before, Nott of Mobile had suggested the mosquito; Finlay of Havana had accepted the idea, but bungled on its application; and the gate stood open. Reed once told me that his orders from Sternberg to find the bacillus icteroides alone stood in his way. Reed was an army man, with the spirit of army obedience, and the search for this "bug" was his main business. Any casual relation of the mosquito to yellow fever lay outside his orders. In after years Carter and I often talked this whole question over, but in 1876, we never dreamed that such conversations would follow our student discussions of the study of medicine. Both of us, under the influence of Cabell and Mallet, determined to go into medicine, but Carter said that he had been at the University of Virginia so long that he was going somewhere else; I said I liked it and was going to stay for my medical course; so, conjoined in sentiment, we parted in person. Carter went to the University of Maryland, and strangely enough neither one of us heard of the other for some twenty years. Then he, as a member of the United States Public Health Service, visited the University of Virginia where I was Chairman of the Faculty.

From long before the Revolution down to the Civil War, yellow fever was the summer plague of our coastal cities and Southern states. The last great epidemic was in Norfolk, Virginia, in 1855; thousands died, and half the physicians engaged in fighting it succumbed. Then came the wonder—there was no yellow fever in the South during the war. The reason was a mystery then, but we understand it now; the Northern fleet, blockading our ports, was our defender against the disease. Immediately after the war, when commerce was resumed with the West Indies and other infected countries, the yellow fever plague returned to most of our far Southern ports. In the late sixties, a dozen or more ports were stricken, and many students at the University of Virginia and other inland centers of learning were unable to go home. Mr. John B. Minor, distinguished head of the Law School, saw his opportunity and opened his summer school of law. Of course, conditions were changed with Reed's abolition of yellow fever, but the impression upon the University remained, and the summer study of law continued. Such men as the late Senator Robinson of Arkansas, Senate leader Alben Barkley of Tennessee, the late Hamilton Lewis of Illinois, and other well-known men gathered here for summer instruction under Mr. Minor.

When I entered the Medical School in 1876, there were but five men on the medical faculty to cover the entire curriculum, and the medical course was given in one year although there were a number of students who did not graduate within that period. A half century earlier, when the University first opened its doors, there was one professor of medicine; fifty-five years after I graduated in 1877, there were thirty-two professors and twenty-two instructors, and the course was four years instead of one.

During my student days, and for ages before that time, medical schools, founded primarily on anatomy, were limited to the season of the year when subjects could be dissected without rapid decomposition, for embalming processes then amounted to little. The result was that most medical schools in America ran from November to March, and the University of Virginia was the first school that I know of in this country having a nine months' or longer session. Our session, therefore, amounted in time to two at other medical colleges, but located as we were near a small town, we had no hospital and no clinical center.

XXX

THE SCHOOL OF MEDICINE, 1876-1877

HAD IT NOT been for my great veneration for Doctor Cabell, I might not have entered upon my medical career when I was just twenty years of age. He taught physiology and surgery; I knew him intimately, and he shaped my life profoundly.

One Sunday, not many years ago, I sat in the University Chapel, looking at the memorial window erected to James Lawrence Cabell, and I then pondered the coincidence of his name, for he was born on August 26, 1813, perhaps on the very day that his parents heard how the *Shannon* sank the *Chesapeake*, and mortally wounded her immortal commander, Captain James Lawrence. That had occurred in June, 1813, and it would take from June to August for Lawrence's "Don't give up the ship" to travel from the high seas off the coast of New England down to the mountain solitudes of Nelson County, Virginia. I am very grateful for the "extra dry" sermon that allowed my mind to wander into these historical researches.

Cabell graduated from the University of Virginia in 1838, and he was a charter member of the Alumni Society, the first ever organized in the South and sixth among the hundreds now existing in the United States. He was soon to become a charter member of the American Medical Association, then in turn, Chairman of the National Sanitary Conference on Yellow Fever,

President of the Medical Society of Virginia, and the first President of the original National Board of Health. In 1858, already an earnest evolutionist, he published *The Testimony of Modern Science to the Unity of Mankind,* a few months before the publication of Darwin's *Origin of Species.* In 1881 he was running neck and neck with Lister in new surgical ideas for in that year was published his *Sanitary Preparation of the Surgical Patient.*

During the Civil War, Doctor Cabell, like several other professors, carried on his classes and also participated in professional work among the wounded. He performed hundreds of operations in the Rotunda at the University.

A scholarly man, a clear thinker, and a profound philosopher, he bore the mint mark of Jefferson's ideas of a medical education, "comparative anatomy, human anatomy and the theory of medicine, in a university atmosphere," with its nine months' session to be followed with clinical material in a city; for he believed that not until then could the student fully appreciate it. James Lawrence Cabell never gave up the ship; with great skill he steered the medical school during the great period of transition.

In the classroom he was the most meticulous master of technical language whom I have ever known. He was a genius for giving his students helpful generalizations during his lecture periods. I recall one of his opening sentences, "When a physiological or normal stimulus is applied to healthy living tissue, the reaction is the function of that tissue." That sort of thing fell flat on students who had not had the preparation that I had been blessed with, but it appealed greatly to me. When physiology classes began, my intimate relationship with Doctor Cabell was renewed, and I was glad that he remembered me and the sickness that had brought us together in the discussion of "man's inhumanity to man."

Under Doctor John Staige Davis and his assistant, Doctor William B. Towles, I studied anatomy. I have always thought that a great teacher was one who could dramatize the essentials against a background of lesser essentials and cognates and bring out the shadows by the light of humor. Old Davis had this quality. He ransacked the earth for medical aphorisms and delivered them with charming naturalness; they might be called

THE SCHOOL OF MEDICINE, 1876-1877

the ten commandments of therapeutics. This was the first one: "When Nature knocks at either door, do not try to bluff her; but night or day, haste away, else your health will suffer."

Doctor Towles, assistant professor and demonstrator of anatomy, caught the best part of Davis's scholarship and charm and added an American homespun of his own that was entrancing. He was, I believe, the only man I ever knew who never showed the slightest repugnance to the human cadaver; if he had a good "stiff" fitted to the subject he was presenting, he would grow as enthusiastic over it as would an artist over some transcendental work of art. Throughout his life the School of Anatomy at the University of Virginia was the best in the country.

We were hard pushed for anatomical material as the state laws were inadequate, and public sentiment was not then cultivated in our favor. We bought, begged, and stole, with the result that our material was used to the utmost. Careless dissection was a crime; every man worked to become a skillful dissector and thus make the most of the material at hand. Our textbook was Wilson's *Anatomy*, a relatively small and unadorned volume compared with the present pictorial editions, but even this was taboo. We heard nothing from the professors or demonstrators except that the one source of knowledge in anatomy was the cadaver. Wilson's *Anatomy* was almost a literal translation of the work of the great French anatomist, Cruveilhier.

In those days a great mural adorned the walls of the dissecting room. Nearly always there were one or more "academs" in anatomy, artists or others after the artistic approach to the human figure, and one of these had drawn in permanent crayon a most surprising scene. The dissecting hall had been built fifty years earlier, and at the back end was a bricklined pit, some thirty or forty feet deep, into which was thrown all anatomical waste— particularly the bodies carved up in "surgery on the cadaver," along with many other fragments, for only the most stalwart bodies were boiled to make proper material for the work in osteology.

The artist had taken as his subject the mouth of this great, nearly filled pit on Judgment Day, and he was an artist almost beyond compare with a sense of humor that literally lapped over. Great clouds emerged from the pit, and rose, and spread out even over the ceiling. On the ceiling section was Old Gabriel with his horn. Down at the mouth of the pit was mere anatomical debris, but a few feet higher the pieces began to get together with a full complement of human motive. Two thoraces were fighting over a pelvic bone. A little farther along a pair were matching femurs, to see which would suit best, but the real *chef-d'oeuvre* was in a cloud that ran under and rose up between two windows. Here were two lovers, the lady minus one tibia, seated on a rock while her inamorato ran back and forth from the *mêlée*, a tibia in each hand and half a dozen extra ones sticking out from the openings in his ribs where he had placed them for easy carriage. Believe it or not, he undoubtedly had a smile on his prognathic facial bones, and she seemed smugly demure as she sat with her sound leg crossed over a legless femur, patiently holding her detached foot in her hands. This drawing was sacred, and although carefully preserved, time, tobacco smoke, and fumes from the boiling caldrons in the cellar were rapidly making away with it.

Doctor James P. Harrison, also a graduate of the Medical School of the University of Virginia, taught the practice of medicine, obstetrics, and medical jurisprudence. He had been in the Navy, was widely traveled, and had seen diseases in all parts of the earth. Beyond earnestness, he had no great gifts as a teacher, but his assigned parallel reading was wide and instructive. It was his great pleasure to accent the influence of the Hippocratic Oath on the medical practitioner's life, and his men left with a high concept of professional duty and a profound and lasting respect for "Old Harry's" lofty purpose and integrity.

The fact that all of these men had European training or had traveled abroad impressed me more than it did some of my fellow students. I had come from a family whose members, after graduation, nearly always made a European tour; and even then I knew that this was in the tradition of Jefferson's university. Most of the original faculty chosen by the founder were either English or Continental scholars, and the drift continued.

I was not old enough to vote in the presidential election, the contest between Tilden and Hayes in November, 1876, but I was

THE SCHOOL OF MEDICINE, 1876-1877

much interested. We did not expect to get the election returns for a day or two; although the telegraph was fully effective then, there was not the demand for news. There were two newspapers in Charlottesville, *The Jeffersonian Republican,* started by a Massachusetts Yankee, and *The Charlottesville Chronicle,* started, I believe, to offset the Republican drift. One was a semiweekly and the other, seemingly, a semi-occasional. The next morning, when "Old Harry" opened his lecture with the sententious quotation "Now is the winter of our discontent made glorious summer by this sun of New York," we knew that he thought that Tilden was elected, and we wondered where he had got his news. Tilden did get a popular plurality of a quarter of a million votes, but Hayes became president, and his administration is chiefly remembered as the period during which "ice water flowed like champagne" at the White House. For weeks before the inauguration Washington was in a turmoil, and the general feeling was intense, but I am glad to say there was no political animosity shown at the University. Real Jeffersonianism, of course, prevented that. Tilden's statesman-like dictum that the offense, however heinous, was not worth another war saved the country and blanketed the Hayes administration with a discredit from which it was never able to recover.

In the spring, Charlottesville had its first fire of sufficient magnitude to call for student help. The town's fire engine, run by manpower, was a four-wheeled truck with long arms folded up on top which, when let down, formed handle bars to work the levers that pumped the water. They could utilize eight or ten men to the side and throw a stream of remarkable power, but, when working earnestly at that job, ten minutes was just about the limit of life. Obviously a couple of hundred athletic boys standing around to relieve the sufferers constituted a considerable asset.

The fire started in a barroom behind what is now called "the old bank building," and it spread to several stores. In those days grocery stores carried liquor wholesale, and the barroom was simply the retail outlet. When a man on horseback arrived at the University to tell the boys that they were needed downtown and said that kegs, carboys, and bottles of spirits were lying around loose, a full contingent responded, and with this additional force the flames were soon checked.

After it was all over some youthful genius conceived the idea of bringing the fire engine up to the University. When the call came to take the engine back to the firehouse on Vinegar Hill every student came to help. Upon reaching the firehouse they elbowed the citizens away from the dragrope and brought the machine, hub deep through the mud, more than a mile to the University. Then the dilemma—what to do with it! They solved this by taking it to the pond, some hundred feet long by thirty feet wide which lay behind the present University Chapel, and pumping in turn until nearly every man in college had exercise enough to last a week. I am glad to say that when they called for volunteers to take the engine back to town in good shape "as a matter of honor," they had all the help they needed.

That was the spring when work was started on "that architectural monstrosity," the Brooks Museum, but at that time the Annex still remained, and of all the architectural evils of the Victorian period in America, that was the worst. I suppose it made the aesthetic soul callous; at all events, I heard no protests against the museum, but when the mansard roof appeared, a certain chilliness crept in. Perhaps the fine collection which it housed later somewhat placated the student body.

Now, as a medical student, I could take part in an event of which I had been merely a spectator during the previous session. While the spring weather was still uncertain we had final exams in anatomy, and that night the medical students unitedly gave a *soirée* and had a bonfire. A pile of seventy-five wooden coalboxes, six feet by four, is as high as a house, and when well soaked in kerosene, you have a bonfire to be proud of. In spite of the uncertainty of the weather, each medical student contributed his own coalbox, and it was a point of honor to steal as many as possible from the law men. To accomplish this, shrewdness, subtlety, and no little courage were demanded.

For that night the ordinary dignities were discarded, and the hard-working student who might not have tasted a drop all year was expected not only to get drunk, but utterly at variance with the prevailing code, *to show it*. In the phrase of the day, "we cut loose the dog." There was a general fund to provide iced kegs of beer, carboys of corn, rye, and that marvellous mixture of these— Bourbon. The *soirée* was on Carr's Hill, and I recall one incident that makes me laugh now, sixty years later. A couple of students noticed that the men were not drinking as much beer as had been expected, and the spirit moved them to play a joke on the class by starting one of the kegs down the conveniently rounded hill to a well-located thicket. In their befuddled minds they planned a subsequent search and the transfer of the keg to Dawson's Row. Great was their indignation the next morning when they located their keg and found that they had started an empty!

Being now an old student I could tell that the time was approaching for the final election of the presidents of the Jefferson and Washington literary societies. As the canvass warmed up, the friends of the candidates worked like beavers, going into the Arcades and Ranges to bring in new members. Just about the two ablest men in college would be chosen for the "final presidency"; jointly they would choose the speaker for Finals; one would introduce him and the other hobnob with him in public about college. Both the men chosen that year are living, one is a college president and the other probably the leading railroad attorney in the country. All the law men belonged to one or the other of the two societies. Another big *soirée* followed this election, the final fling of the season.

Outside of these two big *soirées* there was far less drinking than there is today. This tempts me, now an aging man, to look back and give my experience. It seems to me that every "saint" and every "sot" that I knew at the University is dead. At our reunions, now few and far between, I notice that the serious and sedentary saints are missing, and likewise those of Scotch appetite who took a little drink behind the door once or twice a day but never really knew the joys of intoxication. But those who drank only on such social occasions as they had free and abundant time to give to pleasure are here. The "Saturday night sports," or, to describe the group more exactly, the *"soirée* sports" are the ones who have survived.

With the spring there came a new interest to the University. For the first time since the old flatboat days, boats appeared on the Rivanna; the University of Virginia boat crew were practising in their new boats, "four-oared gigs." At Shadwell, Thomas Jefferson's birthplace, the remains of the old milldam still raised the stream high enough for the crew to get several miles of straightaway and a turn. The racing boats and equipment were the gift of a student, a New Yorker of such quiet tastes that no one suspected his wealth.

Looking back now, from the vantage point of modern medicine, it seems astonishing that life survived at all in that Mid-Victorian Age. Milk was milk, anywhere, and from anything. Sewerage disposal was practically unknown, and when known was discharged anywhere. The old hookworm backhouse encompassed the earth. Diphtheria often swept through whole counties with a mortality of 80 per cent. Here at the University of Virginia, under the aegis of the chairman of the National Board of Health, conditions were somewhat better, but we needed knowledge of the essentials, and that knowledge had not yet come. Pasteur was still wrestling with the problem of micro-organisms, and Koch had not yet laid his finger upon the bacillus tuberculosis. Every day we heard of fellow students with typhoid, malaria, and perhaps others "going into a decline," the ominous advance notice of active tuberculosis. Then we had no clinics, no hospital, and not even a pesthouse for the afflicted, but many a medical student spent his time taking the pulse of his fellow man or watching with concentrated gaze the slow mounting of the new clinical thermometer which I had brought down from the Philadelphia Centennial. Seeing my thermometer and hypodermic, one or two others decided to purchase; but none of us appreciated for a moment the profound change in medicine that an accurate thermometric record would bring any more than we foresaw the evils that could follow the foolish and indiscriminate use of the hypodermic as a "pain reliever."

Throughout the session the medical students, like all others in the University, were hammering away without any knowledge of their grades or marks on previous examinations. That was customary, and no one expected anything else until honors were announced as a result of the final examinations. A student's sole measure of another's intellectual capacity was based on the answers in class. If a man did not answer at all, he "corked"; if he answered fluently, he "curled." But for the man in between, the real man who said what he believed and controversially sustained his argument, appraisal was difficult. Some of the best men in the class were more or less discredited by their fellows because of lack of good delivery. I can recall some who "curled" so beautifully that I thought at the time they should be in the Law School, and a lifetime of experience with them has not changed this impression.

Taking the medical course, as I did, in one year—taking the whole thing together—a very singular sensation is felt at the end of the session. That is produced by the coming together of all the medical subjects which at first seemed utterly unconnected. What connection would the anatomy of the eye have with the humble herb belladonna? By the end of the term we knew that belladonna paralyzed one of the multifarious muscles and left all others untouched and that amyl alcohol took another. I do not believe that there can ever be the same "coming together" in a four-year course without maintaining a general examination covering the whole course—say, an oral one, like ours, which could be ignored by a professor who felt fully satisfied with a man's work.

There was a hazard in those days not so much manifest later. In our class there were three or four men who had remained for several years, always failing the final examinations. These students concentrated on the subjects in which they had failed and otherwise took it easy, in spite of the threatening general examinations. We who carried the entire course for the first time were literally worked to death. Knowing that any breakdown in stamina was fatal, the constant menace of sickness made us uneasy, and we kept away from the sick, a peculiar thing for an embryonic doctor. There was hardly a time when there was not some student ill with typhoid fever for the cause of it was unknown, and this coming together of young men of susceptible age from all over the United States brought it constantly. We accepted it as part of the game. At the same time, there was amongst us a spirit of inquiry and criticism such as that which was manifested by Pasteur in France, and by Koch in Germany.

At last, all was over—the last exam held, the last papers written, "pledged," and turned in. The orals followed—morning, noon and night—one after the other, and when these were finished came the last few days of sustained suspense while everybody waited for the posting of the list.

One morning Doctor John Staige Davis came out of the conference room, walked to the bulletin board, and tacked up a little paper. To a passing student he made the simple remark, "There were only sixteen." This flew like wildfire for we had hoped for twenty, and everyone was afraid to go up and look at that fateful fragment less than four inches square. Finally we persuaded a third-year man—one of whom everyone felt assured—to go up and read the names out loud. He went, and after one glance turned and walked away; so we knew that for him the worst had happened, and then the spell broke. Each of us went up, prepared to take his medicine or not. My name was there, and thus began my calling in a profession on which I can look back a full fifty-five years.

XXXI

THE CLINICS OF NEW YORK, 1877-1878

HAVING SECURED my medical degree, I bought my ticket home and paid a little extra for what was known as a "stopover ticket." I got off at Lynchburg, Virginia, for the day after Commencement the University of Virginia boat crew was to race the Lynchburg crew on the old James River Canal. Having learned from scouts that Lynchburg's time was not as good as ours, every student was confident that he could win on a wager, and practically all the students were there.

It was a side-by-side race of nearly two miles, then they turned in an enlarged basin and rowed back to the starting point, an ideal arrangement for a dramatic view of start and finish from the same seats. All went well until the turn, after that the Virginia crew was hardly in sight, and when it came "limping in" to the utterly bankrupt spectators, the story was told. Charlie Steele of Baltimore, one of our most intelligent and effective oarsmen, had "picked up a crab" at the turn! Needless to say, with several hundred men far from home and bankrupt, his name was an anathema for some time. Fortunately, I had my ticket to Charlotte, no short distance in those days but a train ride of prolonged intensity with a number of stopovers and changes. I survived only by reason of the fact that when I changed to the North Carolina Railroad at Greensboro, I found a ten-cent piece in my watch-fob pocket. I bought a ginger cake six inches square and two inches thick and ate the whole thing.

Charlie Steele became a counsellor and then a partner in the firm of J. P. Morgan and Company, and when he gave his $100,000 bequest to the hospital at the University of Virginia, I felt it was merely in recompense for this ludicrous disaster.

At my father's home in Charlotte, I spent the summer waiting to go to New York for my postgraduate course. Doctor Jones, an elderly physician in that city, was very kind to me. For a man of that period, he had clearly defined concepts of Darwin and the evolutionary theories then under fire; he had enjoyed prolonged training abroad and was strongly against the "rush insanity" of invariable calomel. He sent me on a dozen or more cases in the suburbs of Charlotte and the surrounding country. These were mainly malaria, summer dysentery, and one or two labor cases.

In consultation with Doctor Cabell, I had already blocked out my course for New York, where at that time the best medical school was probably the Physicians and Surgeons at Columbia. Bellevue Hospital, however, was the center of all things medical, so I decided upon the University of the City of New York just across Twenty-third Street from the entrance to Bellevue. My boardinghouse was at the corner of Twenty-second Street and Second Avenue, facing Bellevue Hospital in the other direction, so I was well fixed for concentrated effort.

So high was the standing of the University of Virginia in its scientific training that any student going from there to the University of the City of New York, who registered for five subjects in postgraduate work and stood well on final examinations, would be honored with the degree of M. D. from that institution. I took the Diseases of the Nervous System, Practical Pathology, Orthopedics, Surgery (on the living subject and not the cadaver as at Virginia), and Clinical Diagnosis. In addition to this curriculum, I took some clinical courses under the professors of that field at the Bellevue Medical School. As these courses were outside of their professional work, I did not register at that school. I found there, as graduates and internes, several former University of Virginia students, and they helped in my selections.

THE CLINICS OF NEW YORK, 1877–1878

Under my clinical professors, I attended other hospitals than Bellevue, particularly the New York City Hospital, a new institution on Fifteenth Street, and an "emergency station" as far downtown as Desbrosses Street. For chronic diseases in mass we went across the river to the Charity Hospital on Blackwell's Island. I was not overly surprised when some friends whom I met there told me that they occasionally took a boat and went deer hunting on Long Island.

As an example of our emergency work, I remember a telephone call informing us of a right-angle impact between a tightly-packed streetcar and a three-horse fire engine. I went down with Mr. Erskine Mason, and we found that the two poles of the fire engine had gone clear through the car, fatally wounding three persons. Many more were injured by the impact and ensuing panic.

New York was largely spotted in those days, the Chinese lived down at Five Forks, the Negroes on Twenty-third and a few surrounding streets, and Italians and other Latins in isolated groups. Harlem was unknown, and above Columbia University settlement was sparse.

It was a wide-open city; almost every corner had its barroom, and beer, wine, and whiskey were cheap. On one occasion I, with two brothers from North Carolina, Cornelius and Elisha Battle, found a policeman dead drunk on a bench along his beat. I took his badge, Cornelius his helmet, and Elisha his nightstick, and thus adorned we marched unwittingly into a group of "coppers." I saw them in time to put the badge in my pocket, so I was not involved. As I could come into court with clean hands, I acted as attorney for my friends, assuring the policemen that if they arrested us and we testified how we had obtained our ornaments, nothing could save their fellow officer. They took us to the station house and then, strange as it may seem, let us off. I think the order for our release came from someone higher up.

A favorite song amongst the youth of New York City in those days was:

> I'm a dandy copper of the Broadway Squad,
> A Metropolitan M. P.

And the girls all cry,
As I go by,
"Are you there, Moriarity?"

I made my examinations easily at the end of the session and received a diploma written in florid Latin. My degree from the University of Virginia in plain but stately English pleased me much more. It is significant that my degree from the University of Virginia was dated June 28, 1877, and that from the University of the City of New York, on March 11, 1878. The medical year there was of considerably shorter duration than that of Virginia.

Among the outstanding professors that year were Austin Flint, physiologist and professor of nervous diseases, and Alfred Loomis, practical pathologist—both of them great teachers. I also had John T. Darby, whose practice was extremely wide, as professor of general surgery, as it was called then, which included everything from lithotomy to cataract operations. Lewis Sayre was giving the beginnings of plaster-cast work, and young Keyes was a marvellous instructor in urology. After so many years the general effect is a dream in which these men stand out, figures which have never diminished in the perspective of time.

XXXII

"THE GRAND TOUR," 1881

THE EARLIEST METHOD of medical instruction had been preceptorial, and young aspirants "read medicine," as young lawyers read law, in the office of a successful practitioner. By assisting him in the activities of his profession they were indoctrinated in practice. Where collegiate experience had been acquired, the young doctor was still expected to serve an apprenticeship as assistant to an established physician. In Charlotte these were mostly relatives, and the choice would be to enter into partnership or to hang out my shingle for myself.

Medicine, as practiced in the South in 1879, was largely calomel and quinine, bleeding and blistering. This was the accepted pattern. The doctors dispensed it, the patients expected it, and the faith of both was in accord. The results, to judge from the evidences of longevity recorded on tombstones, were not unsalutary. Nevertheless, typhoid and "summer complaint" were annual calamities, tuberculosis a perennial, and childhood, youth, and maternity bore unnecessary hazards.

My father's uncertain health made it inadvisable for me to be far from him. Preferring to try my wings in a less established field, I started practice in Dallas, Gaston County, North Carolina, a small town about twenty-six miles from Charlotte. This was the center for a country practice in that and adjoining counties. There is no better training for a young physician than the life of a country practitioner. There were then no clinics, hospitals, or laboratories for diagnosis. You read your patient—not a chart—and were the court of last resort between him and his Maker. As a discipline in the virtues of courage, resourcefulness, devotion, and humility, I know of no equal.

At the end of two and a half years, however, I realized that since I was still unmarried, the time for me to do further study and see something of the rest of the world was now. My father and his brothers each had his "grand tour," and for me to study abroad, and above all to observe the foreign clinics and hospitals, was an irresistible attraction. I had considered the possibility of entering the Marine Hospital Service (which was the forerunner of the Public Health Service), but my father generously offered me two years of study abroad; so plans were made at once to leave early in March, 1881.

During 1880, I stopped by the University to visit a friend on Dawson's Row. For some time we had heard quite a batting up of baseballs to cries of "Put one here, Tommy" from the vacant lot in front of House E. When we came out to investigate the hubbub, I saw a trim agile figure, very striking in appearance, standing facing the group and batting balls with uncommon accuracy out to a semicircle of catchers some one hundred yards away. These balls were tossed back to the catchers who passed them to the agile batter. Sitting around on the grass was a silent group watching the proceedings with intense interest. I asked another onlooker who the batter was. "Oh, that's Tommy Wilson, a law student, the best batter in the University." I asked my informant, "Does he always do all the batting? Why doesn't he let some one else bat a while and catch some himself?" "Oh," said my informant, "he never does that. I don't think he *can* catch." Wilson continued his skillful performance as long as I watched the scene. To calls from any part of his circle of receivers, he would toss and bat a ball most accurately into the hands of whoever might call, never too high or too low or inaccessible. It was the unabashed skill of marvellous showmanship —perfect reflex for direction but none for reception—in a way somewhat prophetic of his later career as President Woodrow Wilson.

"THE GRAND TOUR," 1881

He was a student of law under Mr. John B. Minor for almost two years and left after Christmas in 1881. He had come from Princeton where he graduated in the class of '79 with my cousin, Daniel Moreau Barringer.

I sailed from New York early in '81. In the next year and a half I went to the medical centers of London, Edinburgh, Dublin, Paris, and Vienna, applying myself to the study of clinical medicine and hospital administration.

I landed in England and began to perfect the outline of my plans. In London there was much talk of the International Medical Congress to be held there in August. The English had early been the significant leaders in preventive medicine. In advance of other countries their development in manufacture had brought the problems of industrial communities, and their far-ranging navy brought in the problems of infection from tropical contacts. The hospitals in London were of interest, but there were too many friends and compatriots about, and the facility of the language was too great for a young man bent on study to feel that he could concentrate as I desired. I decided to go on to Dublin, from there to Edinburgh, then to northern Germany, and down to Paris to dig in.

Dublin I found to be a city of great charm, less monumental than London, and with a large number of hospitals for different purposes instead of a concentration in one or more. This last is a great advantage for the student but not so happy in administration for the patient. There was the old Blue Coat Hospital, the Misericordiae, the Rotunda, Steevens, the Royal Victoria Eye and Ear, and other charitable institutions. Trinity College, or Dublin University, maintained a high position in the regard of the medical world.

After several days of this visiting, I decided to go out to Phoenix Park to the Dublin Zoo, which had an excellent reputation. In the building for the Carnivora, I gazed with interest into the cage where a leopardess was playing with her two spotted cubs, then I moved to the next which was occupied by a solitary lion. Canvas covered the adjoining cage as the lioness had recently whelped and was not on exhibition. While looking at this superb specimen of *felis leo* who reclined majestically indifferent to spectators, I remembered the Aesop's *Fables* of my Bingham's School days. The Fox's mate had bragged to the Lioness that she had several young in a litter, at least once a year and sometimes oftener, but that the Lioness had only one and sometimes only once or twice in a lifetime. The disdainful reply was, "One, but a lion" ("Unus, sed Leo"). This Latin phrase I quoted half aloud. A gentleman standing by seemed amused, and finding that I was an American physician with a liking for zoology, he said, "If you will come with me, I can show you something of special interest." We entered a side door, and I saw behind the canvas covers a lioness with three cubs, a rare event at all times and phenomenal in captivity. They were still spotted as are all the young of that family which achieve their specific markings later. The gentleman was the curator of the Zoological Garden and a delightful companion. One thing led to another and he showed me the reptile house and other items of special interest; and so two pleasant hours went by. When a gong sounded for closing hour, the curator said, "Outside is the private entrance to my office. It will save a long trip to the admission gate to use this exit." As I stood in the doorway thanking him, two policemen appeared from nowhere and said that I was under arrest. I uttered in amazement, "What for?" They said that there had been a serious riot of Fenians in Phoenix Park, and that all foreigners were under arrest. The curator instantly said, "This gentleman has been with me for the last two hours and I will vouch for his presence." But the bobby replied, "Sorry, Sir, but all visitors are subject to investigation. He must come with us." My friend, the curator, regretted that he could not come immediately with me but said that he would follow as soon as possible; so I started forth under guard, saying sternly to the bobbies, "You can walk behind me if you wish but I will not walk with you," which surprisingly they did. In this fashion I appeared before the magistrate who was conducting a summary court for this emergency. The curator, by now my old and good friend, appeared before I was questioned. He vouched for my time with him, and the magistrate examined my passport, reading aloud to the clerk for recording:

Paul B. Barringer—Citizen of the United States

Age 24	Stature ..5 feet 9 inches
Forehead ....high	Eyes ....hazel
Nose ....small	Mouth ....medium
Chin ....medium	Hair ....light brown
Complexion ....fair	Face ....oval

He glanced sharply back and forth through this identification. Beneath this description I had written:

> If this is found on a corpse answering to the
> above description telegraph or write to
> General Rufus Barringer
> Charlotte, N.C., U.S.A.
> A good reward will be paid.

The magistrate read this last with a grim smile and stated sharply, "A Fenian from North Carolina? Not likely! You are excused." And so I was a free man again. Since my sailing date was imminent, in order to continue my journey, I was obliged to leave at once although for appearance's sake I would have preferred to remain. I thanked the curator heartily and departed. Although I was cleared and at large, I was, however, painfully aware of surveillance even during the later days in London. I was glad to get on to Edinburgh where I spent a week.

The University of Edinburgh had one of the highest ranking medical schools of that day which for years had attracted Southern students. The first medical school in North Carolina, 1866-1877 was called the Edinburgh Medical School. The Royal Infirmary carried many thousand beds and gave excellent clinical opportunity. All of this was very interesting, but my mind was set on study in Paris and Vienna so I pushed on to the Continent and landed in Hamburg.

It was of great interest to be on the land from which my ancestor, old "Pioneer Paul," had come and to see what manner of man he had left behind. I found the Germans of Schleswig-Holstein, Hannover, and Prussia a sturdy, well-built race but as companionable as bulldogs. They were given to more rudeness and impoliteness than the Bavarians and South Germans.

I would as soon go through a horde of savages as a North German customhouse again. The Bavarians are, I believe, more sincerely polite than the French.

I was told on good authority that Barringer was a "Rhineland" name. This is a small duchy lying directly north of Baden and Württemberg and bordered by Alsace-Lorraine, so it sounded quite probable. Since I had to join Judge and Mrs. Victor Barringer later in the summer when they came over from Egypt, I did not dally with sight-seeing but went straight to Paris where I established myself in the Latin Quarter.

The American student, while one of the last invaders of Paris, was much valued as "befo' de War" the denizens of the Left Bank had lived mainly on his credulity and cash. Now in 1881, like so many others, he was going to Vienna. Among the 60,000 students of all kinds in a city of over 2,000,000, there were not more than a hundred Americans registered in the universities where formerly there had been thousands. The few left had been there for some time, one for several years. These figures did not include the art students, of whom there were a large number, but they were not in the Quarter.

Except for Germany, practically every other country was well represented. Outside of France and England, Rumania led off (over 11,000), next Russia, then Servia, Poland, Greece, Italy, Spain, South America, and even Australia. Also in this part of the city lived nearly all the political refugees of Russia, Poland, and other nations. I began to understand why students have played such an important part in the history of Paris, especially her political history. These students averaged about thirty years of age, and most of them were mere birds of passage flying from Paris to Berlin, Heidelberg, Vienna, Göttingen, Munich, and anywhere their interest and cash could take them.

My quarters were simple and adequate; the foreign food, though strange, was not unpleasant. If the meat could have been cooked without oil and if flea powder had been cheaper, I would have been happier.

The infinite thrift of the French was a constant lesson in economy. When I first saw someone buying one cent's worth of meat, I could but imagine a Charlotte grocer's scorn at such an order; but it would make a soup for two. I cannot remember ever seeing a Frenchman at hard work. He apparently sauntered through everything he did but could live for a month on what we waste in a week. Their thrift, however, is equalled by their persistent if casual industry, and were it not for their large standing army they would have rapidly grown wealthy. Every working man or woman wore a blouse or smock that differed for each trade and nearly everybody else was in uniform. As Mark Twain said of this military badge of distinction, "Few escape it."

At one time the superiority of the medical schools of Paris could not be questioned. By the endeavor of a group of able physicians to give to the study of symptoms the same precision as belonged to anatomical observation, and by the combination of these two factors, a new era in clinical medicine was developed. Most of that group were no longer living, but the outstanding inheritor of their genius was Louis Pasteur whose influence, sometimes against the will, was permeating the medical world. He had shed a new light on both medicine and surgery, "aspects of one Art," which had suffered an unfortunate division in the past. His English disciple, Lister, by the study of wound infections had by this time developed antiseptic and aseptic surgery.

It was in this summer of 1881, on June second, that Pasteur completed the experiments which conquered anthrax by vaccination. By his revelation of the relationship of bacteria to disease, he opened the way to the prevention of infection from, and inoculation against, a disease—truly a milestone in the progress of medicine. By conquering anthrax he had saved thousands of sheep and cattle for the French peasant. The government, grateful at last, sent him as their representative to the International Congress of Medicine then meeting in London. There in a special ceremony he was received with acclaim by the ranking scientists, Lister, Tyndall, William O. Priestley, and Paget of England, Virchow and Koch of Germany, and representatives of other countries. A special tribute from royalty was the presence of the Prince of Wales and his brother-in-law, the Crown Prince of Germany. For honors from France there remained only election to the *Académie française* the year following and the foundation of the Pasteur Institute in 1886.

His great friend and associate, Claude Bernard, had died in 1878. As a teacher, which Pasteur was not, he was closer to the medical student than Pasteur. Both were exponents of the experimental method in biology. Bernard's classic words remain the keynote of clinical observation: "A fact is noted: apropos of this an idea is born: in the light of this idea, an experiment is devised, its material conditions imagined and brought to pass: from this experiment new phenomena result which must be observed and so on and so forth."

It was a great regret that I had missed contact with his genius at the Collège de France, where his influence lingered but not his inspiration. The research begun by Louis on typhoid and pulmonary consumption was being ably developed and classified into statistics by his pupil and successor, Gavarret. Alfred Fournier, Médecin de L'Hôpital St. Louis, was revealing the ravages of syphilis in social life; and the great Charcot was at the Salpêtrière. Nevertheless the Golden Age of the French school of clinical medicine was on the wane and the German schools were on the ascent.

After two and a half months of intensive work in Paris, I decided to join a party and take a walking trip through the Franconian Alps before joining my uncle and aunt in Carlsbad. The others were Louis Piella, a South Austrian, Georg Lenin, a Russian, and another American student. We went the usual routes and had the usual experiences, including being caught in a snowstorm and nearly losing our lives. It was an interesting and instructive holiday. The Austrian, the Russian, and I heartily enjoyed all the "vins du pays" and various beers that came our way; but my compatriot, like most Americans, preferred the headier cognac and schnapps, in lieu of whiskey. He devoted himself steadily to their absorption which was probably the prelude to an alcoholic death a few years later. Politics was an infinite discussion, and Piella damned the English with practically every breath; Lenin, however, damned all of Europe, said they would destroy themselves, and that the two future nations were Russia and the United States. I have no reason to believe that he was a relative of their late leader, but I have many times remembered this interesting statement made in the summer of 1881.

We parted after two weeks' time when I went on to Heidelberg. A few days later I met Uncle Victor and Aunt Maria in Carlsbad after eleven years of separation. Time had not cheated them of distinction. He had grown a very imposing beard and side whiskers and looked every inch a judge. She had become very British in accent and dress and enormously stout. The Egyptian climate and love of rich food had seen to that. Hence summers at a European spa were an imperative.

I found their friends most interesting: Mr. William Walter Phelps, the recently appointed Minister to Austria, and his wife; Mr. Phillips, our Consul General at Prague; and a charming Scotch Army officer, Colonel Chalmers, and his sister. There was also a General Evans, the British Commander of the Army of India, who told me that he had travelled much in America and was astounded at the progress exhibited. Speaking of the military prowess of Germany, he said to me that a German had to be made a soldier but that my countrymen were natural soldiers. He felt that the United States with her little standing army was the greatest military power on the globe, so great that the three greatest powers of Europe would hesitate a long time before provoking a quarrel. That from an English general was an impressive statement. Except for our party the hotel was largely filled with British nobility and Members of Parliament, including the Lord Mayor of London who seemed very full of himself. There was great excitement when some M. P. ran away with someone's wife, a lady of title, but to my youthful eye there was very little stirring.

We went on Sunday to the English church and after service met the minister, a very pleasant and likeable young man, by name Benedict Arnold. Since my relatives knew no young people, in fact Carlsbad attracts the mature with ailments, I inevitably saw a good deal of him. He was the great-grandson of our erstwhile Revolutionary general of ill-fame, but far from being embarrassed by his ancestor's career he felt proud of his forefather's loyalty to the Crown by original oath. I suppose he was quite familiar with the text about the one sinner who repented being more valuable than the rest that went to perdition. Nevertheless, I felt it was significant that he was not enjoying an English parish, but perhaps he preferred travel. He asked many questions about the States and said he hoped some day to visit there. I privately hoped that he would travel incognito if he did and never dared tell him that our families had met before. One of my Revolutionary forebears had been captured by General Benedict Arnold, then fighting with Lord Dunmore in Virginia. General Arnold was anxious to learn from this prisoner what was the public sentiment towards him. The prisoner was reticent but when the general promised him not only immunity but release for an honest statement, the reply was, "Sir, we would bury with full military honors the noble leg that bears the honorable scars of Saratoga, but what we would do to the rest of your treasonable carcass, I leave to your imagination." Benedict Arnold made good his word and the young man made good his escape, but this was not a story I could pass on to his namesake. We parted very good friends.

Leaving Carlsbad we went on to Prague, and in the welter of sight-seeing there was one item of special interest. In an old monastery, I saw a theological work written, of course, in Latin by a priest called Barnhardt Baringer, in Frankfort, 1717, A.D. Remembering old Barnhardt at Mt. Pleasant who knew my great-grandfather, I felt these families must have known each other for many years.

Uncle Victor was somewhat concerned over the uncertain situation in Egypt and the increasing power of Arabi Pasha, who was leading a nationalist movement against the British and French financial administrators. His fears were well justified, for in 1882, after the massacre of several hundred foreigners as a result of an uprising for which Arabi Pasha was responsible, the British sent battleships and land forces and thus began their long occupation of Egypt. Judge Barringer's house was destroyed by British gunfire. He lost all his possessions, his library and his nearly completed work on "The Relation of Musselmen and Roman Law." Since all his rare reference works were also destroyed, he never attempted to reproduce this work. He was unable to return to the United States until 1894 and died in Washington two years later.

My uncle and aunt went on to Berlin, happily unaware of the extent of their impending misfortune, and I hastened to Vienna to resume my chosen studies.

XXXIII

A MEDICAL STUDENT IN VIENNA, 1881

THE GERMAN universities at this time were enjoying a freedom which unfortunately they have since lost. Although they were state institutions, the faculties had great academic freedom and the pupils an amazing range of choice in both subjects and instructors. Of course, knowledge of the prescribed subjects must be demonstrated by final examination, but it was a system very flexible for individual talent in teacher and in pupil. Added to this was the native capacity for exhaustive observation and meticulous record of phenomena. The German professor of distinction was not only the director of his own genius, but one able to recognize the specific abilities of his pupils and to direct these into creative observation. In this benign culture research flourished.

The outstanding discoveries in German medicine were by Virchow, the great pathologist in Berlin, whose cellular doctrine, "All cells from one cell" ("Omnia cellula e cellulo") was another milestone in medical history; Koch's revelation of the bacillus of tuberculosis in 1882; Laveran's discovery of the parasite of malaria in 1880; and Ludwig's research on the diseases of the circulatory system. The air was filled with discovery. It was not surprising that the idea of experiment seemed to dominate medicine in this time.

To synthesize these findings as an adjunct to medical practice, the first clinical laboratory for the diagnosis of disease was founded by Von Zeimssen in 1885 at Munich. This idea was followed by others, most notably in 1903 by Johns Hopkins University. By now systematic clinical classes are a part of every efficient medical school, with at least two years of premedical training in academic preparation, and no hospital could function without such a laboratory.

On my arrival in Vienna and before classes began, I heard that there was a call for volunteers of medical training to go down in Bosnia and Herzegovina to combat by vaccination an epidemic of smallpox. These were two provinces which had been Turkish but were now Austrian. Of the trip down and back, the less said the better. It was partly by train, partly by "diligence," as they call their stagecoaches, and partly by horseback and oxcart. The roads may have dated from Caesar but little had been done to them since his day. This was a section presumably comparable to our "backwoods," but in all my travels as a country doctor, I had never seen anything like it. We have in America no analogue to the European peasant, except possibly in some heavily populated portions of the "Black Belt." In some sections of Europe the peasant is little above the brutes. We had but one interpreter and a large mass of frightened people. Fortunately I saw a peasant father using the deaf-and-dumb sign language to his daughter. I spelt out a question in German and got a reply; then with my manual I was able to spell directions which he gave verbally to the others and this seemed to give them confidence. He was quite pleased and very proud, and so was I. Little had I thought that the poor Bingham boy's instruction would ever travel as far as this. After this visit into their provinces I could understand better the snail's pace of the European public mind. Our people may be ignorant, but they are not torpid, for all enjoy self-respect and hope.

The more I think of it the more I am forced to believe the American Constitution "a lucky hit" rather than the outgrowth of political science and thought. Not only was it ahead of its generation then, but it is yet far ahead of the old world.

I settled in Vienna near the Votiv-kirche and not far from the hospital. The room was comfortably fortified for the winter with double windows and an enormous porcelain stove, four feet square and six feet high. Coal was very dear, forty cents a bushel. The first days of new surroundings are always lonely; so when my former complaint, "the chills," dropped in upon me, they were not such bad company as they made me feel quite at home. Strange that English is the only language which has the word "home" in it. The others have merely words expressing a dwelling place. Winter descended rapidly, cold and wet, with fogs that rivalled London in blackness. An early cold snap made my clothing seem as light as a "Georgia Major's." All my surplus cash went into heavy woolens, so my pocketbook was reduced to the zero anticipated. A letter to Uncle Victor found him sailing for Egypt and as low in purse as I. He advised me to apply to Mr. Phelps, which I hated to do, but in a foreign country a broken man must act and that quickly. Mr. Phelps was most kind—as always.

Medicine in Vienna was not so noted for research as for its sound clinical teaching and study of the facts of disease during life and after death. Autopsies were practically routine. In addition, there were many short courses given which made about every phase of medicine available for the visiting student. The wealth of clinical material was so great that one could see in a month more cases of a disease than would be possible at home, even in a metropolitan hospital, for many years.

My professors at the University of Vienna were the distinguished surgeon, Baron Billroth, in Histology and Pathology; Dr. Herman Brehmer in the therapy of chronic tuberculosis; and Dr. Adam Politzer, known affectionately as "Old Politzer," the world famous aurist who is best known for his invention, the Politzer bag, which was used for blowing out the ears before the present mechanical devices came into existence.

In the whole city of over 1,000,000 inhabitants there was only one hospital but that was "kolossal." It filled up six squares solidly, each with a front of six hundred feet, streets not included. For the student, the beauty of the "Spital" was that it was not run for the sake of curing the patient but of instructing the student. Many things in practice seemed simply barbaric and would not be tolerated a day in America. I considered myself most fortunate to have had some years of medical practice, with the responsibilities and relationship of a physician, before studying abroad. Many of my associates had come on from one medical school to another and were less appraising in their point of view.

It was my opinion that the surgeons and physicians of Europe were far more learned and erudite than our own, but that we were better practitioners I was convinced. Any new principle which they elucidated was at first of likely benefit "over the ferry." The anchor of America is our practical application of the *end* (i.e., the welfare of the patient) to the *means* and not the reverse. Even then that gave us supremacy in everything except knowledge.

At least the non-survivors had magnificent funerals. Even the poorest had a guard of soldiers, gorgeous hearse, brass band, priests, boys in white, candle bearers, and lastly, the hired mourners who, even if the purse was ever so small, did their work with praiseworthy sincerity. Only seeing the same ones repeatedly made me realize they were professionals. The number of carriages, frequently empty, following the hearse defined the rank of the deceased, and the "zwei-spannen," or two-horse carriages, gave especial tone.

While the Viennese fulfilled their reputation for gaiety and charm, and their officials for courtesy and politeness, the obvious class distinctions I found very repugnant. Thanks to my uncle and his friends I met a great many more people (mostly likeable) than my fellow students; nevertheless I was quite aware that Americans were regarded as somewhat incomprehensible, slightly dangerous intruders whom the natives could not afford to exclude.

With the lower classes, however, our status was glorified. Merely to say that you were from the "Vereinigten Staaten von Nordamerika" brought smiles and bows as though an angel had descended. They never saw any Americans except the pleasure seekers who were always well dressed and educated, or appeared so, hence they believed that they had only to get to the U. S. A. to be transformed at once into a "tourist." The German peasant sees in you the transformed spirit of an uncle, son, or brother who has departed in search of a fortune, whereas the same spirit is probably still peddling matches or secondhand clothing in the Bowery.

The news of President Garfield's death on the nineteenth of September was published the morning after it occurred. The reaction in Vienna was most interesting. Our American idea of government was revolutionary on the Continent. They considered our country one inhabited by armed mobs who, when they got tired of one set, shot their governors and put in a new set. The tragic assassination of our President seemed a natural incident, but they could not understand how our country could function for so many months without a head. I do not think any European country could have done so. There is no doubt that confidence in our institutions was strengthened abroad by the quiet and patient manners of the American people under this affliction.

The semi-official organs, of course, cited the evils of republican institutions but the popular journals made the good point of posing the question, "If Emperor Francis Joseph I were dead, would Austrian bonds hold their own in the market?" The sense of sorrow in the city, especially among the laboring classes, was almost beyond belief. Mr. Phelps, the American minister, told me that working men would come to the Embassy in their blouses, ask for the minister, walk in, make a German bow, and blurt out in bad German that they had come to say they were sorry. The marble staircase in that residence did not deter them, and Mr. Phelps gave orders that no man who applied to see him should be turned away.

The poor apparently kept to themselves as in all the fine museums and parks which are the glory of Vienna I never saw any except the middle- and upper-classes. One of the papers stated, and from my short observation it seemed true, that the only time a stranger ever saw the rich and poor together was on "All Saints' Day," for them the "Day of the Dead." Big and little, old and young, rich and poor alike, all go to the great public cemetery, the Freidhof, which is considered the largest in Europe. All have lighted tapers and wreaths for decorating the graves of their families. From the widow's mite of a five cent taper to the blaze of light on an archduke's tomb, all was ablaze while the friends and family stood or knelt in silence. It was one of the most impressive sights I have ever seen.

The Kaiser, Franz Josef, as the Viennese called their Emperor, was a man of simple manners and taste and much beloved. The Empress Elizabeth, who was seldom there, was most unpopular and she appeared for only important occasions, such as took place on October twenty-seventh of this year. The whole city was decorated and every one in holiday mood and dress.

Humbert I, King of Italy, and his Queen Margherita made a visit of state to the Emperor and Empress of Austria. This was a visit of great political significance. In making it he quashed the hopes of the "Italia Irredentia" (Unredeemed Italy) party, headed by the physical and political successors of Garibaldi who claimed that a large slice of Austria belonged to Italy. Whatever the value of this visit was to him, it alienated France and England and met with the disapproval of Bismarck.

The culmination of several days of gayety was a military review. Mr. Phelps, as American Minister, had been assigned a box, but because of President Garfield's death he could not attend and was kind enough to present it to me. He warned me, however, that since this was a most important occasion, I would have to be most careful in my guests—extreme decorum and all that. After serious reflection, I decided that my medical compatriots might be a hazard, so I sat in lonely state. It was a spectacular affair, this military review of the armed might of Austria displayed for a monarch who was to be both honored and suitably impressed; a tribute both to and against him. It was a trifle singular to see many regiments which had been famous at Solferino file past the Italian King.

The cavalry, resplendent in plumes, polished brass trimmings, and drawn sabres, was most impressive. At last, the great moment arrived when the visiting majesty was to review a regiment on horseback. The mounting took place right under my box. On foot he was revealed as undersized and unimpressive, wearing some sort of shako built up with masses of cock feathers that tossed in the breeze. The charger which he was to mount, although no doubt well-trained for plumes and tassels, was terrified of the feathers which fluttered like a cockfight under his nose. Perhaps he suffered from some barnyard complex; anyway, the attendant officers struggled and each time the monarch approached, the horse would rear and wheel. It was obvious to my experienced eye that the visiting majesty was no great shakes as a horseman, and after watching this futile exhibition, I found myself shouting, "Take off your hat!" He may have understood English, at least he turned his head and shouted what sounded like "Not to a horse." In that brief moment however, the cock feathers were with the breeze and fell sleek and quiet. The horse calmed down, the monarch mounted, and the final review ended magnificently. I sat in the box in some anxiety for fear of a visit from the gendarmerie, but I think that all were grateful for the incident, and I was not called to account for shouting at a king.

Among the two hundred or more American students in Vienna that year, there were about a dozen Southerners, more than ever before. In fact, they nearly "captured the capital." Mr. Weaver, the Consul General, did much for us in the way of good company. There was a register where all signed their names and addresses, and fortunately a great many young American girls were in town. Every Sunday evening Mr. Weaver and his wife were "at home" with simple refreshments, conversation, and singing old familiar tunes, usually winding up with Moody and Sankey. These weekly evenings were a great boon to the homesick, and all of us were that on Thanksgiving Day and Christmas Eve. One great attraction was the Weavers' little girl, the pet of the American students who regarded her polyglot diction as miraculous. She spoke broken English, excellent French, and fair German. Of course, she was royally spoiled.

The innumerable saints' days of Catholic countries were most disrupting to study; all classes would be suspended, and all foreigners took a holiday. However, there was celebration, of a so-called local deity, that we attended heartily. Tradition had it that a certain lady of the house of Hapsburg, on the way to the altar, lost her wedding veil and would not be married until it was restored to her. Whether for reasons of romance or intrigue it never was found. She became a nun and founded the famous Kloster-Neuburg. From a patron, she became a saint. This *fête* was the three hundredth anniversary of founding, and thirty thousand Viennese went four miles out to the cloister, heard a mass, said an "Ave," and got drunk. The singular feature of this ceremony was that every devout soul had to slide down the side of "the Great Tun," an enormous cask which in the past was miraculously filled with choice wine once a year. Now the miracle would be to see it filled, but full or empty you must slide down, and with the Viennese, we slid too.

Unlike an American crowd, however, everybody drunk or sober was in a good humor and not "on his muscle," as might have been with us. We have the hardest population to control in the world, unless we except some parts of Ireland. There it never occurs to a man to break the law, but with us quite the reverse.

Ordinarily the social life of a student is very limited, but I was most fortunate. However, I found the constant dressing up with white gloves and all that very boring and hard on the purse. The intricacies of correct speech were also fatiguing. There were variations of greeting for every grade of rank. Even the waiter was a "Kellner" in a restaurant, a "Mayar" in a cafe, and a "Diener" elsewhere. Addressing tradespeople you recommended yourself "Ich empfehle mich," but with any of the large group, who have no calling and are classed as *cavaliere* it was to have the honor: "Ich habe die Ehre." They are most punctilious about these salutations. I solved this intricate problem, which would have taken a lifetime to master, by addressing everyone from my bootblack up in the highest rating. The "boots" thought I was quizzing him and Baron Billroth, one of my professors, I am sure classed me as what they called a Social Democrat or Communist. All the Germans used his title, but nearly all foreigners said, "Mein Herr" or "Sir." Since he was a Baron by inheritance and not by honor, he did not seem to mind.

The heart of Vienna is the old "Stadt," once a fortified town. Around this is a street built over the old moat called the Ringstrasse or Ring Street, about two hundred feet wide. It is the great boulevard of that city. At the Ring Theatre, on December eighth, there was a gala performance of "The Tales of Hoffmann" given to a capacity audience. Through an explosion of gas, the theatre was burned with great loss of life, and I had the experience of being an eye witness to what is still classed as one of the catastrophes of all time. Only by chance was I not in the audience as Baron Lapena, the Austrian Judge in Egypt and a friend of Uncle Victor's, had asked me to join him, but I was unable to accept. With a group of American students, I was at the Hôtel de France, an enormous hotel across from the theatre, where there was an American clerk and his room served as a general meeting place.

The theatre was lighted, of course, by gas. When the audience was seated the gas chandeliers were lowered and extinguished, and the footlights were to be lighted before the curtain was raised. Something went wrong when the footlights were turned on. Some say a pocket from a slow leak had formed above the stage and was ignited then; some say that the footlights did not ignite properly. Fortunately, I was not there to secure firsthand evidence. Whatever the cause, there was a terrible explosion which asphyxiated the spectators in the two upper galleries in their seats. Baron Lapena was in the vestibule, haggling over a wrong ticket with the clerk, when the people began to pour out of the auditorium, shouting, "Alles ist verloren, Alles ist verloren," "All is lost," and swept him into the street.

We Americans had rushed out at the sound of the explosion, and as the escaping crowd soon stopped, some of us went into the vestibule. The police said to come out as all were saved, and all waited impatiently for the fire department which was at least a half hour in coming. Just about this time the windows of a front balcony were broken, and people began to pour out, followed by smoke. This was the first sign of fire seen on the outside. We rushed for mattresses, et cetera, and as the height was not over twenty-five to thirty feet, those caught could jump without fatal risk. The few who came this way stated that there were hundreds in the galleries yet, alive and suffocating in the dark. This the police and firemen said was not true, that the informers were scared to death. No one went in (probably fearful of another explosion), and within the next week over four hundred bodies were taken from the upper galleries alone.

One match had saved the twenty or thirty people who jumped

A MEDICAL STUDENT IN VIENNA, 1881

from the balcony. A single light in the intricate stairways would have saved hundreds who in the darkness crushed each other to death, and those who escaped this were smothered. Over seven hundred were missing, so the figure could be put at that. [Editor's note: Official loss, eight hundred and fifty.] Not a soul will ever be punished as the officials said that those whose negligence caused the disaster were all burnt, but the consensus of public opinion is that it was the result of poor inspection, by poor police and a poor fire department.

I had dinner on New Year's Eve with Mr. and Mrs. Phelps. Because of President Garfield's death he had tendered his resignation and expected to return shortly, which was most unfortunate since he was a man of charm and ability. He was also a great admirer of the German character which we many times discussed. In the short time of residence he and his wife had been most popular, in every way distinguished representatives of our country, yet with a change of executive he was obliged to retire. I wish our country had a fixed foreign service. If it were so, it would appeal to me, but to be discarded as soon as you get your place warm would not be to my liking.

I too was pondering the future. My studies abroad had convinced me that there were good things of all lines to be learned in America and that the practical benefit of foreign study (except for special research) was not as great as I had anticipated. Also I decided that to apply what I had learned to medical practice, as I would find it in the section of America to which I would probably return, would be, except in a general way, well-nigh impossible.

On this intricate hypothesis I began to consider making my way homeward in a leisurely fashion through Italy and Spain, staying long enough in a Spanish-speaking country to perfect myself in the language which I had been studying for several months. Except for the newspapers and enough to travel by, I had discarded French as it would be of no use in America, but Spanish would be a needful tongue for Cuba, Mexico, and the rest of our hemisphere.

News of my father's ill-health made it imperative for me to return immediately; so, cancelling all plans for a southern trip,

I secured passage and sailed from Antwerp on the steamer *Rhynland*. This name seemed a strange and felicitous coincidence, and as we pulled out of the harbor, I thought again of my great-grandfather, John Paul Barringer, from what he had escaped, and what he had achieved for his descendants. Once more I was glad to be an American and homeward bound.

PART III
Postscript

XXXIV

DR. PAUL B. BARRINGER

D R. BARRINGER'S personal recollections ended with his return to America. In retrospect the achievements of his life did not interest him as had the preparation for it; hence this postscript. Beyond the basic outline of facts, the tributes and statements of his old students and associates have been used to complete the record.

In Charlotte he found the condition of his father's health too serious to consider leaving him. The problems of medical practice were the same as before. After contact with the world of research, experiment, laboratories, and hospitals the conditions of practice in a domestic setting posed the constant question for a better solution of human welfare. Southern education had been established on a classical basis and was still retarded by the years lost during the Civil War. The gap between this and the demands of the advancement of science in the field of medicine was obvious. In how to close or bridge this gap lay the answer to the question of how best to utilize his excellent training and experience.

This problem was not confined entirely to the South. Only in 1878 was the first course in Pathology, based on the classroom use of the laboratory microscope, given at Bellevue by Dr. William Henry Welch, and eight years later he introduced lectures on Bacteriology at Johns Hopkins University.

In 1882 at his first appearance before the North Carolina Medical Society, Dr. Barringer presented a paper on syphilis, a subject which he had studied in Paris and felt was a much neglected field in Southern practice. This was against the advice of the older physicians as that subject was taboo. At the same meeting he demonstrated the use of his laboratory microscope, and the interest in one seemed to outweigh the disapproval of the other. Nevertheless, many surprising patients appeared subsequently at his office, frequently by the dark of the moon.

In this same year he married Miss Nannie Irene Hannah, the youngest daughter of George Cunningham Hannah of "Gravel Hill," Charlotte County, Virginia. The Hannahs were of Scotch origin, staunch Presbyterians who settled in Lunenburg County, Virginia, about 1755. They are said to have come by way of Barbados, and tradition has it that one of them, a sea captain, assisted in evacuating the women and children from Yorktown during the Revolutionary War.

After practicing in Charlotte, Dr. Barringer accepted in 1886 the position at Davidson College of resident physician with the privilege of starting his own "Preparatory School for Medical Students." This was the long-desired opportunity to fill the gap between Southern education and modern science. He gave courses in Anatomy (on the cadaver), Histology (with the microscope), Physiology, and Biology. The collegiate courses in Physics and Chemistry were improved according to his direction, and the college also agreed to permit any students intending to study medicine to substitute Anatomy and Physiology as electives for college degrees, an early concession to premedical training. In a later year, such students were allowed to substitute selected portions of Hippocrates and Celsus as parallel reading in the Greek and Latin studies of their senior year.

Most of his students were graduates of Davidson College but some were from the U. S. Naval Academy, where in those days there was frequently a plethora of graduates and many were free to enter civil life. One naval student returned to the service and became Admiral Richard H. Jackson. There were two students in '86, eight in '87, fourteen in '88, and twenty-two in '89. Many of these students he sent to the University of Virginia, but more went to New York because Virginia lacked facilities for hospital experience.

In June of 1889, Dr. Barringer was invited to the University of Virginia to give an address at the dedication of the restored Jeffersonian building of the School of Medicine which had been destroyed by fire. On the same visit, at the request of Dr. Cabell who was retiring, he was invited to succeed him as Professor of Physiology and Surgery. This was an honor which touched him deeply and was accepted. General Barringer's health seemed well-established, and the improved railway facilities made the distance less, so he returned to his Alma Mater in September of that year.

At that time the University of Virginia numbered four hundred and eighty-two students, a faculty of twenty-one professors and ten instructors. The Medical School had a registration of one hundred and four students with a staff of four professors, two demonstrators in Anatomy, one instructor in clinical surgery, and one in clinical medicine. These last were local physicians whose services in teaching were the accepted practice of that time even in metropolitan hospitals.

The catalogue announcement had for several years mentioned "a hospital and clinical instruction," but in 1890 this was called a "cottage hospital." The facts were that there was in existence a small building of four rooms entitled the "Piedmont Hospital," built by the charitable ladies of the town for "the poor of the City of Charlottesville, of the county of Albemarle and the contiguous counties." This was situated about a mile from the University, down by the gas tanks, and was known colloquially as a "pesthouse." In consideration for some financial assistance, personally given by several interested members of the faculty, and professional assistance from the medical staff, their students were to receive clinical instruction based on these derelict and frequently malingering inmates. The fear, no doubt gratuitously inspired by the students, of becoming anatomical material for these same young "medics" ultimately blighted this enterprise with a vacuum of patients.

Following Dr. Cabell's method, Physiology was introduced by a series of outline lectures on Histology, but in 1890, for the first time there was work in the physiological laboratory with the microscope, in Practical Histology. A course in Hygiene was presented, and in the study of the Practice of Medicine optional classes were offered in practical Microscopy and Pathology. At the same time a two-year preparatory course for students of medicine was recommended, and in the second year of this training several of the regular medical subjects were covered which would relieve the strain of the arduous one-year program then prevailing.

In 1891 a two-year medical course was required, and a special course in Biology was given by the combined medical faculty. Next year there was a department of Medical Biology teaching Histology, Bacteriology, and later Embryology. By 1895 the required medical course was three years, and in 1898 the present four-year course was instituted. Ophthalmology and Urology had been added, and the faculty had grown to six professors and fourteen demonstrators and assistants. An accredited medical course now carried the many subjects which had formerly been acquired by extensive study and travel; the laboratory work and clinical experience were considered an essential daily background.

The old store which had been used as a medical dispensary was discarded when the first University Dispensary, which included an out-patient clinic, was built in 1895. Its opening year 1200 patients were cared for, but there was still no hospital or nursing staff except that of the college infirmary.

Under Dr. Barringer's direction, the recurrent problem of typhoid was met by a drastic check on the University water supplies, the capping of all open springs and wells on the grounds, and the supervision and enforcement of the necessary sanitary regulations off the campus wherever students boarded or milk for their use was provided. This was a most unpopular innovation with many of the inhabitants but laboratory analysis revealed infection in some beautiful historic springs and valued cold wells.

The State Board of Health, founded in 1872 under Dr. Cabell's direction, had languished for lack of legislative appropriation. After seven years of attrition, the board resigned in a body. In 1893, when fear of Asiatic cholera was current, the board was revived and Dr. Barringer was appointed a member. For this emergency he wrote a pamphlet on cholera, indicating preventive measures, for general distribution.

At that time there was no oculist in Charlottesville for the student body or the residents. Trips to Richmond, Lynchburg, or Washington were expensive and tedious, so Dr. Barringer opened an office for this purpose. This practice was soon so successful that, although highly profitable, he felt it was requiring more time than his other obligations would permit; and so it was ultimately turned over to a former student who had studied in this field.

Early in 1895, General Rufus Barringer died at his home in Charlotte where he had returned after being a patient at the Johns Hopkins Hospital, then coming to the front in modern medical practice.

On Sunday morning, October 27, 1895, the University was devastated by a catastrophic fire which the primitive fire equipment was unable to control. Fanned by a high wind it burned out the Rotunda, the crowning glory of the "academic village," and also the classrooms and public hall which were in the Annex, an ugly four-story building attached to it. This unparalleled tragedy was thought a body blow to the institution but by the afternoon, arrangements were made for the erection of temporary lecture rooms, laboratories, and a working library. No lectures were lost in any department. In the following June of 1896, Dr. Barringer was elected Chairman of the Faculty by his colleagues, and this executive position, in spite of frequently tendered resignations, was confirmed annually by the Board of Visitors until his firm retirement in June 1, 1903.

These were exceedingly full and difficult years. In addition to the teaching responsibilities of his professorship, which carried as well three months of duty as college physician, there was the increasingly heavy executive work as Chairman of an expanding University. The funds contributed after the calamitous fire were used for the restoration, under the architectural direction of Mr. Stanford White, of the Rotunda, the building of an academic hall, auditorium, and two flanking buildings for Physics and Engineering, enclosing Mr. Jefferson's Lawn.

Rubble brick from the Annex of the Rotunda was used for the more permanent construction and enlargement of the University Dispensary. This building now included a waiting room, operating amphitheater, drugroom, three examination rooms, with quarters for resident internes upstairs. The additional space was desperately needed as the annual attendance was then over three thousand patients, and by 1901 it had reached twelve thousand. The need for a hospital was imperative.

One of the architects of the new Congressional Library, Mr. Paul J. Pelz, was willing to draw up the plans, for a slender fee, on the chance that the building would take place. Although the Board of Visitors had given permission for solicitations for this purpose, funds were slow in acquisition. One donor withdrew a subscription of $1,000 because she would be contributing to a "pesthouse on the University grounds," but another Virginia woman, Mrs. Nancy Langhorne Shaw, later Lady Astor, gave the first $600 which made possible the excavation of space for a foundation. This empty space, which waited two years for the building to cover it, filled with rains and was dubbed "Barringer's Frog Pond." In 1901, however, the first building of the University of Virginia Hospital was completed in which all functions of a hospital were incorporated, "Omnia cellula e cellulo."

As a teaching hospital the greater space was given to wards for white and colored patients who provide that voluntary clinical material which is the life of a medical school. The private rooms were few and simple. Quarters were also provided for a group of student nurses who were trained by the chief nurse, Miss Florence Besley, in addition to her other duties. The staff of Negro orderlies was headed by Stuart Fuller, now doorman and major-domo, the only surviving veteran of the original personnel.

Additional flanking buildings were added in the next two years. Since then the development has gone steadily on to the present Medical Center of five hundred beds, one pavilion of which carries its founder's name. Like all teaching hospitals, it serves the suffering public of every race, creed, and color. It carries an annual attendance of approximately fifteen thousand bed patients while the out-patient department has expanded to nearly

61,000 per year. It draws not only from every county in the state of Virginia but has patients from nearly all other states of the Union and from as far south as Argentina and as far west as Hawaii.

To Dr. Barringer's share in establishing this great hospital, the late Dr. Roy K. Flannagan paid the following tribute:

"Dr. Paul B. Barringer will deserve to be remembered at the University of Virginia throughout time as the father and, I may say, nursemaid, and in the truest sense the founder of our University Hospital. For he started it from literally nothing and accomplished its erection under the most deeply discouraging circumstances of the ridicule and reactionary conservatism of those who would apparently keep the old school just as Jefferson built it, even if the University had to shrivel as a consequence in the competition of a modern world. Jefferson was no conservative— no real builder ever is. That hospital, small as it was in its beginnings, saved Virginia's Medical School—the capstone of its University's glories, and to Paul B. Barringer goes full credit for his indefatigable and successful efforts in demonstration of the possibility of building a clinic there. Dr. Barringer's vigorous handling of the situation of the University, following the fire of 1895 that destroyed the Rotunda and so much of its teaching property, his refusal to be discouraged—rallying its Alumni, renewing its spirit, rapidly finding the money and rebuilding, furnished a stimulus that from that day to this has never flagged. ...He was an heroic figure in a time when a man of heroic stature was needed."

His interests ranged far beyond the bounds of his profession or of his University. He felt strongly his obligation as a citizen. The problems facing the Negro race in making the adjustment from their prewar status to American citizenship were of deep and abiding concern, and he made numerous addresses on this subject.

When the Tri-State Medical Society was formed, he had advised that since each state, North and South Carolina and Virginia, had its own medical society which covered the general needs of practice, this new organization should devote the first day of its meeting to some subject of broad general interest to the profession—such as, the general increase in inebriety and nervous diseases, the problems of the Negro race, or other factors in public health. By request he read in February of 1900 a paper on the influence of heredity in the Negro entitled "The American Negro: His Past and Future." In March of the same year, before the Southern Educational Board, he presented "The Sacrifice of a Race," an analysis of the alarming vital statistics of this transplanted people. He stated, "The history of the Negro as a race is one of profound pathos."

This was followed in 1901 by "Negro Education in the South," given before the Southern Educational Association in Richmond, Virginia. Observing that the total status of the South was inseparable from the status of 40 per cent of its population, the Negro race, he warned against the increasing sentiment for assigning to Negro education only what he produced as a taxpayer as economically unwise and unworthy of the South. "It would be better to double the subscription and get better teachers... base his franchise upon property qualification and give ... a legitimate stimulus to work.... Let us make the taxpayer and not the politician the racial ideal. The temptation to spend is inherent in the human race; to learn to save is to cultivate man's highest power, the power of inhibition." When this address was published in *The Educational Review* of that year, the editor, Dr. Nicholas Murray Butler, wrote him that he considered it "the most statesmanlike contribution since the [Civil] War."

In 1901 Dr. Barringer accepted an invitation from the Chicago Club to meet with the Negro leader, Booker T. Washington, in a discussion of this problem. The following letter, hitherto unpublished, reveals the tenor of this meeting:

"Grand Union Hotel
New York City
March 13, 1901

"Dr. P. B. Barringer
University of Virginia
Charlottesville, Virginia
"My dear Sir:
"Since we met in Chicago I have thought much concerning

your earnest words, and the more I consider what you have said, the more I am sure that on the vital points connected with the elevation of our race, there is not so much difference between us as I feared there was. I am very anxious to get better acquainted with you and your views. I feel that in working together we can accomplish much towards the solution of the problem which is so dear to the hearts of all of us. The whole matter weighs upon me heavily day and night.

"The suggestion which you made of a conference between Northern and Southern people where the whole matter can be studied, not from a sentimental standpoint, but where the cold, hard facts can be carefully weighed, will accomplish much good, and I hope that you can see your way clear to encourage such a conference.

"I have asked my publishers to send you a copy of my book, 'Up from Slavery,' which I hope you will find time to glance through.

"Yours truly,
Booker T. Washington"

In the field of general education Dr. Barringer realized the profound necessity of university leadership. Addressing the Accomac Teacher's League in 1900, he advised that "when one considers that for every hundred boys of college age in America, but one is in college ... and in the South a still smaller proportion, we must see that the end [of education] is not yet reached. Our colleges and schools must grow and develop to meet the coming demand, which is as certain as the continued growth of this country."

The School Review, edited by the School of Education of the University of Chicago, in the December, 1902, number reported:

"There is no State in the Union that has been evincing such an interest in education during the past year as the 'Mother of Presidents.' The meeting of the Constitutional Convention made it necessary that the educational interests should be thoroughly investigated and the best parts conserved. This discussion has borne fruit, and one of the best and most statesmanlike utterances has just been made by Professor Paul B. Barringer, Chairman of the Faculty of the University of Virginia. The opening and closing paragraphs are specially interesting and will give our readers a fairly adequate idea of the prospects for better and higher education in Virginia.

"'I take the position regarding the public schools of Virginia that there is but one course that can offer hope for this State, and that is a complete, general, non-sectarian system of education, such as was proposed by Mr. Jefferson one hundred and twenty-five years ago—a system of elementary schools, a complete system of public high schools or academies, and a University. This is exactly the system which has made the States of the North and West what they are today in wealth and power, and it has been the lack of such an educational machine which has caused Virginia to drop from her one-time position of primacy in wealth and influence to the position which she now occupies—some twenty-five from the top in a total of forty-five states.

"'I believe in changing the University to fit the public schools, and changing the public schools to fit the University. Let us have an organic connection throughout the whole, so that a stimulus applied at any part will be felt throughout the whole system. When this is done, Virginia will once more take her natural place in the galaxy of states, and will prosper as she never has prospered before. The spirit of Jefferson is here, and here will come the strong, the virile, and the free. The University will shine as a city that is set upon a hill, and all things will turn toward the light.'"

Of this period Dr. William A. Lambeth, a former student and for many years an associate as professor of Hygiene, stated that "his creative talent and power of organization largely effected the present coordinated relation existing between the public schools and the University.... The changes in the material equipment of that institution from one-half million dollars to one million dollars tested Dr. Barringer's abilities as a financier... and here again he was equal to the occasion....Perhaps no one individual has been called upon for effective work in so many fields, teaching, executive, disciplinary, all complicated by delicate relationships and rendered difficult by custom and indefinite responsibilities and authority.

"When Chairman of the Faculty two great results marked his efforts; the organic connection of that institution with the public school system and the creation of the present Hospital of the University of Virginia."

He felt definitely that the Arts and Sciences were above politics and should bear no intrusion from this field. With the increase of grants of money from foundations, state and federal sources, this was not an easy policy to maintain. The need for assistance was great, but the question of ultimate freedom in appointments and policies was a primary consideration to be most carefully guarded.

Despite the demands of professional life, he never lost his boyhood interest in natural science. When President Theodore Roosevelt was the guest of the University in 1902, he and Dr. Barringer found a mutual interest in the crossbreeding of cattle for the perfection of a hardy far-ranging type or, better still, the domestication of adapted types of animals useful to man in a similar environment. This letter from South Africa, where after his retirement, President Roosevelt was big-game hunting, is written in pencil on yellow paper and contains a suggestion which, despite its hypothetical value, has probably remained speculative:

North of Kenia
September 10, 1909

Dear Mr. Barringer,
All right, I'll pay special heed to the elands; they surely ought to be domesticated; their ordinary habitat is like the southern great plains of our West.

Sincerely yours,
Theodore Roosevelt

His early fondness for snakes was shared with Dr. Howard A. Kelly of the Johns Hopkins University whose first scientific training was as a naturalist. In 1902 Dr. Barringer published a monograph on "The Poisonous Reptiles of the United States, and the Treatment of Their Bites" which is still a classic. One of his students is the well-known herpetologist, Colonel Martin L. Crimmins, Inf., U. S. A., who carried his knowledge of snake venom into the realm of medical therapeutics.

Early in his life, the Marine Hospital Service had been considered as a career, and Dr. Barringer had watched its growth into the Public Health Service with close attention as an infinite field for scientific usefulness. In 1798 Congress had authorized a Marine Hospital Service to provide medical care for sick and disabled American seamen. The first such hospital was built at Norfolk, Virginia, in 1800, the second at Boston, in 1802, and later others were added at important sea and lake ports. Naturally the medical officers stationed at these hospitals were the first to encounter epidemic diseases such as cholera, yellow fever, and smallpox coming in from other countries. This same year the Marine Hospital Service was granted authority by Act of Congress to cooperate with the local health associations in the control of disease which led to official quarantine regulations. This authority was increased in 1893 to assist in controlling from state to state the spread of all factors inimical to human health. By 1902 an hygienic laboratory was established in Washington for the increasingly necessary research, and the name was changed to Public Health and Marine Hospital Service. In 1912 authority over the pollution of navigable streams and lakes was added to the diseases of man, and the name was abbreviated to the Public Health Service. Two successive chiefs of this service were former students of Dr. Barringer, Surgeon General Rupert Blue and Surgeon General Hugh S. Cumming.

Late in life, at the age of sixty-one and in retirement, Dr. Barringer was most grateful to be called into active duty by the Public Health Service during World War I. This was to fight influenza and typhoid among the coal miners of western Virginia in order to keep up the production necessary for war. Whatever other honors had come his way, in his old age none was more valued than a card from the Surgeon General, a routine token of appreciation thanking him for this patriotic assistance and signed by one of his "old boys," Hugh S. Cumming.

Preventive medicine he saw was a field of increasing importance. In this connection he had written in 1903 concerning "An Unappreciated Source of Typhoid Infection," in which he called attention to the appalling infection of railroad tracks by the elementary system of human waste disposal which in turn polluted the watersheds of our cities and towns. The Pennsylvania Railroad had this article printed for distribution among its employees and made drastic changes in its methods of disposal.

Dr. Barringer lived to see this dread disease, with which the hospital had been largely filled in previous summers, become so rare, except in the rural districts, that it was possible for medical students to graduate without the experience of seeing a single clinical case.

By 1903 the University had increased to six hundred and fifty students, with a faculty of twenty-nine professors and thirty instructors. Desiring to be relieved of the increasing burden of executive work, Dr. Barringer retired from the faculty chairmanship in order to devote himself to the further development of the Medical School which now numbered one hundred and sixty-four, approximating its highest registration; he also wished to take up the research necessary to rewrite his textbook on Physiology which, published in 1894, he knew was imperatively in need of revision and development.

In the Chairman's annual report to the Board of Visitors, tendering his resignation, he recommended the continuance of the "school" system as having produced superior work from professor and student and which, with the honor system, had made it possible for the University to face competition on a lower financial allowance than other institutions. He advised the creation of deans at additional salaries to assist in the discipline and organization necessary to the increasing student body.

With the growth of the University and the increased academic expansion in relation to the general education of the state, the Board of Visitors decided at last to make a long considered change in Thomas Jefferson's system of organization. After the chairmanship of Professor James Morris Page for one year, Dr. Edwin Anderson Alderman, President of Tulane University, was elected the first president of the University of Virginia in 1904.

Dr. Barringer's plans for writing and research, however, were interrupted. Unfortunately a reputation as an executive is hard to discard, and in 1907 he accepted the presidency of Virginia Polytechnic Institute at Blacksburg, Virginia. As the State Agricultural and Mechanical College, there was great scope for scientific contribution. There he gradually brought the entrance requirements to the fourteen Carnegie Units, fortified the B. S. courses in all the technical schools, and enlarged the Agricultural Department. He also advocated the surrender of those B. A. and M. A. degrees which were based on classical courses as he felt they duplicated, at the expense of the state, similar courses which were being given at the University. He was an early advocate of dairying as a solution for Virginia's agricultural problems, and the emphasis which he laid on the improved breeding of milk cattle and the corollary plant and grass breeding has been a development of financial value to the State.

When Lord Bryce, the British Ambassador, was invited to address the National Agricultural Union, meeting at Raleigh, North Carolina, in 1909, Dr. Barringer was asked by Bennehan Cameron, President of the State Fair, to give the "Response from the South." After the usual oratorical amenities, he described the new era of the South, saying, "Our poverty is passed and the days of prosperity are close at hand... and to whom is this prosperity due? It is due to the heroic efforts of the survivors of the late war and the youth now grown to manhood who were trained under them. What have these our people done? They have lifted a war scarred and blasted section, in the chaos of subverted social order, and they have done all this by working out their own problems in their own way."

After six busy and effective years at this institution, where he cemented more completely its connection with the Departments of Agriculture of the state and the nation, he retired to his country place near Charlottesville. There, after establishing a dairy farm, he led the busy life of a private citizen.

Retirement was a word without meaning for a man of his temperament. The capacity for physical endurance had necessarily become less, but the mental horizon remained for as Hall said of him, "his mind ranged... the universe in search of the varied knowledge that would satisfy his innate yearning to know. He was interested in the earth and in what grows out of it; but most of all in his fellow mortal, who lives upon the spheroid terra; in his origin, in his behavior, in his aspirations and in his destiny. The years did not enroll him amongst the decrepits; he remained forever young, and his spirit dwelt among the young and their unfolding minds.... He brought by inheritance and by inculcation all that was best of the antebellum South into the self-assertive new day.... He did not repine for the dear...dead days; his heart was in the present and in the unfolding future."

By training and experience he had preceded the day of the specialist—although he recognized the imperative and valued the evolution of that type of mind and its proper training in response to the demands of modern medicine and modern science.

A most companionable father, he gave much time and close attention to the education and development of his children. It was a large family: six sons, Rufus, Paul Brandon, George Hannah, Victor Clay, Thomas Cunningham, and John; and four daughters, Anna Maria, Margaret, Eugenia Morrison, and Alma Worth. When they were grown and scattered, finding the management of so large a place too arduous, he moved closer to his beloved University.

There although an old man he was constantly in touch with a group of young students, medical and otherwise, who daily stopped by for a chat about their problems or some angle of development in thought or experiment that Dr. Barringer might suggest. Always preferring the out-of-doors to the confines of any house, he sat by preference under a favorite white oak tree, at all hours and in all weathers, pipe in hand, holding an open forum for youth.

This companionship was not reserved for human beings only. He possessed a profound reverence for the right to existence and dignity of every living creature—a friendship with life which made him a true citizen of the world; and beyond, this affection extended to the stars, whose place and arrival, even when sight had failed, he knew with unfailing accuracy, "old friends that will never fail."

The enjoyment of life transcended old age which was met with humor and philosophy. The following extract from one of his occasional ventures into rhyme shows both qualities:

This hardly noticed change of view,
This mild distrust of ventures new,
This growing urge to hoard the coin,
These sometimes twinges 'bout the loin,
    Can this be Age, the foe?

This growing tendency to sit
And dream, of days when I was fit
To do—and did—the work of ten,
These reveries of "now" and "then,"
    Can this be Age, so soon?

This drawing nearer to the wife,
This lessening desire for strife,
This holding fast to friends of old,
This treating strangers "much too cold,"
    Can this be Age, that comes?

I see no sudden change of state,
No red mark in life's book of fate,
But many things, each as a feather,
All show, when balanced up together,
    That this is Age, that's here.

    * * * * * *

But mark you, Age, you silent hound,
That thought, unknown, to run me down,
Not quite so fast—don't cut across,
You trail at heel, I'm still the boss,
    To heel, Old Age, come along!

On the philosophic side, one of his most charming essays entitled "Our Old Friend Death," defined his acceptance of finality:

"Death, the real, the ultimate, the inevitable, is but a conservative factor in the final evolution of all living things, and as such should not be and is not dreaded when it comes at the proper hour and in a natural form.

"The old tree posed on its decaying roots, awaiting the storm for its fall, has no fear of the crash nor the decay which is to follow.

"The old worn beast of the field which feels the approach of death seeks out some dark, cool, and comfortable but isolated spot, and there quietly and seemingly with contentment, awaits the inevitable end.

"The old man, the fires of youth burnt out, the appetites of life largely satiated, slowly and complacently withdraws himself within the bounds of a special kingdom called old age and awaits, with anticipation rather than fear, the final flicker of the spark in the embers of life. . . .

"It is an end, natural, legitimate and right. . . . Death will come . . . as a friend."

A man of peace, the only one in the successive generations of his family who had never borne arms in combat, he lived to see his grandsons begin their preparation for service in World War II. On January 9, 1941, came the "awaited friend." His wife survived him by three years.

Whatever may have been the achievements in his calling as a physician or scientist or executive, he would prefer to be remembered as a teacher of men; and so one of his "old boys" best describes him:

"To listen to Dr. Barringer and to watch his vivid chalk illustrations, ranging from the mysteries of modern plumbing to the distribution of the vagus nerve, grow out on the blackboard, was an experience never to be forgotten. He had the facility of making his words live before the eyes, exhibiting the talent of a born teacher, words tapestried with anecdote and humorous allusions from history, literature and rich colorful experience. His genius as a teacher impressed me most and stands out in my mind ahead of any other aspect of his truly distinguished career, beyond even that of his great administrative ability. Fine administrators are more or less plentiful; teachers of Dr. Barringer's quality, in my experience, have been scarce."

To discover and direct responsive young men of talent is the hope of every devoted scientist, and his reward is in their success. Such men, however, have marked themselves for fame; there are others whose abilities are not so assured. Out of his own rich experience in living and generous understanding, he had the perception, sometimes in the face of academic disapproval, to see that the vital and frequently nonconformist student possessed qualities of value; that frequently innate curiosity and a capacity for adventure, when directed into the proper fields, could lead to creative production and the leadership of men. These individualists, many of them now men of renown, whom space prevents from defining by name, are scattered all over the country in various callings. Their profound affection and constant correspondence kept him in touch with his and their expanding world. Dr. Hall states truly that:

"The college student who occupied no place in 'Old Paul B.'s' charitable esteem did not belong in student life.... The relationship existing between him and his students was highly personal —a spiritual state—that is disappearing from all school life, to the impoverishment of the student and the teacher. In the hundreds of former students, the spirit of 'Paul B.' will shine as noble influence forever, for the great teacher becomes always one of the world's immortals."

INDEX

ABBOTT, Judge, 42
Abram, 26, 27, 29, 94
Alcohol, 81-82, 189-90
Alderman, Edwin Anderson, 269
Allison, "Wash," 40, 82
Allison family, 82, 154
Alston, Lavinia M., 78
Ambroselli, 209
"American Negro: His Past and Future, The," 264
Anatomy, Wilson's, 221
Anderson, Jimmy, 45
Andrews, Alexander Boyd, 79
Arabi Pasha, 242
Arnold, Benedict, 241-42
Arnold, General Benedict, 242
Atkins, Smith, 109
Atlantic, Tennessee, and Ohio Railroad, 71-73
Audubon, John J., 89
Avery, Alphonso C., 16, 17
Avery, Hattie, 93
Avery, Susan Morrison, 6, 16, 17, 36, 71

BACHMAN, John, 70, 88-91, 161, 183, 193, 207
Baird, Spencer F., 161, 183
Baldwin, Mary, 186
Baringer, Barnhardt, 242
Barkley, Alben, 218
Barksdale, Lena, v
Barnhardt family, 22
Barringer, Alma Worth, 271
Barringer, Anna Maria, 271

Barringer, Anna Morrison, 4, 8, 35, 63, 82, 93, 186
Barringer, Anne Cucullu, 105
Barringer, Betty, 45
Barringer, Catherine Blackwelder, 146
Barringer, Daniel L., 41
Barringer, Daniel Moreau, 41, 78, 80, 81
Barringer, Daniel Moreau, Jr. (Dick), 80, 164-65, 167, 235
Barringer, Elizabeth Brandon, 4
Barringer, Elizabeth Eisemann, 144-45
Barringer, Elizabeth Weathered, 80
Barringer, Ella, 79
Barringer, Eugenia Morrison (mother of P. B.), 4, 16, 24, 73-74
Barringer, Eugenia Morrison (daughter of P. B.), 271
Barringer, George Hannah, 271
Barringer, John (son of P. B.), 105, 271
Barringer, John (cousin of P. B.), 78, 79
Barringer, John (son of "Pioneer Paul"), 145
Barringer, John Paul ("Pioneer Paul"), 21-23, 87, 124, 143-46, 237
Barringer, Katie, 45
Barringer, Lavinia Alston, 78
Barringer, Lewin Weathered, 80
Barringer, Lizzie, 80
Barringer, Margaret, 271
Barringer, Margaret Long, 82, 141, 142, 163

Barringer, Maria Massey, 5, 33, 43, 46, 70, 83, 100, 102, 106, 125, 137 ff., 238, 241, 243
Barringer, Nannie Irene Hannah, 258
Barringer, Paul (grandfather of P. B.), 4, 81
Barringer, Paul (cousin of P. B.), 79
Barringer, Paul Brandon, Jr., 271
Barringer, Rosalie Chunn, 17, 33, 70
Barringer, Rosie, 80
Barringer, Rufus, marries Eugenia Morrison, 4; letter from Federal prison, 111-14; returns from prison, 114; serves in the Confederate Army, 115-24; Civil War letters, 116-17, 117-19; interview with Lincoln, 121-23; mentioned, 23, 141, 142, 151, 163, 179, 193, 194, 233, 253, 261
Barringer, Rufus (son of P. B.), 271
Barringer, Thomas Cunningham, 271
Barringer, Victor (cousin of P. B.), 79
Barringer, Victor Clay (uncle of P. B.), 5, 40-47, 61, 74-75, 77, 80, 82, 83, 86, 88, 90, 99, 100, 102, 106, 109, 125, 130, 142, 238, 241, 242, 243, 246
Barringer, Victor Clay (son of P. B.), 271
Barringer, William, 78-79
Barringer, William, Jr., 79
Baseball, origin of, 127-29
Bassinger, Kate, 6
Bates, Mr., 103
Baths (watering places), 177
Battle, Cornelius, 231
Battle, Elisha, 231
Battle brothers, 154
Bayard, Jim, 182
Bechtler, Christopher, 88
Bechtler gold pieces, 57, 88, 125
Bees, 48
Bell, Alexander Graham, 215-16
Benjamin, Judah P., 102-4
Bernard, Claude, 240
Besley, Florence, 262
Billroth, Theodor, 246
Bingham, Belle Worth, 152
Bingham, Dr., 34, 85
Bingham, Robert, 152, 166, 167
Bingham, Robert Worth, 152
Bingham, William, 151 ff., 165, 166
Bingham's School, 151 ff., 202, 207
Birds of North America, 161, 183
Black, Clausell, 126
Blackwelder, Catherine, 146

Blockade, effects of, 48 ff.
Boeck, Leopold C., 204-5
Borden brothers, 154
Boston, visit to, 140
Boutwell, Judge, 42
Branding, of murderer, 86
Brandon, Elizabeth, 4
Breckinridge, John C., 102, 104
Brehmer, Herman, 246
Brevard, Alexander, 10
Brickmaking, 57-59
Brock, Dr., 180, 187
Brown, John Edmunds, 16
Brown, Laura Morrison, 16
Bryce, Lord, 270
Blue, Rupert, 268
Bull Run, General Barringer's letter from, 38-39
Burns, Uvalde, 187
Burton, General, 4, 96
Butler, Nicholas Murray, 264

CABARRUS, Stephen, 23
Cabarrus County, formed in 1793, 23
Cabell, James Lawrence, 206-7, 217, 219-20, 230, 259, 260
Callithump, 196
Cameron, Bennehan, 270
Camp meeting, 135-36
"Can This Be Age?" 272
Carter, Henry Rose, 217
Chalmers, Colonel, 241
Charcot, Jean Martin, 240
Charlottesville Chronicle, The, 223
Cheek, Colonel, 116, 118
Chemistry, study of, 203
Cherokee Indians, 37, 167
Chesapeake, 219
Chess game, with Jefferson Davis, 100
Chunn, Mr., 69-70
Chunn, Rosalie, 17, 33, 70
Chunn family, 37
Clavin, Ned, 171
Clay, Henry, 41
Cock fighting, 79, 168-74, 210-11
Collis, Charles H. T., 121, 123
Concord, early village of, 4-5
Confederate Navy Yard, 97
Cook brothers, 153
Coon hunting, 182
Cotton gin, 31-32
Coues, Elliott, 161
Coxe, Mr., 70
Crew, University of Virginia, 226, 229
Crimmins, Martin L., 267

INDEX

Cruveilhier, Jean, 221
Cucullu, Anne, 105
Cucullu, Ernest, 104-5
Cumming, Hugh S., 268

DABNEY, Charles, 200
Darby, John T., 232
Darwin, Charles, 4, 220, 230
Davidson, Isabella, 14
Davidson, William Lee, 19
Davidson College, founding of, 19-20
Davis, Jefferson, 94, 98-101
Davis, John Staige, 220, 221, 228
Deaf-mute alphabet, 153
"Death, Our Old Friend," 272-73
Derr family, 22
De Vere, M. Schele, 206
Dialect, Negro, 65-66
"Diking up," 208
Dixie Cookery, 137
Dublin, hospitals, 235; zoo, 235-37
Duelling, 210
Duke, Washington, 163-64
Dunnington, Francis P., 203

EDINBURGH, clinic visited, 237
Educational Review, The, 264
Eisemann, Elizabeth, 144
Elizabeth, Empress, 249
Ellen, Little, 100
Ellen, Old, 99, 106
Emerson, Ralph Waldo, 211-12
English, study of, 158
Europe, travel in, 233-54
Evans, General, 241
Exodus, quoted, 62
Explosives, making of, 53

FANNING, David, gang of, 145
Fillmore, President, 81
First Corinthians, quoted, 62
First North Carolina Cavalry, 34-35, 38, 115, 116
Fish, Hamilton, 41, 42
Flannagan, Roy K., tribute to Dr. Barringer, 262; mentioned, vi
Flint, Austin, 232
Flints, 49
Foard, Hiram, 82, 83, 126
Foard, Noah, 82, 141
Foote, H. I., 119-20
Forney, Peter, 10, 133
Fournier, Alfred, 240
Fox, Doctor, 34
Franz Josef, Kaiser, 249

Fraternities, at University of Virginia, 198
Fuller, Stuart, 262

GARFIELD, President, death of, 248
Gaslight, 8
Gauge, railroad change of, 191-92
Gibson, Doctor, 83
Gibson, Mattie, 83-84
Gildersleeve, Basil, 206
Gold, discovery of, in North Carolina, 88
Gordon, Armistead C., Jr., vi
Gordon, Colonel, 116
Graham, Eliza Ann, 101
Graham, Isabella Davidson, 14
Graham, John, 146
Graham, Joseph, 10, 13-14, 132, 133, 134, 179
Graham, Mary, 4, 7, 20, 24, 134
Graham, William A., 20-21, 43, 80, 88, 166
"Great Snow of 1857," 3
Greeley, Horace, 141
Grier, Margaret Barringer, 45

HALL, James K., tribute to Dr. Barringer, 274; mentioned, vi
Hall, Will, 126
Hamburg, visit to, 237
Hampton, Wade, 79
Hannah, Cunningham, 258
Hannah, Nannie Irene, 258
Hannah, Ruth, 104
Harris, Betty Barringer, 45
Harris, Edwin, 45
Harris, Lydia, 90
Harris, Wade, 126
Harrison, Burton H., 100, 101
Harrison, Fairfax, 101
Harrison, James P., 193-94, 211, 222-23
Hayes, Rutherford, 216, 222-23
Herndon, William Lewis, 21
Hill, Daniel Harvey, 17, 73, 168
Hill, Eugenia, 73
Hill, Harvey, 8
Hill, Isabella Morrison, 8, 16, 71, 73, 74
Hill, Joe, 73
Hill, Randolph, 73
Hilliard, Billy, 37
Hog killing, 30-31
Hoke family, 27
Holmes, George L., 206
Hughes brothers, 154
Humbert I, 249-50

Hunter, Doctor, 93
Hunter, Humphrey, 26

IRWIN, Harriet Morrison, 5, 17, 74
Irwin, James, 17, 71, 72
Irwin, John, 71, 72, 95-97
Itch, 47

JACKSON, Anna Morrison, 6-8, 16, 70, 73, 74, 93-94, 96
Jackson, Julia, 70, 93
Jackson, Mary Graham, 6
Jackson, Richard H., 258
Jackson, "Stonewall," letters of, 6, 68-69; mentioned, 6, 7, 8, 17, 73, 92, 132, 133, 134
James River and Kanawha Canal, 7, 229
Jefferson, Thomas, 194, 195, 200, 201, 202, 204, 209, 226, 266, 269
Jefferson Debating Society, 199, 211, 225
Jeffersonian Republic, The, 223
Jerry, 81
Johnston, Albert Sidney, 26, 30
Johnston, Joseph E., 98, 102, 104
Johnston, Sidney, 26, 59
Johnston, William, 101, 103
Johnston, William Preston, 100
Jones, Doctor, 230
Jones, Horace, 181

KELLY, Howard A., 267
Kenmore University School, 177 ff., 202
Keyes, Edward L., 232
King's Highway, 10
Kinsolving, Mrs. Lucien L., v
Kirkpatrick, Reverend, 61
Kirk's Tories (Kirk's Lambs), 69
Koch, Robert, 226, 239, 244

LACY brothers, 154
Lambeth, William A., tribute to Dr. Barringer, 266-67; mentioned, vi
Lane, James Henry, 141
Latin, study of, 157-58, 180
Laveran, Charles L. A., 244
Lawrence, James, 219
Leather tanning, 55
Lee, Robert E., 118, 119, 206
Lee, W. H. F., 118
Lenin, Georg, 240-41
Lewis, Hamilton, 218
Lice, 47
Lilly, Doctor, 160

Lincoln, Abraham, assassination of, 102; interview with Rufus Barringer, 121-23
Lister, Joseph, 220, 239
Logan, Doctor, 103
Long, Margaret, 82, 141, 142, 163
Loomis, Alfred, 232
Lubbock, F. R., 100
Ludwig, Karl F. W., 244
Lutheran Church in the Carolinas, History of the, 145
Lynch, Major, 175
Lyrbrand, Mart, 171

McBEE family, 27
McBride, Major, 107-8
McDairmed brothers, 154
McDonald, Mr., 99
McDonald family, 82
McDowell, Robert, 10-12
McGuffey, William, 206
McKesson family, 36
Main royal, 172
Mallet, John W., 203, 213, 216
Mallory, S. R., 101
Mandy, 63, 64
Margherita, Queen, 249
Marriages, Negro, 63-64
Marshall, Chief Justice John, 196
Marshall, Tom, 195
Mason, Erskine, 231
Massey, Maria, 5, 33. See Maria Massey Barringer
Mathematics, study of, 159, 181
Matthews, Luke, 199
Maury, Matthew Fontaine, 131
Meade, General, 120
Meade, Hodijah, 141
Means, General, 45
Means, Katie Barringer, 45
Means brothers, 154
Mebane, Doctor, 155
Medicine, study of, 214-15, 219-32, 244-54; preceptor in, 230; first school in N. C., 237; Preparatory School (Davidson), 258; pre-med (U. Va.), 260; microscope, 257, 258; biology, 258; bacteriology, 260; histology, 258, 260; syphilis, 258; embryology, 260; ophthalmology, 260; urology, 260
Melchoir family, 22
Merrimac, 72
Merrimon, A. S., 81
Microscope, classroom use of, 257

INDEX

Military training, 153-55
Miller, Samuel, 201, 202
Minor, John B., 198, 206, 218, 235
Montgomery, Walter A., v
Monticello, 178
Moore brothers, 154
Morgan, Sam, 163
Morrison, Alfred, 17
Morrison, Anna, 6, 16. See Anna Morrison Jackson
Morrison, Eugenia, 4, 16, 24, 73-74
Morrison, Harriet, 5, 17, 74
Morrison, Isabella, 8, 16, 71, 73, 74
Morrison, James, 73
Morrison, Jim, 19
Morrison, Joseph Graham, 17, 132-35
Morrison, Laura, 16
Morrison, Mary Graham, 4, 17, 20, 24, 134
Morrison, Robert Hall, 16, 19-20, 24, 26, 27, 61, 62, 87, 94-95, 134, 179
Morrison, Robert Hall, Jr., 94
Morrison, Susan, 6, 16, 17, 36, 71
Morrison, William, 17
Mortar and pestle, 56
Mount Vernon, 178

NAT, 63
Negro dialect, 65-66
"Negro Education in the South," 264
Negro marriages, 63-64
Negro passes, 64
"New ground," 28-30
New York, University of the City of, 230-32
Nitrates, 53
North Carolina, University of, 40-41, 179
Nott, Josiah Clark, 217

OCCUPATION army, 107-8
Opossum hunting, 182
Origin of Species, 220
Osborne, Frank, 141
Osborne, James W., 140, 141
Osborne, James W., Jr., 141
"Our Old Friend Death," 272-73
Owen, Doctor, 187

PAGE, James Morris, 269
Page, John R., 204
Paget, James, 239
Paris, study in, 238-40
Parker brothers, 154
Parrot, Mr., 188
Pass, Negro, 64

Passenger pigeons, 183-85
Pasteur, Louis, 226, 239, 240
Patton, Mrs., 37
Pedro, Dom, 215
Pelz, Paul J., 262
Perry, Matthew Calbraith, 21
Peyton, Green, 194
Phelps, William Walter, 241, 246, 249, 253
Phifer, Caleb, 23
Phifer, Charles, 99
Phifer family, 22, 82, 154
Philadelphia, trip to, 137-39
Philadelphia Centennial, 213-16
Philips, Charles, 81
Phillips, Charles, 109
Phillips, Consul General, 241
Phyllis, 5, 6, 8, 9, 26
Phyllis, Old, 26
Piella, Louis, 240
Piercing of ears, 62-63
Pigeons, passenger, 183-85
Plank Road, 16-17, 20, 24
Poe, Edgar Allen, 200
"Poisonous Reptiles of the United States, and the Treatment of Their Bites, The," 267
Politzer, Adam, 246
Pool, Solomon, 179
Poppies, scraping of, 52-53
Priestley, William O., 239

RABBIT hunting, 160-61, 183
Ransom, Robert, 42, 115-16
Reagan, John R., 104
Reed, Walter, 217, 218
Relation of Musselmen and Roman Law, The, 242
Rivers, Harvey James, 9, 14-15
Robinson, Joseph Taylor, 218
Robinson brothers, 153-54
Rogers, William Barton, 213
Roosevelt, Theodore, letter from, 267
Ropemaking, 55-56
Ruffin, Judge, 82

"SACRIFICE of a Race, The," 264
Saints' Days, 250-51
Sanitary Preparation of the Surgical Patient, 220
Santos, Julio Romano, 205, 216
Sayre, Lewis, 232
Scabies, 47
School Review, The, 265
Scott, Alice, 86

Scott, Doctor, 46, 130
Scovillite Tories, 145
Sermons, on slavery, 61 ff.
Shannon, 219
Shaw, Nancy Langhorne, 262
Sheridan, General, 118, 119, 120
Sherman, General, 98, 104
Shipp, Robert Johnston, 10, 26, 30, 50
Singleton, Governor, 170
Slavery, sermons on, 61 ff.
Slaves, purchase of, 10-12
Smallpox, 46-47, 245
Smith, E. Kirby, 98, 104-5
Smith, Sandy, 84
Snake heads, 72
Soap, 50
Soirees, 224-25
Sprunt brothers, 154
S'Quash, 10-15, 26
Stage coach, 35-36
Steele, Charlie, 229-30
Stoneman, General, raid of, 92-94, 98; mentioned, 89
Stough, Sheriff, 5, 85, 86, 87
Strode, H. A., 179, 180, 181, 184, 185, 187, 188, 193, 194, 201
Strode, Mrs. H. A., 182, 187
Strother, Mr., 187
Stuart, J. E. B., 79, 116
Sutter, John Augustus, 87
Sutter, Rheinholdt, 87, 92, 144
Swain, Eleanor, 109
Swain, Governor, 109
Swineford, Oscar, vi

TATE, Charlie, 164, 167, 168, 170-71
Tate family, 36, 154, 168
Taylor, Zachary, 41, 81
Telegraph office, 75
Telephone, demonstration of, 215-16
Temperance Society, 208-9
Testimony of Modern Science to the Unity of Mankind, The, 220
Thermometer, "L-armed," 214, 226
Thorburn, C. E., 101
Thornley, Doctor, 50
Thornton, William M., 204, 205
Thornwell, Doctor, 27, 30
Tilden, Samuel, 216, 222-23
Tournament, riding in a, 174-76
Towles, William B., 220, 221
"Transformations du Monde Animal, Les," 185
Tryon, Lord, 143, 145
Twain, Mark, 239

Tyler, Lyon Gardiner, 200
Tyndall, John, 239

"UNAPPRECIATED Source of Typhoid Fever, An," 268
University of North Carolina, 40-41, 179
University of the City of New York, 230-32
University of Virginia, visit to, 188-90; study at, 193-212; description of in 1875, 195; fraternities at, 198; crew, 226, 229
University of Virginia Magazine, The, 199, 212

VANCE, Dave, 164, 165, 167
Vance, Zebulon, 80
Vance brothers, 154
Velocipede, 129-30
Venable, Charles, 202, 205, 206, 211
Venable, Frank, 200
Vienna, medical studies in, 244-54
Virchow, Rudolph, 239, 244
Virginia, University of, visit to, 188-90; study at, 193-212; description of in 1875, 195; fraternities at, 198; crew, 226, 229
Virginia Military Institute, 6, 7, 17, 73, 132
Viviparous Quadrupeds of North America, The, 89
Von Zeimssen, 245

WALKING trip, 240
"Wash," 106
Washington, Booker T., letter from, 264-65
Washington Debating Society, 199, 211, 225
Weathered, Elizabeth, 80
Weaver, Consul General, 250
Webb, W. R., 119-20
Welch, William Henry, 257
Welsh main, 173
Wertenbaker, William, 200
Wheeler, Joseph, 90, 94, 95
Whippings, 156
White, Stanford, 261
Wilson, Woodrow, 234-35
Wood, J. Taylor, 100
Worth, Belle, 152

YANDELL, Doctor, 105
Yankee Jim, 43, 63, 86, 102, 106
York, Bill, 4
Young, Mrs., 76

www.ingramcontent.com/pod-product-compliance
Lightning Source LLC
Chambersburg PA
CBHW020301010526
44108CB00037B/275